MW01618630

Course Author

Rabbi Zalman Moshe Abraham

JLI Course Development Team

Editorial Review Board

Printed in the United States

The Rohr Jewish Learning Institute
822 Eastern Parkway, Brooklyn, NY 11213

(888) YOUR-JLI/718-221-6900
www.myJLI.com

Oasis in Time

The Gift of Shabbat in a 24/7 World

The **Rohr Jewish Learning Institute**
gratefully acknowledges
the pioneering support of

George and Pamela Rohr

SINCE ITS INCEPTION
the **Rohr JLI** has been
a beneficiary of the vision, generosity,
care and concern
of the **Rohr family**

In the merit of
the tens of thousands of hours of Torah study
by **JLI** students worldwide,
may they be blessed with health,
Yiddishe Nachas from all their loved ones,
and extraordinary success
in all their endeavors ❧

עוֹד יְנוּבוּן בְּשֵׂיבָה דְּשֵׁנִים וְרַעֲנַנִּים יִהְיוּ

(תהלים צב,יד)

לכבוד ר׳ שמואל שיחי׳

THIS COURSE IS DEDICATED
WITH LOVE AND ADMIRATION TO

Mr. Sami Rohr

לאורך ימים ושנים טובות

on the occasion of his eighty-fifth birthday
in tribute to his years of visionary philanthropy
and support for Torah study.

May he continue to go from strength to strength
enjoying health, happiness and prosperity,
bringing joy and blessing to others
as he receives joy and blessing from his family and loved ones

מיט געזונט און מנוחה.

Endorsements for **Oasis in Time**

"The French theorist Bernard Stiegler has written that in today's technological age we are experiencing a collective loss of *savoir faire* and *savoir vivre*: the loss of an understanding of how to be and how to live. Communication technologies orient us to the urgent and the efficient, rather than to the meaningful and the humane. The *Oasis in Time* course promises to provide a much-needed respite. Drawing upon ancient traditions, the immersive and contemplative experiences of this program can help us to develop the much-needed habits of mind and spirit necessary to address ourselves to these troubled times. I am pleased to recommend it."

Lynn Schofield Clark, PhD
Associate Professor and Director,
Estlow International Center
for Journalism and New Media,
University of Denver
Author, *Parenting in a Digital Age*

"In today's world of confusion and loss of direction in life, which manifests in young people adopting self-destructive habits, JLI is a beacon of light that can guide people to the safe haven of true happiness."

Rabbi Abraham J. Twerski, MD
Psychiatrist, Founder and Medical Director
Emeritus of Gateway Rehabilitation Center,
Pittsburgh, PA,
Author of 60 books on self-esteem,
personal growth, dependency recovery,
and Torah commentaries

"Shabbat is as relevant today as it was in the desert thousands of years ago. You'll be so energized and productive the next day you'll accomplish more than if you'd worked right through it. So go ahead, unplug."

Ken Goldberg, PhD
Craigslist Distinguished Professor of New Media
University of California at Berkeley
Co-founder, Berkeley Center for New Media

"Shabbat is a gift in my life. Personally, it provides a safe space: a retreat where I can contemplate about the past week, re-energize my spirit for the week ahead, and spend precious time with my beloved family. In business, it has set my company apart from the competition, garnered respect and loyalty from our customers, and brought unprecedented growth.

I highly recommend JLI's new course this spring, *Oasis in Time.* I encourage you to learn about this millennia-old Jewish tradition and how it can enhance your life on the mystical, psychological and social levels."

Elie Horn and Family
CEO, Cyrela Brazil Realty
São Paulo, Brazil

"I light candles to welcome Shabbat. It brings me so many blessings and peace. I encourage you to explore this special mitzvah this spring with JLI's course, *Oasis in Time*. I know JLI's classes will be a source of inspiration and help make your life brighter and the world around you a more peaceful place."

Paula Abdul
Pop singer, dancer, choreographer,
and TV personality

"My family came to America to escape religious persecution and anti-Semitism in the former Soviet Union. Here I found my calling as a professional boxer—and as a Jew. I decided that if anyone wants a 'whupping' from me [on Saturday], they got to wait until after sundown. From the day I stopped fighting on Shabbat, my career took off. I began to win championships. Shabbat blesses the whole week for me. It gives me the purpose and inner strength to do what I need to do. JLI's course, *Oasis in Time*, examines how Shabbat restores balance in our personal lives and in the world. Learn about Shabbat with JLI. This is our identity. This is our day."

Dmitriy Salita
Professional boxer
North American Boxing Association
Light Welterweight Champion, 2005

"I had a life that anybody would have wanted. But after retiring from the NFL, somehow something didn't feel right. I was starved for inspiration. As an athlete, I had inspiration, but as a human being, I didn't. I felt lost when the cheering stopped. It was not until my first Shabbat experience that things started to change. As a football player, I loved the games, the challenge, the competition, the camaraderie. But today I get a charge from different things. Even the feeling of coming out of the tunnel at Lambeau Field, home of the Green Bay Packers—beautiful blue sky, the smell of beer and brats in the air—can't compare to the rush of Shabbat. Find your inspiration—learn about Shabbat with JLI."

Alan Shlomo Veingrad
Former NFL offensive lineman
of the Green Bay Packers and Dallas Cowboys,
winner of Super Bowl XXVII

"My parents always told me, 'If you take care of Shabbat, Shabbat will take care of you.' Shabbat has charted the course of my life. It has been the backbone of my energy and my power throughout my basketball career. I encourage you to attend JLI's upcoming course, *Oasis in Time,* and learn how Shabbat can provide direction and motivation to use your talents to create a better, more spiritual world."

Tamir Goodman
Professional basketball player (retired)

"Shabbat is one of the greatest gifts of Judaism, and it can be appreciated on so many levels, each level building on the one before it to create a true harmony of spiritual, ethical, and personal growth every single week. *Oasis in Time* layers learning about the beauty of Shabbat in an intimate and comprehensive fashion. The wisdom contained has the potential to truly transform your life, your relationships, and your concept of purpose on this Earth. That's a mighty task, but it is easier than we think. I implore you to learn about Shabbat, put it into practice, and watch the miracles begin."

Mayim Bialik, PhD
Actor and Neuroscientist
Star of 1990's TV series, "Blossom"
Amy Farrah Fowler on TV series,
"The Big Bang Theory"

Course Foreword

by United States Senator Joseph Lieberman

The Rohr Jewish Learning Institute generously invited me to share with you some of my thoughts about the beauty and importance of Shabbat, the Sabbath, and the blessings I have found it to bring to my life. For me, Sabbath observance is a gift because it is one of the deepest, purest pleasures in my life. It is a day of peace, rest, and sensual pleasure. It engages the senses—sight, sound, taste, smell, and touch—with beautiful settings, soaring melodies, wonderful food and wine, and lots of love. It is a time to reconnect with family and friends—and, of course, with God, the Creator of everything we have time to "sense" on the Sabbath. Sabbath observance is a gift that has anchored, shaped, and inspired my life.

The Sabbath is an old but beautiful idea that, in our frantically harried and meaning-starved culture, cries out to be rediscovered and enjoyed by people of all faiths. It takes the form it does—its laws and customs—because from ancient days, generations of rabbis and sages have been transmitting, refining, and elaborating traditions that define Sabbath observance. These traditions build fences around the Sabbath to protect it as a day of faith and rest. The Sabbath is an organic entity reflecting centuries of thought and experience. It is not an arbitrary contrivance. Some ordinances have seemed meaningless in the past, but have been revealed in their full meaningfulness in modern times. I constantly seek the wisdom of Sabbath practices, and I'm rarely disappointed by what I find. If the cost is an occasional inconvenience or discomfort—like getting soaked on the walk home from the Capitol—I consider that a small price to pay for all that the Sabbath gives and teaches me.

Hadassah and I sometimes speak of a place beyond time called "Shabbatland." In many ways, the Sabbath is an entirely different place from the one in which we live our weekday lives. It's a place out of time, away from clocks and watches, bound only by the natural movements of the sun. Whether I am spending Shabbat in Washington, D.C., or in my hometown of Stamford, Connecticut, entering the Sabbath is like stepping into a different world, one that is defined not by geographical boundaries but by faith, tradition, and spirituality.

"On Shabbat," Rabbi Menachem Mendel Schneerson, the Rebbe of the Chabad movement, said, "we cease to struggle with the world, not because the task of perfecting it is on hold, but because on Shabbat, the world *is* perfect; we relate to what is perfect and unchanging in it."

In the Bible, we are given the text of the fourth commandment twice: once in Exodus, when Scripture narrates the revelation of God to the children of Israel at Mt. Sinai, and again three books later in Deuteronomy when Moses repeats the story of the Sinai revelation to the Israelites in the desert forty years later. The wording of the commandment in these two accounts is different.

Exodus emphasizes the role of the Sabbath in commemorating the creation of the world and in acknowledging and honoring God as Creator. We are told there to "remember" the Sabbath, to remember particularly that the world has a purposive Creator. We are not here by accident. We are here as a result of God's creation.

The second recording of the commandment to observe the Sabbath is in the context of God's liberation of the Jewish people from Egypt. It is an affirmation that God not only created us but that He continues to *care* about His creation and about human history:

> And remember that thou wast a servant in the land of Egypt, and that the Lord thy God brought thee out from there with a mighty hand and a stretched out arm: therefore the Lord thy God commanded thee to keep the Sabbath day. (Deuteronomy 5:15)

The Exodus led to the revelation at Sinai in which the commandment to remember and guard the Sabbath is given, and with the law came the responsibility each of us has to become God's partners in shaping, improving, and ultimately perfecting human history.

The Talmud contains a wonderful teaching, namely, that if everyone observed two Sabbaths in a row, the Messiah would come and preside over the redemption of humanity. On the surface, this vision seems inconsistent with other talmudic teachings that the appearance of the Messiah will be totally unexpected, perhaps even unrecognized at first. So what did the rabbis mean when they said that two globally observed Sabbaths would bring in the Messianic Age? I think they were saying that the Sabbath has the power to mend the breaches that separate human beings from each other and from God, and that closing those two breaches will create the conditions for redemption.

If all of us would just stop and observe one Sabbath, and then another, in perfect unity with God and one another, then the world would be redeemed.

Until then, each day of Sabbath rest that you choose to observe will give you a taste of the world to come. The Sabbath is truly a gift. A gift from God. The gift of rest. I hope and pray that you will accept it and let Sabbath rest enrich your life.

The prophet Isaiah taught beautifully about a future time when everyone will observe the Sabbath:

> Also the sons of the stranger, that join themselves to the Lord, to serve Him, and to love the name of the Lord, to be His servants, every one that keeps the Sabbath and does not profane it. . . . Even them will I bring to My holy mountain, and make them joyful in My house of prayer. (Isaiah 56:6–7)

Then, in the concluding verses of his book, Isaiah pictures how it will be in that blessed future:

> And it shall come to pass, that every new moon, and every Sabbath, shall all flesh come to bow down to the ground before Me, says the Lord. (Isaiah 66:23)

In our time, I believe, the Sabbath is a gift that is desperately needed. It is God's gift to everyone who chooses to accept it. That is what this program is about—exploring concepts that are important to us as Jews and that I think we can share with all mankind.

Joseph Lieberman

March 2011

Table of Contents

Lesson 1

The Gift

Introduction

Who has not felt the excitement of receiving an exquisite gift? Memorable gifts fulfill our needs and our desires in ways that, perhaps, we would not have achieved on our own. They provide surprise and delight.

We treasure gifts for the joy they give us, but we also treasure them because of the people who gave them to us. Gifts tell us that the givers care enough to take the time to think about us and what makes us happy. Most of all, they reflect that those who love us decided to share a bit of themselves.

Shabbat is called God's special gift to the Jewish people. We will discover why in this lesson, as we unwrap the gift of Shabbat together.

The Gift

Text 1

אמר לו הקדוש ברוך הוא למשה:
מתנה טובה יש לי בבית גנזי ושבת שמה, ואני מבקש ליתנה לישראל, לך והודיעם.
תלמוד בבלי, שבת י,ב

God said to Moses, "I have a precious gift in My treasure house called Shabbat and I desire to give it to the Jewish people; go and inform them."

Talmud, Shabbat 10b

מתנה טובה יש לי בבית גנזי ושבת שמה

Text 2

זָכוֹר אֶת יוֹם הַשַּׁבָּת לְקַדְּשׁוֹ.
שֵׁשֶׁת יָמִים תַּעֲבֹד וְעָשִׂיתָ כָּל מְלַאכְתֶּךָ.
וְיוֹם הַשְּׁבִיעִי שַׁבָּת לַה׳ אֱלֹקֶיךָ
לֹא תַעֲשֶׂה כָל מְלָאכָה אַתָּה וּבִנְךָ וּבִתֶּךָ עַבְדְּךָ וַאֲמָתְךָ וּבְהֶמְתֶּךָ.
שמות כ,ח–י

emember to sanctify the day of Shabbat.

Six days you shall labor and perform all your work.

But the seventh day is Shabbat for the Lord your God, you shall perform no work—neither you, your son, your daughter, your manservant, your maidservant, nor your beast.

Exodus 20:8–10

Question for Discussion

In what way can Shabbat rest be termed a gift? What benefit might there be to taking a full-day's break from work?

Pragmatic Rest

Lucrative Rest

Text 3

ויגדל משה ויצא אל אחיו וירא בסבלתם (שמות ב,יא). מה ראה, ראה להם תקנה לשעבודם כדי שינפשו ופרש להם הלכות שבת לנוח ולהנפש . . . נכנס אצל פרעה אמר לו אני רואה מלאכת שלך עתידה להבטל. אמר לו המלך כיצד. אמר לו לפי שאין קצבה לעבודתם . . . אם יהיה עבד לאדם שאין לו קצבה במלאכתו אינו מת. אמר לו הן. אמר לו משה אלו עבדיך אם אין אתה נותן להם ריוח במלאכתם הם מתים. אמר לו פרעה כבר מניתיך על מלאכת שלי, לך עשה להם כשאתה רואה.

בראשית רבתי א,ו–ח

oses grew up and went out to his brothers and saw their suffering" (Exodus 2:11). What did Moses see? He saw a solution that would allow them to recover from their burden. He told the Jewish people about the laws of resting on Shabbat. . . . Then he went to Pharaoh and said, "I see that your enterprise is going to fail."

Pharaoh said to him, "Why is that?"

Moses replied, "Because there is no limit to their work. . . . If a slave works incessantly, won't he die?"

Pharaoh agreed.

Moses then said to Pharaoh, "These people are your slaves; if you give them no respite, they will die."

Rabbi Moshe Hadarshan (11th century). Leader of French Jewry, renowned for his contribution to midrashic literature. In his commentaries on Scripture, Rashi frequently quotes from Moshe Hadarshan's *Yesod*, a work of scriptural expositions that is no longer extant. Another of Rabbi Moshe's works is *Bereishit Rabati*, a midrashic anthology on the Book of Genesis. In this work, Rabbi Moshe draws upon his vast store of knowledge and remarkable creative ability to develop the central ideas of the Midrash by comparing and connecting them with other relevant verses and passages.

Pharaoh said, "I have appointed you as the overseer of my work. Do with them as you see fit."

Rabbi Moshe Hadarshan, *Bereishit Rabati* 1:6–8

Text 4

בעשותו מלאכה בשאר ימי השבוע יזדרז בה בהעלותו על לבו כי תקרב אליו עת המנוחה . . . וכן אחר עבור יום המנוחה, יצא למלאכתו בזריזות. כי הרואה שאין לו מנוחה יעשה מלאכתו בעצלה ועל כרחו.

דרשות רבינו יונה, פרשת ויקהל

A person who considers that a period of rest is approaching will work with enthusiasm . . . and after the day of rest passes, the person will return to work with [renewed] zeal. But if a person sees no upcoming rest, the work will be done lethargically and begrudgingly.

Rabbi Yonah of Gerona, Homilies, *Parashat Vayakhel*

Rabbi Yonah ben Avraham of Gerona (d. 1263). Born in the late 12th century in Gerona, Spain. A talmudist and teacher of ethics, he also served as dean of the yeshivah in Barcelona. He was a cousin and friend of Nachmanides, and a teacher of the Rashba and Re'ah. Authored works on Tanach, Mishnah, and Talmud, but is most famous for his *Sha'arei Teshuvah*, a work on ethics and repentance.

Leisure Rest

Text 5

Rabbi Moshe ben Maimon (1135–1204). Better known as Maimonides or by the acronym Rambam; born in Cordoba, Spain. After the conquest of Cordoba by the Almohads, he fled Spain and eventually settled in Cairo, Egypt. There, he became the leader of the Jewish community and served as court physician to the vizier of Egypt. His rulings on Jewish law are considered integral to the formation of halachic consensus. He is most noted for authoring the *Mishneh Torah*, an encyclopedic arrangement of Jewish law, and for his philosophical work, *Guide for the Perplexed*.

ענין השבת טעמו מפורסם ואין צריך לביאור, כבר נודע מה שבו מהמנוחה עד שיהיה שביעית חיי האדם בהנאה ובמנוחה מן העמל והטורח שלא ימלט ממנו קטן וגדול.

מורה הנבוכים ג,מג

The concept of Shabbat is well recognized and requires no explanation. The rest it affords is understood; one-seventh of the life of every person, whether small or great, is spent in enjoyment and rest from toil and trouble.

Maimonides, *Guide for the Perplexed* 3:43

Learning Activity 1

What are the five activities/pursuits outside of work that you most enjoy?

1.

2.

3.

4.

5.

Text 6

והרב המורה זכר עוד תכלית אחר למנוחת יום המקודש הזה והוא כדי שיהיה לישראל שביעית הימים במנוחה ועונג מעולמם.

ויותר ראוי לומר כדי שיהיה להם שביעית הימים פנוי ללמוד התורה האלהית . . . וכן אמרו חכמינו זכרונם לברכה לא ניתנו שבתות וימים טובים לישראל אלא ללמוד בהם תורה.

אברבנאל, שמות כ

In the *Guide for the Perplexed,* Maimonides mentions another purpose for Shabbat rest—that the Jewish people should have a seventh of their life dedicated to pleasure, as well as rest from their worldly concerns.

However, it would be more appropriate to say that a seventh of their days should be free for the study of the divine Torah. . . . Indeed our sages have said, "Shabbat and holidays were given to the Jewish people for no other reason than for them to study Torah."

Rabbi Don Yitschak Abarbanel, Exodus 20

Rabbi Don Yitschak Abarbanel (1437–1508). Born in Lisbon, Portugal; rabbi, scholar, and statesman. Abarbanel served as a minister in the court of King Alfonso V of Portugal. After intrigues at court led to accusations against him, he fled to Spain, where he once again served as a counselor to royalty. It is claimed that Abarbanel offered King Ferdinand and Queen Isabella large sums of money for the revocation of their Edict of Expulsion of 1492, but to no avail. After the expulsion, he eventually settled in Italy where he wrote a commentary on Scripture, as well as other venerated works. He is buried in Padua.

Text 7

Herman Wouk (1915–). American novelist and playwright. Born in New York City to a Jewish-Russian immigrant family. When the U.S. entered World War II, he joined the Navy, serving in the Pacific Theater for four years. Wouk's wartime experiences gave him the material and background for his bestseller and Pulitzer-Prize-winning *The Caine Mutiny* (1951). *This Is My God* (1959) was his best-selling affirmation of faith in traditional Judaism, penned after much self-examination and exposure to many non-religious influences. His later works include the novel *Inside, Outside* (1985), which discusses Judaism in private life and in politics, and *The Will to Live On: This Is Our Heritage* (2000).

Leaving the gloomy theatre, the littered coffee cups, the jumbled scarred-up scripts, the haggard actors, the shouting stagehands, the bedeviled director, the knuckle-gnawing producer, the clattering typewriter, and the dense tobacco smoke and backstage dust, I have come home. It has been a startling change, very like a brief return from the wars. My wife and my boys, whose existence I have almost forgotten in the anxious shoring up of the tottering ruin, are waiting for me, gay, dressed in holiday clothes, and looking to me marvelously attractive. We have sat down to a splendid dinner, at a table graced with flowers and the old Sabbath symbols: the burning candles, the twisted loaves, the stuffed fish and my grandfather's silver goblet brimming with wine. I have blessed my boys with the ancient blessing; we have sung the pleasantly syncopated Sabbath table hymns. The talk has had little to do with tottering ruins. My wife and I have caught up with our week's conversation. The boys, knowing that the Sabbath is the occasion for asking questions, have asked them. The Bible, the encyclopedia, the atlas, have piled up on the table. We talk of Judaism, and there are the usual impossible boys' queries about God, which my wife and I field clumsily but as well as we can. For me it is a retreat into restorative magic.

Saturday has passed in much the same manner. The boys are at home in the synagogue, and they like it. They like even more the assured presence of their parents. In the weekday press of schooling, household chores, and work—and especially in a play-producing time—it often happens that they see little of us. On the Sabbath we are always here, and they know it. They know too that I am not working, and that my wife is at her ease. It is their day. . . .

My producer one Saturday night said to me, "I don't envy you your religion, but I envy you your Sabbath."

Herman Wouk, *This is My God* [Boston: Little Brown and Co., 1987], pp. 45–46

Transcendent Rest

Commemorative Rest

Text 8a

כִּי שֵׁשֶׁת יָמִים עָשָׂה ה׳ אֶת הַשָּׁמַיִם וְאֶת הָאָרֶץ אֶת הַיָּם וְאֶת כָּל אֲשֶׁר בָּם וַיָּנַח בַּיּוֹם הַשְּׁבִיעִי עַל כֵּן בֵּרַךְ ה׳ אֶת יוֹם הַשַּׁבָּת וַיְקַדְּשֵׁהוּ.

שמות כ,יא

For [in] six days the Lord made the heaven, the earth, the sea, and all that is in them, and He rested on the seventh day. Therefore, the Lord blessed the Shabbat day and sanctified it.

Exodus 20:11

Text 8b

משרשי מצוה זו שנהיה פנויים מעסקינו לכבוד היום, לקבוע בנפשותינו אמונת חדוש העולם שהיא חבל המושכת כל יסודי הדת . . . ובמנוחתינו בשביעי זכר לנו בחדושו של עולם, כי כשישבתו בני אדם כולם ביום אחד בשבוע וישאל כל שואל מה עילת זאת המנוחה. ויהיה המענה כי ששת ימים עשה ה׳ וגו׳.

ספר החינוך, מצוה לב

Sefer Hachinuch is a work on the 613 commandments, arranged in the order of the *mitzvot's* appearance in the Torah. Four aspects of every mitzvah are discussed in this work: the definition of the mitzvah and its sources in the Written and Oral Torah; ethical lessons which can be deduced from the mitzvah; basic laws pertaining to the observance of the mitzvah; and who is obligated to perform the mitzvah and when. The work was composed in the thirteenth century by an anonymous author who refers to himself in the introduction as "the Levite of Barcelona." It has been widely thought that this referred to Rabbi Aharon Halevi of Barcelona (Re'ah); however, this view has been contested.

Among the reasons for this mitzvah is that in honor of the day [of Shabbat], we should be free from our work so that we can impress upon ourselves the belief in God as Creator of the universe, which drives all the tenets of our faith. . . . When we rest on the seventh day, we will recall the Creation of the world, for when all people rest on the same day of the week, and one asks, "What is the cause for this rest?" the answer will be, "For in six days God created, etc."

Sefer Hachinuch, Mitzvah 32

Text 9a

וְזָכַרְתָּ כִּי עֶבֶד הָיִיתָ בְּאֶרֶץ מִצְרַיִם וַיֹּצִאֲךָ ה׳ אֱלֹקֶיךָ מִשָּׁם בְּיָד חֲזָקָה וּבִזְרֹעַ נְטוּיָה עַל כֵּן צִוְּךָ ה׳ אֱלֹקֶיךָ לַעֲשׂוֹת אֶת יוֹם הַשַּׁבָּת.

דברים ה,טו

And remember that you were a slave in the land of Egypt, and the Lord your God brought you out from there with a mighty hand and with an outstretched arm; therefore, the Lord your God commanded you to observe the day of Shabbat.

Deuteronomy 5:15

Text 9b

ומלבד זכירת חדוש העולם יש בו זכירת נס מצרים. שהיינו עבדים שם ולא היינו יכולים לנוח בעת חפצנו במנוחה. והא-ל הצילנו מידם.

ספר החינוך, מצוה לב

Aside from reminding us of the Creation of the world, Shabbat also reminds us of the miraculous Exodus from Egypt: we were slaves there and we were not able to rest when we wanted, but God saved us from their hands.

Sefer Hachinuch, Mitzvah 32

Text 9c

כמו מלך אחד שבנה מדינה והלך ולקח עבדים והוציאם לחרות והושיבם בתוכה . . . ראוי שיקבע להם זכר ליום שבנה המדינה . . . ובעבור זה צוה עליהם לשמור את יום השבת להורות על חדוש העולם ועל יציאת מצרים מעבדות לחרות.

ספר העיקרים ג,כו

This can be compared to a king that founded a state, bought slaves, freed them, and settled them there. . . . It is fitting for him to mark the day the state was completed. . . .

For this purpose God commanded the Jewish people to observe the Shabbat: to attest to the Creation of the world and their Exodus from slavery to freedom.

Rabbi Yosef Albo, *Sefer Ha'ikarim* 3:26

Rabbi Yosef Albo (ca. 1380–1444). A Spanish rabbi and philosopher; a student of Rabbi Chasdai Crescas. Albo is renowned for his philosophical work *Sefer Ha'ikarim* (Book of Principles). The work stresses three fundamental aspects of Jewish belief: faith in the existence of G-d, Torah from Sinai, and reward and punishment.

Question for Discussion

Why is it important for us to recall both of these events —the Creation and the Exodus?

Text 10a

הֲלוֹא יָדַעְתָּ אִם לֹא שָׁמַעְתָּ אֱלֹקֵי עוֹלָם ה׳ בּוֹרֵא קְצוֹת הָאָרֶץ לֹא יִיעַף וְלֹא יִיגָע.

ישעיהו מ,כח

Do you not know? Have you not heard? God the Lord is everlasting, He is the Creator of the ends of the earth, He neither tires nor wearies.

Isaiah 40:28

Text 10b

לא בעמל ולא ביגיעה ברא הקדוש ברוך הוא את עולמו.

בראשית רבה כז,א

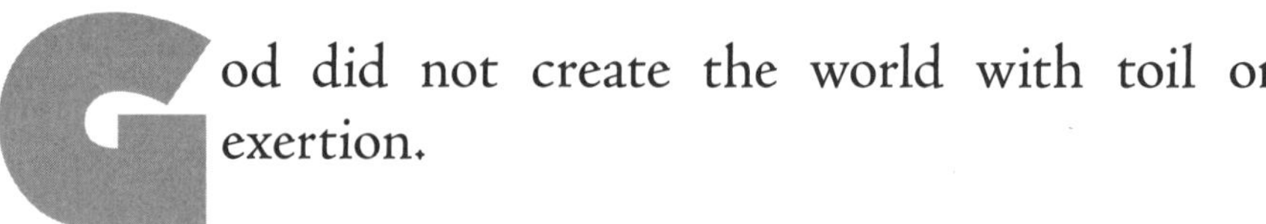

God did not create the world with toil or exertion.

Midrash, *Bereishit Rabah* 27:1

Text 11a

וַיְכַל אֱלֹקִים בַּיּוֹם הַשְּׁבִיעִי מְלַאכְתּוֹ אֲשֶׁר עָשָׂה
וַיִּשְׁבֹּת בַּיּוֹם הַשְּׁבִיעִי מִכָּל מְלַאכְתּוֹ אֲשֶׁר עָשָׂה.
וַיְבָרֶךְ אֱלֹקִים אֶת יוֹם הַשְּׁבִיעִי וַיְקַדֵּשׁ אֹתוֹ כִּי בוֹ שָׁבַת מִכָּל מְלַאכְתּוֹ.
בראשית ב,ב–ג

By the seventh day, God completed His *melachah* that He did, and He abstained on the seventh day from all His *melachah* that He did.

And God blessed the seventh day and He hallowed it, for thereon He abstained from all His *melachah*.

Genesis 2:2–3

Text 11b

דע כי יש הבדל בין מלת עבודה ובין מלת מלאכה, עבודה כולל כל המעשים שאדם עושה, ואפילו אין במעשהו ענין המצטרך לידיעה וחכמה, גם אינו משנה דבר במעשהו ולא מתקן דבר, כמו לשאת משאות אבנים, לרוץ ממקום למקום . . . וכל אלה הדברים לא יפול עליהם שם מלאכה . . . ואין שם מלאכה נופל אלא על המחדש דבר בענינים הטבעים ומשנה אותם במעשהו ממה שהיו, ועל ידי החדוש הזה יהיה תקון הדבר, הן שיבנה הן שיהרוס, תמיד ישנה, וכשיש במעשהו תקון ליישוב העולם הרי זה מלאכה.
הכתב והקבלה, שמות לה,א

Know that there is a difference between the word *avodah* and the word *melachah*. *Avodah* refers to all of a person's actions, even if the action does not require knowledge or wisdom. In addition, if nothing is being changed or fixed by the action, for

Rabbi Ya'akov Tsvi Mecklenburg (1785–1865). German rabbi and scholar; served as rabbi in Königsberg, East Prussia. In 1839 he published *Haketav Vehakabalah*, a work on the Torah that defends the views of traditional Judaism against the critiques of the "Enlightenment" movement.

example, when carrying loads of stone or running from place to place . . . we do not use the term *melachah*. . . .

The term *melachah* only applies when someone creates something new from raw materials, changing it from its previous state and improving it. Whether building or destroying [in order to rebuild], there must always be a change. When a person's work makes the world more habitable, it is called *melachah*.

Rabbi Ya'akov Tsvi of Mecklenburg, *Haketav Vehakabalah*, Exodus 35:1

Learning Activity 2

A. Enumerate the differences between *avodah* and *melachah*:

Avodah	*Melachah*

B. Cite some examples that fit each category:

Avodah	*Melachah*

Text 12

כל מעשה אלהים שעשה בששת הימים נקראים מלאכות לא עבודות . . . ולכן אלה המלאכות כולם אסורים לנו לעשות ביום השבת . . . לא מצינו לא תעבוד ביום השבת . . . ויצא לנו מזה שמותר לטלטל בשבת שולחנות וכסאות אוכלים ומשקים . . . כשהם לצורך עונג שבת; וכן מותר לרוץ כל היום מבית לבית וכיוצא, אף על פי שהן עמל וטורח לפי שאינן אלא עבודות, והשם יתברך לא אסר עשיית העבודה זולת המלאכה, ולכן החורש כל שהוא והזורע כל שהוא והכותב שתי אותיות בשבת, ואף על פי שאין בכל זה עמל וטורח, כבר חלל את השבת לפי שעשה מלאכה.

הכתב והקבלה, שם

All of the work that God did during the six days of Creation is called *melachah,* not *avodah.* . . . Therefore, we are forbidden to do *melachah* on Shabbat. . . . We don't find a prohibition that says, "Don't do *avodah* on Shabbat." . . .

Consequently, it is permitted to carry tables and chairs, food and drink . . . when they are needed for the enjoyment of Shabbat. Similarly, it is permitted to run from house to house all day, and so forth. Despite the fact that there is toil and trouble, it is *avodah*—and God did not forbid *avodah,* only *melachah.*

On the other hand, although there is no toil and trouble when one plows just a bit, plants just a bit, or writes just two letters on Shabbat, it is a desecration of Shabbat because *melachah* was done.

Rabbi Ya'akov Tsvi of Mecklenburg, ibid.

Learning Activity 3

You receive the following question from a friend. Based on what we have learned so far, how would you respond?

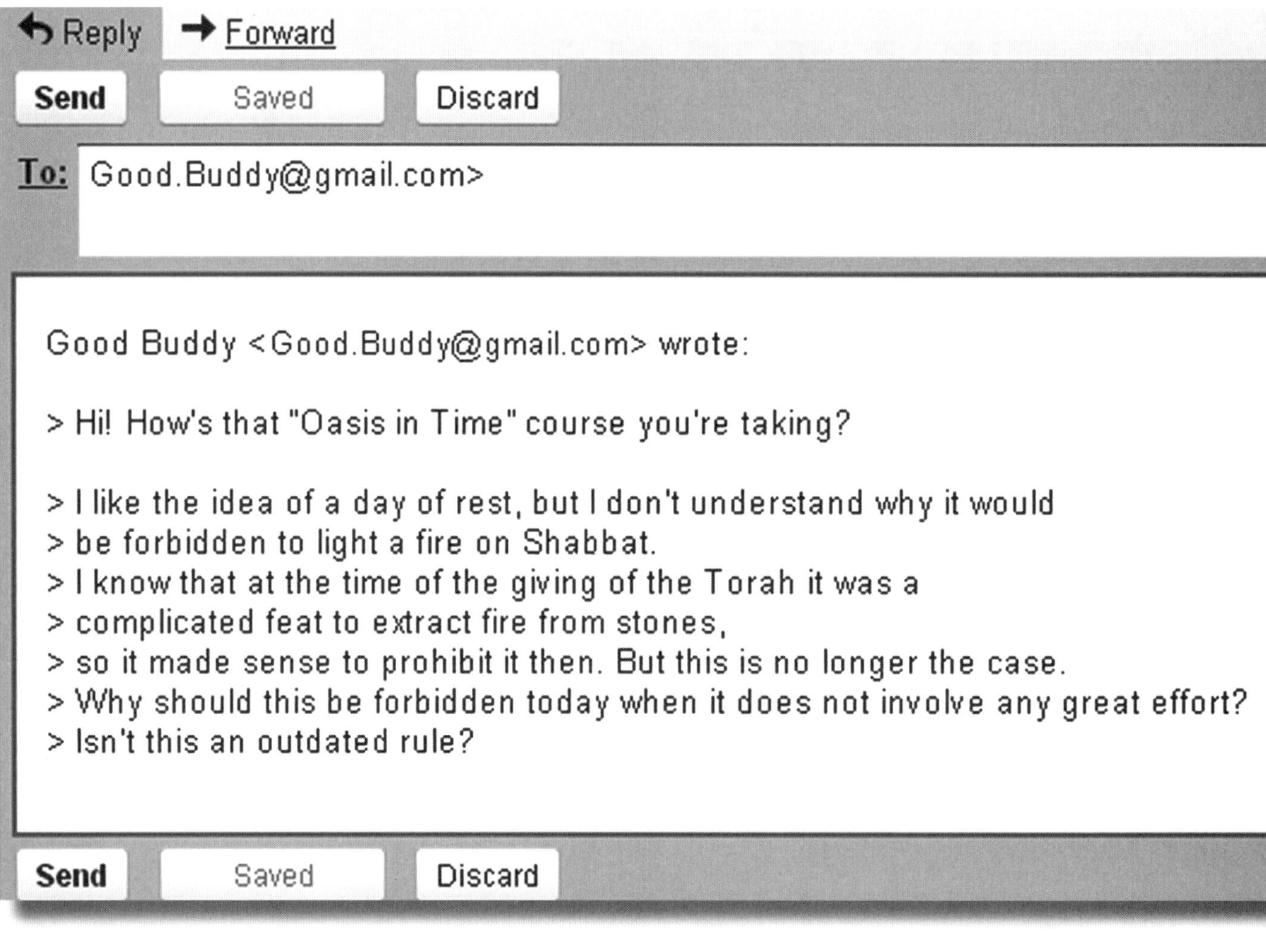

Cosmic Rest

Text 13a

על דרך משל כאדם השובת ונח ממלאכתו אשר עשה שבשעת מעשה היה שכלו ומחשבתו מלובשים במעשה ההיא ואחר כך כששובת חזרו שכלו ומחשבתו למקורן.
לקוטי תורה, דרושים לשבת שובה סו,ג

Rabbi Shne'ur Zalman of Liadi (1745–1812). Chasidic rebbe and founder of the Chabad movement, also known as "the Alter Rebbe" and "the Rav." Born in Liozna, Belarus, he was among the principal students of the Magid of Mezeritch. His numerous works include the *Tanya*, an early classic containing the fundamentals of Chasidism; *Torah Or; Likutei Torah*; and *Shulchan Aruch HaRav*, a reworked and expanded code of Jewish law. He is interred in Hadiach, Ukraine, and was succeeded by his son, Rabbi Dovber of Lubavitch.

This is comparable to a person who pauses and rests from the work he has performed. While he was working, his mind and thoughts were engaged in that action. Later, when he rests, his mind and thoughts revert to their source.

Rabbi Shne'ur Zalman of Liadi, *Likutei Torah, Derushim LeShabbat Shuvah* 66c

Text 13b

וכך על דרך זה בשבת עולה החיות שנמשך בששת ימי המעשה בעשרה מאמרות שנברא העולם לבחינת המחשבה.
ולכן שבת אותיות תשב שענין שבת וענין תשובה הכל אחד דהיינו חזרת הדברים למקורן.
לקוטי תורה, שם

Similarly, on Shabbat, the energy that was engaged during the six days of Creation—that is, the ten utterances with which the world was created—ascend to the realm of thought.

Therefore, the word *Shabbat* shares the same letters at the word *tashuv,* return, for the concept of Shabbat and the concept of return are the same, the reverting of things to their source.

Rabbi Shne'ur Zalman of Liadi, ibid.

Reprise: The Gift

Learning Activity 4

We have noted that the appreciation of the gift of Shabbat is a lifelong journey. Below is a summary of some ways in which the benefits of Shabbat rest have been explored in this lesson. Place an asterisk next to the three benefits of Shabbat that are most important to you right now.

Shabbat can help me maintain my physical health.

Shabbat can help me prevent mental burnout.

Shabbat can give my mind a break from work, enhancing my creativity.

On Shabbat, I can stop thinking about work and enjoy life.

On Shabbat, I can spend quality time with my family.

On Shabbat, I can spend time in prayer, study, or meditation.

On Shabbat, I can become conscious of my inherent value.

On Shabbat, I can contemplate God as the Creator of the world.

On Shabbat, I can come to the recognition that God continuously provides for the world.

On Shabbat, I can recall that I am created in the divine image.

On Shabbat, I can recall the unique mission of the Jewish people.

On Shabbat, I can experience God more strongly.

On Shabbat, I can feel the intrinsic holiness of the day.

Key Points

1. God gave the Jewish people the Shabbat and called it a gift. This gift offers us multiple benefits and opportunities.

2. Shabbat can help maintain physical health and prevent mental burnout. It can also help us maintain a positive work attitude and enhance our creativity.

3. Shabbat frees us from the burdens of work and gives us the time needed for family and spiritual pursuits.

4. Shabbat reminds us that our inherent worth is larger than our accomplishments.

5. The Torah tells us to rest on Shabbat so that we will remember that God is the Creator of the universe. By working for six days each week and resting on the seventh, we reenact the process of the Creation.

6. Our rest follows the pattern of God's rest. God's rest is the cessation from creative accomplishment, not the cessation of exhausting labor. Thus, we refrain from creative accomplishment, not exhausting labor.

7. Every Shabbat the world is elevated from the realm of God's speech to the realm of God's thought. This makes Shabbat an intrinsically holy time when the entire universe is more attuned to its Creator.

8. When we refrain from work on Shabbat, we are better able to access the transcendent nature of Shabbat.

Additional Readings

A Jewish Ethic of Leisure

by **Rabbi Norman Lamm**

In his *Utopia*, published in 1516, Sir Thomas More predicted a situation that no doubt amused the practical men of his time: a nine-hour day and sixty-hour workweek. From the point of view of the proportion of work to leisure in the pattern of contemporary society, we are living a utopian existence. Whether the results of this new apportionment of our time are actually proving "utopian" is altogether another question.

The New Leisure

Today, almost all of us are members of the leisure class, a designation no longer confined exclusively to a particular aristocratic elite. Leisure is gradually replacing work as the basis of culture. "Literally a revolution has occurred—a turning around—for what was on the periphery is now at the heart of man's daily existence."[1] Even our work is more leisurely than ever before, if we except those professions in which tension and anxiety are part of the warp and woof of the work itself. The Protestant ethic has weakened, and in place of the admiration accorded work and diligence in and for themselves, a new leisureliness has taken hold, what David Reisman, in his *Individualism Reconsidered* (New York: Free Press of Glencoe, 1964) has called, "the modern cult of effortlessness."

A cultural transformation of this sort must have religious as well as social and economic consequences. For the problem of leisure is the problem of how we use time, and the problem of time is the problem of life itself. It simply will not do to continue considering the problem of leisure as frivolous, relegating it to resort entrepreneurs, travel agents, and summer-camp head counselors. "Leisure is part of man's ultimate concern. It is a crucial part of the very search for meaning in life, inasmuch as the social malaise of our time has been diagnosed as anxiety and boredom, alienation and meaninglessness."[2] Whether we consider leisure as a theological problem *per se*, certainly the profound changes it can cause in a person's outlook and disposition represent a challenge to religion and require that guidance be provided in adjusting to the changing economic conditions and social patterns. In short, it is desirable that efforts be undertaken to develop a Jewish ethic of leisure.

A Leisure Explosion?

Before proceeding any further, it is best to clarify the empirical situation: is there indeed a sudden excess of leisure to raise serious problems for us? On the face of it, there certainly is a leisure explosion. President John F. Kennedy announced at the beginning of the seventh decade of the twentieth century that the major domestic challenge of the 1960s would be that of automation, and he included in it not only the economic problems raised by the subsequent unemployment and need for retraining, but also the deeper and subtler problem of the utilization of this newfound leisure. Towards the end of that decade, the Southern California Research Council predicted that by 1985 the typical worker in the United States would have the choice of a 25-week vacation, retirement at age 38, or a 22-hour workweek—a truly frightening situation for the typical American who spends Sunday morning at church praying for eternity and in the same rainy afternoon is at his wits' end because he cannot attend or watch the ball game on TV and has no idea what to do with his time! While the forecast has proven quite premature, despite the intervening dawn of the information and electronic age, the problem has remained disturbing even decades later.

[1] R. Lee, in *Religion and Leisure in America: A Study in Four Dimensions* (Nashville, Tenn.: Abingdon Press, 1964).

[2] Ibid.

Yet, a caveat should be inserted here. Despite what has been said above, so richly supported by popular wisdom, not all experts agree that the situation is so happy as to constitute a threat. In a research study sponsored by the Twentieth Century Fund, it was found that, the unemployed and part-time worker aside, the typical American is working only a few hours, if any, less than his counterpart worked a hundred years ago. Moonlighting, travel to and from the job, making necessary home repairs, and so on, leave almost as little time for full leisure as a century ago. The conclusion is that "the more time-saving machinery there is, the more pressed a person is for time."[3] (Actually, the paradox is not a new one. John Stuart Mill noticed the failure of "labor-saving devices in the 1860s, and so did Samuel Butler.)[4] In a leading article in a prestigious business journal, one writer laid to rest all the predictions as to the sudden abundance of leisure time in the foreseeable future. The United States will continue to have a "scarcity" economy, and "the prospect of greatly reducing the hours on life's treadmills remains nothing more than a prospect." The more time we save in making goods, the more time we spend in providing services. Hence "for a long time we'll probably have to work as hard as ever."[5] Closer to our own times, the almost instantaneous contact by e-mail, fax, and mobile phones has "saved" time and yet imposed a burden by the implied demand for an immediate reply; and the spending of innumerable hours in front of the television and at the personal computer is almost a prerequisite for being "informed."

Nevertheless, all this having been noted, there is little doubt that we do have sufficient leisure around to warrant our attention and concern, whether more or less than in the past, and whether or not more can be expected in the future. The problem may not get worse, but it is bad enough. Furthermore, leisure is not an affliction peculiar to "affluent" societies alone. The distinction between work and leisure as two separate states appears to be universal. The Dutch linguist Huizinga has observed, in his *Homo Ludens*, that every language he examined had a different word for work and a different one for play, the distinction thus pointing to something innate rather than socially acquired and conditioned. Furthermore, while the full-time workingman may have little significantly increased leisure time, there has been a redistribution of available time that has served to create a special problem for those least capable of solving it. Free time goes increasingly to those with the least resources to enjoy it: the worker suddenly laid off, with no money to enjoy his new free time, and early retirement at a time of increasing longevity, or longer vacations for those whose educational backgrounds have not prepared them for a life of cultivation of the mind. At the same time, those best equipped to use leisure creatively—scholars, thinkers, the managers of wealth, and the like—are the ones who today work long hours.[6] There is a real element of tragedy in the otherwise comical situation described by Robert Browning:

> When a man's busy, why, leisure
> Strikes him as wonderful pleasure;
> Faith, and at leisure once is he?
> Straightaway, he wants to be busy.

Leisure has become for us, and possibly has in some measure always been, a source of anxiety and worry.

Leisure as a Problem

The problem of leisure is of crucial importance for our society. Historians have hinted ominously at the relation between the fate of a civilization and the way its members use or abuse their leisure. It might seem frivolous to suggest that, for instance, the future of Western civilization hinges on the success of the bowling or golf industry. Yet it is quite reasonable to assume that the vigor and toughness of a nation is displayed in its choice of leisure activity, which is more descriptive of its inner character than work, for the character of its work may be dictated by necessity rather than by choice. The communal uses of leisure may well make or break a culture, revealing its inner moral worth and determining its cultural growth or decline for a long time to come.

---

3 S. Degrazia, *Of Time, Work and Leisure* (New York: The Viking Press, 1962), p. 329.

4 J. Barzun, *Science: The Glorious Entertainment* (New York: Harper and Row, 1968), p. 257.

5 G. Burck, "There'll Be Less Leisure Than You Think," *Fortune*, March 1970.

6 A. Heckscher, "Reflections on the Manpower Revolution," in *American Scholar*, Autumn 1964.

The notion that a person's true character is revealed in his disposition of his "play" time is anticipated in the Talmud,[7] which tells us that a man's character can be tested in three ways: *be-khiso, be-khoso, u-ve-kha'aso*, by his pocket—is he a miser or is he a spendthrift? by his cup—how does he respond to the temptation of alcoholic excesses? and by his temper—can he control himself in the presence of provocation? These three provide a guide to what kind of person one is. However, there is a fourth test according to some, a fourth index of character or personality: *af be-sehoko*, also by his "play"—how does he use his leisure? That will reveal the essential quality of a man.

Our major problem is that boredom—the concession of failure in the confrontation with the challenge of leisure—leads to the erosion of meaningfulness in life. There is a straight road that leads from ennui to anomie. The bored man seeks to escape the world where free people choose and decide, and seeks instead the deadening environment of noisy and gaudy entertainment that will anesthetize the quest for meaning which goes unanswered within him. A wise psychiatrist speaks of an "existential vacuum" revealing itself in the state of boredom.

> Now we can understand Schopenhauer when he said that mankind was apparently doomed to vacillate eternally between the two extremes of distress and boredom. In actual fact, boredom is now causing and, certainly, bringing to psychiatrists more problems to solve than is distress. . . . Think, for instance, of "Sunday neurosis," that kind of depression which afflicts people who become aware of the lack of content in their lives when the rush of the busy week is over and the void within themselves becomes manifest. Not a few cases of suicide can be traced back to this existential vacuum. Such widespread phenomena as alcoholism and juvenile delinquency are not understandable unless we recognize the existential vacuum underlying them. This is also true of the crises of pensioners and aging people. . . . Moreover, there are various masks and guises under which the existential vacuum appears. Sometimes the frustrated will to meaning is vicariously compensated for by a will to power, including the most primitive form of the will to power, the will to money. In other cases, the place of frustrated will to meaning is taken by the will to pleasure. That is why existential frustration often eventuates in sexual compensation. We can observe, in such cases, that the sexual libido becomes rampant in the existential vacuum.[8]

The situation, then, is frightening enough as is. Considering the predictions of yet more frustration (or better, blank time), especially when due to early retirement, the dangers become awesome. If these predictions indeed become a reality in the next few years, as they show every promise of doing, what in heaven's name will our people do with all that spare time? Cultivate the soul and mind? or dull their brains and fill their cranial cavities with that ceaseless flow of tripe and terror that issues from television and other channels of mass communication? or, worse yet, will they seek the cheap thrills of social, moral, and legal delinquency?

Work and Rest

Now, one cannot speak of *the* Jewish view of leisure. The situation has simply never presented itself in just those terms to allow the most authoritative expositors of Judaism to pronounce on it and allow a consensus—or several of them—to develop. What we must do is refer to the sources and make a modest attempt at adumbrating the outline of a Jewish ethic of leisure. There is no suggestion here of thoroughness in examining these sources, merely a gathering of some major passages and opinions and an attempt to organize them coherently and make explicit some of the values which have not heretofore been brought out into the open.

It is well known that the Rabbis of the Talmud did not disdain manual labor. Indeed, most, if not all, of them were engaged in various occupations in order to earn their livelihood;[9] the rabbinate first emerged as a pro-

---

[7] *Eruvin* 65b.

[8] V. E. Frankl, *Man's Search for Meaning* (Boston: Beacon Press, 1992), pp. 169 f.

[9] Some of the references to well-known Talmudic sages as craftsmen or laborers are as follows: *Yoma* 35b (Hillel); *Shabbat* 31a (Shammai); *Megillah* 17b, Rashi (R. Simeon ha-Pakoli); *Shabbat* 49a (R. Yosi b. Halafta); *Berakhot* 28a (R. Joshua); *Ta'anit* 23a (Abba Hilkiah); *Pesahim* 113b (R. Hanina

fession in the Middle Ages. Yet, work was looked upon as something necessary, not an autonomous virtue. There are values that transcend that of work, such as the study of Torah. R. Simeon b. Yohai exposed an apparent contradiction between two Scriptural verses. In Deuteronomy (11:14), we read that we are to gather in our corn and oil and wine, implying that we are to do the work. In Isaiah (61:5) the promise is given to the "mourners of Zion" that strangers will tend their flocks and foreigners till their soil. How do we resolve the contradiction? The verse in Isaiah refers to the times the Israelites perform the will of God, the one in Deuteronomy to when they fail to perform His will.[10] Work is thus a necessity, not a blessing.[11]

However, to skip a whole period of history, the desire for leisure time (other than for the study of Torah) did not win the unrestrained enthusiasm of Jewish thinkers. Saadiah Gaon, in developing his theory of character on the Platonic model, which requires a well-rounded personality fulfilling all potentialities in harmony, and which abjures one-sidedness, speaks of the excessive striving for "rest" (which is essentially the same as leisure) as one such one-sided aberration. Granting that leisure is necessary for physical and mental recovery, and is the aim of religion as well—witness the Sabbath and holidays—it nevertheless is a vain and empty goal if taken by and for itself. It has meaning only as the aftermath of strenuous exertion and hence is ancillary to work but can never replace it. Taken without work, it is mere laziness, and the consequences of idleness need not be belabored. Yet, Saadiah recognizes that it is not quite so simple, not so black-and-white. In his last comment on the subject, he acknowledges that it is natural to find the soul inclining towards rest or leisure, because the Creator must have implanted it there, since Scripture considers it a premonition or anticipation of the serenity and tranquility which will characterize eternal life.[12] The eschatological note rescues leisure from faring any worse at the hands of Saadiah.

Leisure and the God Idea

It is fair to say, I believe, that Judaism takes the middle road, staying clear of either extreme. If we take the idea of *imago Dei* seriously, then it is legitimate to prescribe for the human "image" what holds true for the divine Creator; anthropology summarizes theology. The Jewish conception of God rejected the full implications of both the Aristotelian and the Neo-Platonic conceptions. Aristotle's Prime Mover was not a living God; He was impersonal, eternally introverted, unrelated, indeed, catatonically incapable of relationship. He was, as a distinguished philosopher of history has called him, an "eternal paralytic."[13] The God of Aristotle was one who never created, never worked, was always at rest and in leisure—on a perpetual and infinite vacation—as He contemplated Himself for all eternity. The Neo-Platonic God, however, created, but He created because He had to. Emanationism denied divine freedom. God emanated existence because it was in His nature to do so, and not as the result of a free choice. This Deity is an unceasing worker, a slave of His own creativity. He is a God who never takes a vacation, a God who knows no rest or leisure. The God of the Bible was neither the one nor the other—or, perhaps, both the one and the other. A God of freedom, He both "worked" and "rested," created and ceased creating. The pattern of work and leisure for man, affirming both in correct proportion, is an act of *imitatio Dei*.

Man needs both. Without work, he lacks self-approval and an opportunity for the catharsis of his aggressive instincts. Without leisure, his emotions are starved, his

---

and R. Oshaiah); and many others. Other statements revealing a positive orientation to labor include: *Avot* 1:10, 2:2; *Kiddushin* 29b, 82a; *Gittin* 67b; *Nedarim*, 49b, *Sanhedrin* 29a.

10 *Berakhot* 35b. The resolution by the Talmud is somewhat problematical; see Maharsha, *Hiddushei Aggadot*, ad loc. However, see R. Zadok ha-Kohen of Lublin, *Peri Zaddik* (to *Lekh Lekha*).

11 Cf. *Eruvin* 13b. It is erroneous to conclude, however, that the Bible considered this necessity for labor as a curse, because Adam was punished by having to earn his bread by the sweat of his brow (Gen. 3:17-19). The meaning of these verses is that the work will not be rewarding, that the labor will be disproportionate to the prize. Adam was originally placed in the Garden of Eden "to work it and keep it" (Gen. 2:15), implying the naturalness, as it were, of work.

12 *Sefer Emunot ve'Deot* 10:16.

13 H. A. Wolfson, *The Philosophy of Spinoza*, (Cambridge, Mass.: Harvard University Press, 1948), II, p. 346 f.

selfhood stunted, his identity diminished.[14] "Study [of Torah] unaccompanied by work must ultimately fail and bring on sin."[15]

The Holiness of Time

A more direct approach to the construction of an ethic of leisure would be through a consideration of the value Judaism places on time. For leisure means greater availability of time, and time is man's most precious possession. The drama of existence in Judaism is essentially temporal. The encounter between man and God is captured not so much in holy places as in sacred moments. A number of writers have emphasized the priority that Judaism grants to time over space: from Jewish theologians, especially Abraham Joshua Heschel who has approached it both poetically and philosophically; to Christian theologians, such as Harvey Cox, who, in his *The Secular City*, recognized the concept of *sæculum* against *mundus* as the Biblical conceptual framework; and Jewish historians such as Salo Baron, who begins his monumental work with attention to the preference of Judaism for the historical over the agricultural-geographical explanations of the festivals. In this they are no doubt correct. The Halakhah offers ample support for this thesis. Some forms of *kedushat ha-zeman* (holiness of time) are unconditional, though others are not. Thus, while the holidays are dependent upon the calendar, which must be determined and sanctified by the Jewish court acting on behalf of the Israelite people, the holiness of Sabbath remains absolute and unconditional. Its sanctity is promulgated by God, not by man. Its designated time cannot, therefore, be changed by any human agency. *Kedushat ha-makom* (holiness of space), contrariwise, is always conditioned upon human agency. A synagogue is holy only because people pray there. A Torah scroll is sacred only if the scribe's intentions were pure and thoughts holy while writing. Even the Talmudists, who maintain that the sanctity of the Holy Land is enduring and can never be abrogated, agree that initially its sanctity required the act of *kiddush*, of dedication or sanctification by human beings. The holiness of time was fixed even before Sinai: the Sabbath was decreed at Marah. The holiness of place was undetermined even after Sinai. "To the place which I will show thee" is how God refers to the Temple site in the Bible. Holiness is more a temporal than a spatial quality. The event has a greater claim on *kedushah* than does locale. One may conceivably live a whole life in one room and never have access to a holy place. However, one cannot live a week without experiencing, or being subject to, the holiness of time.

What is sacred, however, can be desecrated. If time is precious, then its misuse is a calamity. Danger is always the natural concomitant of opportunity. It is this ambivalence, this attitude of risk towards time, that must characterize our approach to leisure, which is simply available time. It is good or bad, creative or destructive, all according to our own orientation towards it.

Sabbath Rest

Now, if time is the concept which serves as the criterion for an ethic of leisure (or, more precisely, a theology of leisure), and the Sabbath is the expression *par excellence* of the holiness of time, then it is important to search in the complex of Sabbath itself for some closer identification of leisure. The pattern of "six days shalt thou work" and the seventh day as a Sabbath does indeed represent a pattern for work-leisure. Upon further investigation, we may find one specific concept that not only directly speaks of leisure on the Sabbath, but that is paradigmatic for leisure in general, and that may serve as a model for an ethic of leisure. That concept is *menuhah*, Sabbath "rest."

The central precept of *Shabbat* is, of course, the refraining from indulging in *melakhah*, in creative changes in nature, the halakhic definition of "work."[16] A corollary, however, is "rest." The Bible, in the second version of the Ten Commandments, requires observance of the Sabbath "that thy manservant and thy maid-servant may rest as well as thou."[17] This means that on *Shabbat* one must not work in the ordinary, lay sense of the term: not go to offices or schools or stores. Apparently, this resting is a purely negative act. It is a vacation, a

14 Barzun, *Science*, p. 258.

15 *Avot* 2:2.

16 For the implications of the prohibition of *melakha*, see Chap. VI. of this book.

17 Deut. 5:14.

day off. However, that this is not at all so may be seen from the significance of *menuhah* as emphasized throughout the Sabbath liturgy. Three times we pray, "God and God of our fathers, be pleased with our rest (*menuhah*) . . . ," as though *menuhah* were a form of *avodat ha-Shem*, as are sacrifices. Obviously, we are not dealing with a mere self-indulgent vacation, anthropomorphically invoking God's maternal approval of our concern with our health. The *Minhah* prayer, which celebrates the qualities of *menuhah*, concludes its central portion on this note: " . . . and by means of [Israel's] *menuhah*, they sanctify Thy Name." Sabbath rest is thus nothing less than a vehicle for the observance of Judaism's most illustrious precept, *kiddush ha-Shem*, "the sanctification of the divine Name." But to "sanctify the Name" means to act in such a manner, generally before gentiles, that glory will redound to Judaism and enhance the Name (i.e., reputation) of the God of Israel in the world.[18] Obviously we are dealing with something far more fundamental than just taking a day off from work every week. There lies within *menuhah* a concept that Jews must teach to all humankind (unlike the halakhic observance of the prohibition of *melakhah,* which was covenanted only for Jews), and the appreciation of which will add to the glory of God and Torah. We are dealing, in other words, with a Jewish ideal of *universal* import and relevance. As such, its implications must extend beyond that of relaxation.

The positive quality of *menuhah* is revealed in the talmudic aggadah concerning the translation of the Torah into Greek, the Septuagint.[19] One of the changes agreed to independently by each of the 70 translators concerned the verse: ". . . on the seventh day God finished His work which He made; and He rested on the seventh day."[20] If God *finished* His work on the seventh day, that implies that He worked into the Sabbath day. Hence, to avoid this error, they translated, ". . . on the *sixth* day God finished his work . . ." Now this may serve to clarify the problem in Greek; what, however, of the original Hebrew? The Rabbis answer with a parable which indicates that the culmination of all creation was created on the Sabbath day: *menuhah*, rest.[21] Obviously the definition of "rest" or leisure is not mere passivity or time off, simple relaxation, but something far more significant and novel, something which requires *creation* and that itself is the culmination of all previous creations.

This the Greeks did not understand. The pagan mentality could not grasp that *menuhah* has positive content. Even Hellenistic-Jews were misled as to this interpretation of *menuhat Shabbat*. They understood the Sabbath as an opportunity to refresh oneself the better to be able to work the next six days—almost a capitalistic dispensation: I will let you take one day off, but get a good rest so that you can produce more the following week.

Leisure as the Purpose of Creation

However, the authentic Jewish view is not that the Sabbath was created for the six days, thus reducing *menuhah* to the character of a vacation, but that the six days were created for the sake of the Sabbath; that, as indicated, the *menuhah* was itself the apex of the order of creation. The point is corroborated by Rabbi Don Isaac Abrabanel, the great Spanish exegete and thinker, in his commentary on the very first word of the second chapter of Genesis. We read, *Va-yekhulu ha-shamayim ve'ha-aretz*—"the heaven and the earth were finished." *Va-yekhulu* is translated as "finished." That is not its only meaning. *Va-yekhulu* also comes from the word *takhlit* or "purpose." In English, as in Latin and Greek, the same double meaning occurs. Thus, the word "end" has two meanings: conclusion and also purpose, as in "means and ends." Similarly, in Hebrew the word *takhlit* means both conclusion and purpose. Hence, *va-yekhulu ha-shamayim ve'ha-aretz* not only means "heaven and earth were finished," it also means "heaven and earth attained their *takhlit*, their purpose." That *takhlit* or purpose was *Shabbat*. So do we say in our Friday night prayer: "You sanctified the seventh day, *takhlit ma'aseh shamayim va'aretz*, as the purpose of the creation of heaven and earth." The prooftext follows: *Va-yekhulu ha-shamayim* . . . .

18 See my article on "*Kiddush* and *Hillul Hashem*," in the *Encyclopedia Judaica, 1974 Yearbook*, pp. 194–206.

19 *Megillah* 9a.

20 Gen. 2:2.

21 Genesis Rabba 10:10, according to Rashi in his commentary to the Pentateuch. See *Matnot Kehunah*, ad loc.

The same perspective on the relation of Sabbath to the workweek is indicated by the medieval German mystic, Rabbi Yehudah He-Hasid: "One who goes to sleep on the Sabbath should not say, 'Let us sleep so that we can do our work when the Sabbath is over,' but rather let him say, 'Let us rest, for today is the Sabbath.'"[22] An eminent talmudist of the nineteenth century, commenting on the variation between the Decalogue as recorded in Exodus and the one recorded in Deuteronomy, maintains that *zakhor*, "remember" the Sabbath day, means that during the entire week we are to put aside choice provisions for the Sabbath; and *shamor*, "observe" or "keep" the Sabbath day, is its negative—that we must not fail to lay up supplies for the Sabbath during the workweek. Both intend, therefore, that the six days are in preparation for the seventh. According to this idea, we understand the relevance of the verse "Six days shall you labor and do all your work, and the seventh shall be a Sabbath for the Lord your God." Work during the six days becomes a duty and a virtue because it is a preparation for the seventh day. *Shabbat* is the purpose of the whole week.[23]

Clearly, then, the more genuinely Jewish conception is not that we have *menuhah* on the Sabbath in order the better to work on the other days, but we work in order to rest, in order to participate in *menuhah*.

What is the content of *menuhah*, such that it makes *Shabbat* the purpose of the rest of the week and comprises the universal dimension (as an act of the sanctification of the Name) of Judaism's most distinctive religious institution?

The answer, I believe, lies in this. *Issur melakhah*, the prohibition of labor, implies the cessation of our activities imposed by us as creative personalities upon the natural world. However, authentic *menuhah* requires that on the Sabbath we direct these creative changes not onto nature but onto ourselves, spiritually and intellectually. *Menuhah* is not a suspension of our creative energies for one day of the week, but a refocusing of our creative talents upon ourselves. The difference between the prohibited *melakhah* and the recommended *menuhah* lies not in the *fact of* creativity, but in the *object* of one's creative powers: oneself or one's environment, the inner world or the outer world.

Hence, *menuhah* is now seen as religiously enforced leisure, a model for all leisure activity, defining leisure, optimally, as creativity turned in on oneself.

The Misuse of Leisure

With the above in mind, we may now turn to an analysis of the forms of leisure, in the hope that this classification will offer us the beginnings of a more detailed Jewish ethic of leisure. In Hebrew, we find not one but three terms for leisure, each of which has a different value and different signification within the context of *menuhah*.

The first of these is *sehok*, or play. The term is frequently used in rabbinic literature as a euphemism for the three cardinal crimes: unchastity, idolatry, even murder, in the sense of tormenting a victim. *Sehok* is the *misuse* of leisure. It indicates a debilitating kind of idleness, a useless and degenerate play. So, when two English researchers discovered that the chief diversion of young English people is increased sexual itineracy,[24] they confirmed what the Jewish Sages warned of many centuries ago. "*Sehok* is primarily sexual immorality," said the Rabbis.[25] The exact definition of *sehok* was a matter of dispute between two first-century Sages, R. Eliezer and R. Simeon b. Gamaliel.[26] The problem concerned the enforced idleness (*battalah)* of a housewife, either because of an abundance of servants or because her husband vowed not to benefit from her personal labors. Both Rabbis agreed that the situation was intolerable. R. Eliezer maintained that even if she had a hundred maids, she ought to do some work in the household, "for idleness leads to *zimah*, unchastity." R. Simeon, dealing with the case where the husband vowed to abstain from benefiting from his wife's work, decreed that he must divorce her and grant her *ketubah* (dowry

22 *Sefer Hasidim*, ed. R. Margoliot, Jerusalem, Mosad Harav Kook 1957, p. 228, #226.

23 R. Naphtali Zevi Judah Berlin, *Ha'amek Davar* to Deut. 5:12.

24 B. S. Rowntree and G. R. Lavers, in *English Life and Leisure* (London, New York: Longmans, Green, 1952).

25 *Tanna de-vei Eliyahu Rabbah* 13.

26 *Ketubbot* 59b.

and settlement), "for idleness leads to *shi'amum.*" This last word, in modern Hebrew, usually means "boredom"; in all probability, that is its original meaning in the Mishnah. Soncino translates it "idiocy," which is a shade too harsh a rendition of Rashi's translation of the word as *shiga'on*. Maimonides' translation of *shi'amum* as *behalah*, which means a kind of frightened confusion, would locate the term somewhere in between the two. Indeed, the Sages anticipated a modern discovery: boredom may lead to mental breakdown. The mind cannot long maintain its integrity if unoccupied and unstimulated. Moreover, boredom is the principal product of idleness. R. Simeon preferred divorce to idleness or misused leisure that can lead only to gross violation of the wife's psychological integrity.

According to the Talmud,[27] the difference between the two Tannaim occurs in a case where the wife spends her time at dog races and other such "leisure" activities. Here only R. Eliezer's stricture would apply, for the element of *zimah* or immorality may certainly enter into the situation. R. Simeon, however, would be lenient, because since there is not total idleness there is no danger of *shi'amum*. The Talmud decides in favor of the stricter opinion, that of R. Eliezer.

The *sehok*-misuse of leisure is thus objectionable both morally and psychologically. When there is nothing to do, you do what you ought not to do. One may add that the Rabbis knew this from a careful reading of history. They were no strangers to Imperial Rome and its social and moral patterns. In Rome, the day's work was usually done by noon or shortly thereafter, with the rest of the time spent in pleasure and amusement. More than half the days of the year were holidays. It is probably that the Rabbis saw a cause-and-effect relation between this excessive and misspent leisure and the immorality of Rome which they so deplored. The relation between *sehok and zimah* is all too obvious.

God's Rest

Turning now from *sehok* to the positive content of leisure, we find two words in Hebrew, both Sabbath-associated words. When the Torah described God as "resting," it says *shavat va-yinafash. Shavat* (He rested) is similar to the word *Shabbat*, and it means to refrain from work. *Shevitah* (the noun, which in contemporary Hebrew also means a strike) is a period in which we desist from work. The negative, passive aspect is immediately evident. The second word is *va-yinafash* (noun: *nofesh*). This signifies another form of leisure. *Va-yinafash* or *nofesh* comes from the word *nefesh*, the soul, the spirit.

Hence the concept of *menuhah* contains one or both of these ideas. The negative understanding of *menuhah* (or leisure) we may call *shevitah*, cessation of activity. The positive we may call *nofesh.*[28] (We are not using *shevitah* in a pejorative sense, because both of these signify proper uses of leisure.) Before proceeding to define more carefully the human significations of these

27 *Ketubbot* 61b.

28 This definition of *nofesh* (see further in text) seems to be belied by II Samuel 16:14, where we are told of King David and his people arriving weary: *va-yinafesh sham*, "and he rested there." At first glance, the word as here used has a purely physical connotation, as opposed to *ayefim*, tired. However, the verse must not be taken out of context: David's sagging morale was a result of his pursuit by his son Absalom, and his humiliation by Shimi. *Va-yinafesh* may then refer not so much to his physical fatigue as to his psychological rehabilitation after suffering indignities. The remaining verse, where *nofesh* is used in verbal form, is most enlightening. God gave the Sabbath, the Torah teaches (Exod. 23:12), so that thy ox and thy ass can *yanuah* (rest, from *menuhah)*, and so that the son of thy maidservant and the stranger may *va-yinafesh*. The concept of Sabbath rest is thus not the same for animal and for man. For animals the Sabbath achieves, maximally, *menuhah* (of the form *shevitah*), the kind of "leisure" that will free the animal from the enforced labor to which it is subjected by its human masters and will allow it to exercise its own "individuality," which in this case means to graze, drink, breathe, and fulfill its other biological functions without interference. One cannot, of course, speak of development and transformation with regard to an animal's self or character. With regard to humans, however, the Torah changes its terms. The structure of the sentence is parallelistic, in keeping with the biblical literary style, but that fact does not diminish the significance of the specific words used by the Bible. The "son of thy maidservant and the stranger" may also experience, on a human level, *menuhah* (of *shevitah*). However, Sabbath rest, the archetype for leisure time, has a more creative function for human beings: *nofesh*.

two terms, it is best to recall that although Sabbath observance need not be considered altogether an act of *imitatio Dei*, at least in the limited sense of the practice of *menuhah* it may be regarded as just that. Since the terms *shevitah* and *nofesh* are used of God in the biblical text, they must be understood in the first instance as divine attributes and then, *mutatis mutandis,* as categories of the human use of leisure.

Actually, not much change is required, and it will be seen that the definitions of *shevitah* and *nofesh* in Exodus 31:17 follow logically from their formulation as human categories. In the early part of Genesis, we find God appearing in three phases, two of them explicit. "In the beginning God created" initiates the period of God's creativity. Implied is a precreative phase in which God existed by Himself. The term *shavat va-yinafash* now indicates the transition from the second period to the third, from the creative phase to the postcreative. Here the two words *shevitah* and *nofesh* are both identical and divergent. They are identical in that His "rest" means a return to the first stage, equating the precreative and the postcreative phases *in regard to His creativity.* God steps out of His role as Creator. However, there is a difference. The creation itself introduces a new, dynamic element into the divine life. The universe, and the freedom He granted its intelligent creatures, implies an element of the unpredictable, of surprise and contingency.[29] This freedom, or contingency, is inextricably bound up with the idea that in withdrawing from the divine act of creation (*mi she-amar le-olam dai),* He gave man the mandate to continue the initial act of creation as an ongoing process. This is the new element in the total picture which makes the third phase of God's life different from the first and which, essentially, makes time and history irreversible. *Shevitah* implies the restoration of God, in relation to Himself, to the initial precreative phase. There are, from the point of view of *shevitah,* essentially only two chapters in the divine biography. *Nofesh* makes the third, postcreative stage qualitatively different from the first or precreative. God must now deal with man who is himself a creator, who continues the process initiated by God in His second phase. *Nofesh* is a characteristically theistic element. Deism could accept the concept of *shevitah*, for it would indicate a resignation by God from the material universe, an introversion and an abandonment of the world as though it has never existed. The concept of *nofesh*, however, posits an ongoing dialogue between the Creator, after His initial act, and His creature-creators. Only of a personal God can we say *va-yinafash.*[30]

Shevitah

Having suggested the content of the two terms as divine attributes, we may now turn to their meanings as human terms. *Shevitah* means that a man ceases his usual labors, and this respite from routine activity allows him to rediscover himself by emerging from the workweek. With man overinvolved in and overwhelmed by his set pattern of work, his dignity is threatened. He begins to identify himself by the functions he performs in society or family and turns him into an impersonal cipher, like a beast of burden that can be just as easily replaced by another function-bearing animal that happens to be technologically efficient. By disengaging from his environment with nature, with society, with business, man is permitted self-expression. His real "self" comes to the fore. He does not have to be busy taking notes or selling or buying or fighting. By means of *shevitah* on his Sabbath day of "rest," he can start expressing the essential self that lies within. *Shevitah* is thus the use of leisure to *restore* one's individuality in all its integrity. By pulling out of the routine of weekday involvement, I confront myself in order to find out who I am. Leisure helps me resolve my "identity crisis." By getting away from my normal activities, which harness me into the measured responses of a Pavlovian, completely deterministic way of acting during the week, my inner, original ego emerges; I can rediscover myself when I am taken out of the matrix of these challenges and the responses which are expected of me. In this sense, *shevitah* exploits the limits of my character and my potentialities. (As we shall see shortly, it *exploits* them but it cannot *expand* them.) It is the desirable result of available time not wasted in *sehok.*

In practical terms, leisure is a time for games. Leisure refers not only to *time*, but also to the *nature* of the

29 See end of chap. 1 in this book.

30 See further on this, chap. VI in this book.

activity.[31] You can drive a car and driving is part of your work, because you are a cabdriver; but you can drive and consider it leisure. You can just think and regard that thinking as work if you are a professor or a student; but you can also think and feel it is a delight and a joy—whether you are a taxi driver in the one case or an intellectual in the other. Leisure is a game activity in the highest sense. We place a person in a new environment, in new conditions, allow him to bring out unsuspected skills that were heretofore latent in him, to express himself in new ways, whether of esthetics or athletics or any other way to which he is unaccustomed during the week.

Nofesh

From here, we go to the next step, *nofesh. Nofesh* is more than self-*discovery;* it is the use of leisure for self-*transformation.* Paradoxically, it is in a sense more passive than *shevitah.* Instead of activity for the purpose of self-*expression,* it may require a certain kind of personal, inner silence in which you make yourself available for a higher *impression.* It is the incorporation of the transcendent rather than the articulation of the imminent. You try to respond to something that comes from without, from above. *Nofesh* means not to fulfill yourself but to go outside yourself, to rise beyond yourself; not to *discover* your identity, but rather to *create* a new and better identity. *Nofesh* requires of us that we take our creative talents, which during the week are applied to impersonal nature or unengaged society, and now turn them inward and create a new, real self. This is the inner and deeper meaning of *menuhah:* it is *re-creation*, not relaxation.

Tradition speaks of an interesting phenomenon concerning the Sabbath. During the week, everyone has a *neshamah*, a soul. However, on *Shabbat*, we receive a *neshamah yeterah*, an "additional soul." This suggests an undeveloped facet of personality, a spiritual dimension, of which we remain unaware in the normal course of events. On *Shabbat* (in the *nofesh* sense of a *menuhah),* we are given the time to enrich ourselves by developing or creating this spiritual dimension. Hence, whereas *shevitah* implies the development of a latent, preexistent talent, *nofesh* means the creation of a novelty within the personality, bringing in something new, transforming the self by growing into a *neshamah yeterah.*

The question is how is this done? The act of *shevitah*, of expressing oneself, is something in which psychologists and social workers are expert. The more difficult challenge is: how do you transcend yourself, how do you effect *nofesh*?

Doing Nothing

Perhaps the first answer should be, do nothing. By simply removing the distractions and the obsession with work that chokes off creativity during the week, man's innate propensity for self-creativity may come to express itself quite naturally. When Alexander the Great asked Diogenes whether he could do anything for him, the famed philosopher replied, "Just stand out of my light." Hasidim of the great R. Nahman of Bratslav used to set aside an hour a day known as the Dead Hour, in which all business would be set aside and nothing structured would be permitted, in order to allow the repressed soul to come to the fore; dead to the world and alive to oneself. *Shevitah* itself may lead quite effortlessly, at least with some people, to a *nofesh*-use of *menuhah*. Perhaps someday we shall know how to heighten creativity. Until then, one of the best things we can do for creative men and women is to "stand out of their light."[32]

The Study of Torah

Second, and more important, Judaism provides its classical answer to the ideal *nofesh*-utilization of leisure time. It is the intellectual way: the study of Torah. "The Sabbaths were given to Israel in order that they might study Torah."[33] The Sabbath, both as a specific day and as the model for an ethic of leisure, is the occasion for study.

31 "Leisure is the state of being free of everyday necessity. . . . The man in this state is at leisure and whatever he does is done leisurely"—Sebastian Degrazia, in *Of Time, Work, and Leisure.*

32 J. W. Gardner, *No Easy Victories* (New York: Harper and Row, 1968), p. 50.

33 J. T. *Shabbat* 15:3.

The ancient Greeks regarded the use of leisure for contemplation as a central element in their culture. The Greek word for leisure, *schole*, is the origin (via the Latin *schola*) of our word "school." In the period of Socrates, Plato and Aristotle, the idea of leisure meant being engaged in something desirable for its own sake—the composition of music or poetry, conversation—and above all it meant the exercise of the speculative faculty and the cultivation of the mind. Contemplation was for Plato and Aristotle the way to truth, and the *via contemplativa* was therefore cherished more than the *via activa*.

Modern civilization, however, is too action oriented to adopt the peripatetic ethic as a way of life for leisure expression.[34] Study is more active than contemplation as such, and hence more accessible to it. (Nevertheless, we must not underestimate the value of leisure for education, not only as simply available time, but also as a necessary component of the educational process. Scott Buchanan has pointed out that Socrates was not only a noisy questioner, but also a great *brooder.* "This is a good description of teaching: brooding, almost in the literal sense, the way a hen broods over her chickens."[35])

More important, intellectual development has never been enough for the Jew; it must be informed with moral purpose. Such moral-oriented study is what is meant by *talmud torah.*[36]

For the Jewish tradition, the study of the Torah is the highest value; it outweighs all other commandments.[37] The moral quality of Torah study is indirect. One need not study only with the specific intention of knowing how to practice, although one must never study with the intention that he will *not* carry it out in practice.[38] It is a most unusual idea in the history of religion; an entire people is commanded to study not only so that they may know what to believe or how to observe, not only so that they may survive and perpetuate themselves, but also because study itself has an innate value, because it is by itself the supreme value for which other things are propaedeutic, only means leading to this end. Torah is thus, primarily, an intellectual activity, but one informed with moral purpose and infused with religious meaning. So important is the study of Torah that one scholar of the second century, R. Ishmael, explains that only because the Bible explicitly tells us, "if ye shall hearken diligently unto my commandments . . . I will give the rain of your land in its season . . . that *thou mayest gather in thy corn and thy wine and thine oil,*"[39] are we permitted to work during the week. If not for this verse, a man would never be permitted to work, to "gather in" his "corn and wine and oil." Why not? Because he would be obliged to do only one thing all his life, namely, to study Torah, "to meditate in it by day and by night,"[40] For Jews, the study of Torah is not something you do when you take time out of your "normal" activity. Rather, what we are wont to call our "normal" activity is the time that we take off, legitimately or illegitimately, from what normative Judaism considers our major activity, the study of Torah. That is why the Talmud speaks of the need for a special dispensation to engage in work other than Torah.

Constancy of Study

Study was considered not a dispensable virtue, but one that if one fails to do it, one is guilty. *Bittul Torah*, the neglect of study, when circumstances allow study to take place, is a cardinal sin. Thus, the Rabbis taught that one ought not to engage in frivolous conversation with a woman lest such flirtation lead him to neglect his studies, and this will cause him to "inherit Gehinnom."[41] For this reason, the Halakha regards man's normal state that of preoccupation in the study of Torah; every other activity is a temporary distraction. Thus, although every

34 See G. C. Taylor, "Work and Leisure in the Age of Automation," in *Main Currents in Modern Thought* (May-June 1966), p. 118.

35 *Embers of the World: Conversations with Scott Buchanan*, ed H. Wofford, Jr. (Santa Barbara, Cal.: The Center for the Study of Democratic Institutions, 1970), p. 50.

36 See chaps. III, VI, and VII of my *Torah Lishmah: Torah for Torah's Sake in the Works of R. Hayyim of Volozhin and His Contemporaries* (Hoboken, N.J.: Ktav, 1989), Excursus I.

37 *Pe'ah* 1:1.

38 N. 35 above, and see chap. VIII, "Scholarship and Piety."

39 Deut. 11:13-14.

40 *Berakhot* 35b.

41 *Avot* 1:5.

other blessing pronounced over the performance of a commandment must be followed immediately by the act of *mitzvah* so that if one is interrupted between blessing and performance with some profane activity it must be recited again, this does not hold true for the blessings recited in the morning over the study of Torah.[42] The commandment to study Torah is thus total; it applies to all times and takes precedence over all other activities.[43] This general principle is expressed programmatically by Maimonides,[44] who divides the day into twelve hours—three for working and nine for studying. This idea may appear unusual to moderns because of its time allotment, but it is an illustration of the fact that there is in Torah enough material to occupy a man's mind for a full lifetime, and that Judaism sees Torah study as the Jew's major occupation. Because it is also a *mitzvah*, or morally infused intellectual labor, it is more than innately worthless, time-filling "plowing of parched fields," a sort of "make-work" scheme for idle minds. Rather it is the kind of pursuit that can change a man's life and redefine for him, progressively, his place in the universe and his relations with his God.

We must attempt to find leisure expression not only in the standard ways to which we are normally accustomed, through games, skills, esthetics, art, song, choreography—although these too must never be overlooked, for these are legitimate as the *shevitah* aspect of *menuhah*. Indeed, simple relaxation can have religious significance. Maimonides[45] tells us that upon arising each morning a man "must know before whom he lies." However, we also must progress beyond this and find an outlet in the most creative activity known to Israel, namely, study.

Leisurely Study

Now, when I say that *nofesh* requires that we use leisure for Jewish learning, I do not mean necessarily scholarship of the professional kind, or the kind of education our children get in school, which is, under the best circumstances, routinized. Perhaps we may have to devise a form of game-oriented study, something I believe is already available on the Internet. We mentioned earlier that the same activity can be of the nature of work or that of a game. In the history of Jewish scholarship, there is a long story of reaction during the last three hundred years or so against the Talmudic methodology called *pilpul*, subtle dialectics (pejoratively called "hair-splitting"), the tendency to pull together disparate ideas from all corners of the earth and build difficult, abstract, and abstruse conceptual structures. Those who opposed *pilpul* believed in straight and unencumbered analysis. One would be hard put to find anyone reckless enough to venture a defense, let alone advocacy, of *pilpul* today. In truth, *pilpul* has been unfairly maligned, for this is the way the intellect "plays," the way the mind indulges in its delightful games and exercises. I can lug cartons of dresses up seven stories and not like what I am doing, but if I go to the gym and I do the same kind of exercise playing basketball, I enjoy it. Similarly, the mind can think along straight analytic terms and doing so is part of its "work," but when it relaxes and spins off ideas in the stimulating patterns of dialectic, the process is a happy game, a leisure-type thinking. Perhaps we have to rediscover that technique for our own times, especially for the highest kind of leisure activity, *nofesh*.

Conclusion

Surely, the finest expression of the quest for leisure as the fundamental element in Jewish aspiration comes from the closing paragraphs of Maimonides' immortal code, the *Mishneh Torah*,[46] where leisure and its proper uses are portrayed as the essence of the Messianic vision:

> The Sages and Prophets did not hope for the coming of the Messiah in order that they might rule over the world, or have dominion over the other nations, or that they might be glorified by other

42 *Tosafot*, s.v. *she-kavar*, *Berakhot* 11b, and see *Shulhan Arukh, Orah Hayyim* 47, esp. *Turei Zahav* (8). R. Jair Bacharach (Responsa *Havvot Yair*) considers the earning of a livelihood as an indirect form of "engaging" in Torah, since it is a means of allowing study to continue; hence the verb *la'asok*, rather than *lilmod* in the formula of the blessing.

43 See my article on the study of Torah in *Ha-Pardes*, vol. 28, no. 11.

44 *Hilkhot Talmud Torah* 1:12.

45 *Guide for the Perplexed* 3:51.

46 *Hilkhot Melakhim* 12:4, 5.

> peoples, or in order to eat and drink—but that they be free to engage in the study of Torah and its wisdom, without anyone to oppress them or distract them, so that they might thereby deserve the life of eternity.
>
> In that time [of Messiah] there will be neither famine nor war, neither envy nor competition. Goodness will be available in great abundance, precious things as commonplace as dust. And the business of the entire world will be only to know God. Therefore will Israelites be great sages, knowing the hidden things, and comprehending the knowledge of their Creator, insofar as humans are able. As it is said, "for the earth will be full of the knowledge of the Lord as the waters fill the sea."

Faith and Doubt: Studies in Traditional Jewish Thought, 3rd ed. (Jersey City, NJ: Ktav, 2006), ch. 7, pp. 184–207
Reprinted by permission of the publisher, KTAV Publishing House, Inc., © 2006 Rabbi Norman Lamm

The Shabbat Experiment: Limiting or Liberating?

by **Lisa Sugarman**

So consider this (and I mean really take a minute and think this through): No e-mails. No telephones (yes, that includes cells). No TV. No iPods or laptops. No driving. No radio. No electronics whatsoever. Period. For 24 hours. Imagine giving up everything with an on-off switch. Could you do it? And why would you want to? Would it restrict or release you?

Well, a few months ago in this column I opened my big mouth and admitted to the entire town of Marblehead that every once in awhile I fantasize about chucking all the devices and gadgets in my life just so I could remember what real life feels like. Not permanently, just sort of a reboot for the soul.

Ever since I put it out there it's been on my mind. I wanted to make it happen, but the timing never seemed to be right. Plus, I'd be lying if I said I wasn't a little intimidated by the thought of giving everything up. It sounded great in theory, but when you think about the actual ramifications it ends up looking like a pretty outrageous idea, especially considering how most of us live our lives day to day. We're constantly either refreshing, updating or checking something, and if we're not doing that we're chauffeuring someone somewhere or making a call or using a gadget that's supposed to make the quality of our life better.

But does it?

So when the e-mail came in from my daughter's Hebrew school, Chabad, a few weeks ago inviting people to take The Shabbat Challenge I knew someone was sending me a sign that this was my shot. So I took it.

For anyone who doesn't know what's involved in "keeping Shabbat," it means that every week, from sundown on Friday to sundown on Saturday, Jews all over the world unplug. Fifty-two weeks a year. And for those 24 hours, they stay unplugged. They eat, they rest, they reflect, many pray, they spend time with family and friends, and they recover physically and spiritually from their week.

Chabad picked the weekend in late January, and they spelled out the rules: driving, not OK; board games, OK; power, not OK; walking, OK (it's a long list). So for one, full day my family would flip the master breaker and go completely dark. And we decided that if we were going to do it we were going to go all in, which for a Reformed family who practices the most liberal form of Judaism that was WAY in. The fact that it was temporary definitely took the edge off. But it was still intimidating no matter how you looked at it.

So we picked which lights would stay on for the full 24 hours; we unscrewed the light bulb in the fridge so it didn't go on when we opened the door; we cooked everything before sundown on Friday night; we unplugged every device; we picked out all our board games and books. And then it came.

And it was painless.

Without really even noticing, Shabbat settled in and the vibe of our whole house shifted. It was a quietude that was defined by the fact that we knew it would last, even for only a day. All the pressure was gone. The anticipation of rushing or fussing or preparing had disappeared. Once we committed to the challenge, everything was surprisingly easy. And it became shockingly obvious that we all carry around a very misplaced sense of urgency—when there's actually very little that we can't do without.

My brother-in-law gave me the best analogy right before sunset. He said, "There's a beauty created in the quietude of the Sabbath that's difficult to describe or capture otherwise. You need to focus on that quietude rather than on the things you might otherwise be doing."

Then he put it in terms that I could really understand. He said that my sister-in-law made some amazing salsa the other night and also some homemade tortilla chips with a hint of lime. He said he noticed the hint of lime when he ate the chips without the salsa but then forgot all about it once he started dipping into the fiery salsa. After the salsa was gone, he said he started eating the chips dry again and realized how much he liked that subtle hint of lime that was invisible in the context of the salsa. He said the same thing goes for the Sabbath. Enjoy removing the noise to find the quietude that's always there waiting to be revealed.

OK, so we may have bent the rules a little and taught our girls how to play Texas Hold'em to pass the time (gambling can't exactly be promoted on Shabbat, but it's a game, and games are OK). But since flexibility is the real root of Reformed Judaism we cut ourselves some slack.

We also stayed in our pajamas until 4 in the afternoon, getting dressed only to walk down to Preston Beach to see the sunset. And by that point, even the sound of the cars on the road seemed a little intrusive because we were used to such a comfortable quiet. It was a little surreal, at least for me, feeling so far away from home even though I was right there—probably because everything felt so different.

In the end, the 24 hours flew by and we all ended up with much more than we bargained for. It gave us a clarity and peace that would be tough to duplicate any other way. And it changed each one of us somehow, too. My girls said they were shocked at how fast the time went by and how "not boring" the experience was. And my husband, who would sleep with an earpiece in if he could, said he felt amazingly liberated to shut everything down and just walk away. And for him that's big.

Now this doesn't mean we're going all in and making this a weekly thing, but it definitely gave us all something to think about. It showed us that there's a place we can always go to get away—far away, like a "staycation" for the spirit. And those are in right now, aren't they?

So it's ironic: After all that, the real challenge was letting the Sabbath go. Who knew?

The Marblehead Reporter, Feb. 10, 2010
Reprinted by permission of the publisher

Lesson 2

Beginning with the End in Mind

Introduction

Are you a spontaneous person? Do you like diving straight into the action? Or do you prefer spending your time thinking and preparing your next move?

Abraham Lincoln said, "If I had eight hours to chop down a tree, I'd spend six sharpening my axe."

In this lesson, we will look more closely at how we prepare for Shabbat, and how those preparations impact the way we personally experience this special day.

Why Prepare?
Introduction

Text 1

One can never speak enough of what Shabbat was like in the shtetl—and what it did for its inhabitants. The Shabbat helped people endure the other six days of the week, often gray and dark, heavy with sorrow and anxiety. Hence the waiting for Shabbat, which actually began much earlier. Thursday evening or early Friday morning, the housewife would already be busy preparing the hallah, gefilte fish, and cholent, the traditional elements of a Shabbat meal in the shtetl. The white tablecloth, the white shirt: everything had to be ready. . . . We couldn't wait for her arrival.

In the stores, business was conducted with haste. Sellers and customers were equally in a hurry to go home. Men would go to the ritual bath, the *mikvah*, then dress and prepare to be worthy of welcoming the Shabbat, already on the horizon. The first to spot her would be the beadle, the shammash: he would go around [to] stores and homes shouting *"Yidden, greit zicht tzu Shabbes!"*—Jews, ready yourselves for the Sabbath! Or a variation on the same theme: *"Yidden, s'is bald Shabbes oif der velt!"*—Jews, it's almost Sabbath in the world!

Elie Wiesel, *Wise Men and Their Tales* [New York: Schocken Books, 2003], p. 328

Elie Wiesel (1928–). Professor of the humanities at Boston University. Born in Sighet, Transylvania, at the age of fifteen he was deported by the Nazis to Auschwitz. Wiesel is the author of more than 40 books of fiction and non-fiction, including the acclaimed memoir *Night*, which has been published in more than 30 languages. In 1986, Wiesel won the Nobel Prize for Peace. Soon after, Wiesel and his wife established the Elie Wiesel Foundation for Humanity. For his literary and human rights activities he has received numerous awards including the Presidential Medal of Freedom and the U.S. Congressional Gold Medal.

Pragmatic Considerations

Text 2a

מי שטרח בערב שבת יאכל בשבת, מי שלא טרח בערב שבת מהיכן יאכל בשבת.

תלמוד בבלי, עבודה זרה ג,א

One who labors before Shabbat shall eat on Shabbat;

But if one does not labor before Shabbat, from whence shall he eat?

Talmud, Avodah Zarah 3a

מי שטרח בערב שבת יאכל בשבת

Text 2b

איזה הוא עונג . . . שצריך לתקן תבשיל שמן ביותר ומשקה מבושם לשבת הכל לפי ממונו של אדם, וכל המרבה בהוצאת שבת ובתיקון מאכלים רבים וטובים הרי זה משובח.

רמב״ם, הלכות שבת ל,ז

Rabbi Moshe ben Maimon (1135–1204). Better known as Maimonides or by the acronym Rambam; born in Cordoba, Spain. After the conquest of Cordoba by the Almohads, he fled Spain and eventually settled in Cairo, Egypt. There, he became the leader of the Jewish community and served as court physician to the vizier of Egypt. His rulings on Jewish law are considered integral to the formation of halachic consensus. He is most noted for authoring the *Mishneh Torah*, an encyclopedic arrangement of Jewish law, and for his philosophical work, *Guide for the Perplexed*.

What is meant by delight? . . . A person must prepare a particularly sumptuous dish and a pleasantly flavored beverage for Shabbat—commensurate with one's financial means. The more one spends for Shabbat and the more good food one prepares, the more praiseworthy it is.

Maimonides, *Mishneh Torah*, Laws of Shabbat 30:7

Text 2c

יש לטעום בערב שבת את התבשילין שנעשו לשבת.

קיצור שולחן ערוך עב,ז

Rabbi Shlomoh Ganzfried (1804–1886). Hungarian rabbi and authority on Jewish law. Best known for his *Kitsur Shulchan Aruch*, a user-friendly summary of Rabbi Yosef Caro's *Shulchan Aruch* and the observations of subsequent halachic commentators. This highly acclaimed work quickly became a classic, a mainstay in every Jewish home. Rabbi Ganzfried was born in Uzhhorod (today part of Ukraine), and after being orphaned at a very young age was adopted by Uzhhorod's chief rabbi, Rabbi Tzvi Hirsh Heller. Eventually Rabbi Ganzfried was appointed *dayan*—chief rabbinical magistrate—of Uzhhorod, a position he retained until his passing.

On Friday, it is proper for one to taste the foods that were cooked in honor of Shabbat.

Rabbi Shlomoh Ganzfried, *Kitsur Shulchan Aruch* 72:7

Honoring Shabbat

Learning **Activity 1**

There are certain tasks that we are eager to delegate to others, while there are others we would rather do ourselves, even if others could easily do them for us.

What might make someone want to personally engage in a task?

Tasks I Do Myself	Why I Do Them Myself
Tasks I Delegate to Others	**Why I Delegate Them to Others**

Text 3a

ויתקן את הבית ויציע את המטות, ויפרוס מפה על השלחן ותהא פרוסה כל יום השבת . . . וישמח בביאת השבת, ויחשוב בדעתו אלו היה מצפה שיבוא אליו איזה אדם יקר וחשוב איך היה מתקן את הבית לכבודו, ומכל שכן לכבוד שבת מלכתא.

קיצור שולחן ערוך, שם

One should clean the house, make the beds, and spread a tablecloth over the table to remain there the entire Shabbat. . . . One should rejoice at the arrival of Shabbat, thinking to oneself, "If I were expecting an important guest, imagine how I would prepare my home! All the more so in honor of the Shabbat queen."

Rabbi Shlomoh Ganzfried, ibid.

Text 3b

ישתדל שיהיו לו בגדים נאים, וגם טלית של מצוה נאה לכבוד שבת . . . שלא יהא מלבושך של שבת כמלבושך של חול. ואפילו אם הוא בדרך בין הנכרים ילבש בגדי שבת, כי אין המלבושים לכבוד הרואים אלא לכבוד השבת.

קיצור שולחן ערוך עב,טז

One should try and have elegant clothes and also a beautiful *talit* in honor of Shabbat . . . so that the Shabbat garments should not be like the weekday garments. Even if one is on the road among non-Jews [who are not celebrating Shabbat], one should wear one's Shabbat clothes, because the clothing is not for the honor of one's company, but rather in honor of Shabbat.

Rabbi Shlomoh Ganzfried, *Kitsur Shulchan Aruch* 72:16

Text 4a

רבי אבהו הוה יתיב אתכתקא דשינא ומושיף נורא. רב ענן לביש גונדא . . . רב ספרא מחריך רישא. רבא מלח שיבוטא. רב הונא מדליק שרגי. רב פפא גדיל פתילתא. רב חסדא פרים סילקא. רבה ורב יוסף מצלחי ציבי. רבי זירא מצתת צתותי. רב נחמן בר יצחק מכתף ועייל מכתף ונפיק, אמר: אילו מקלעין לי רבי אמי ורבי אסי מי לא מכתיפנא קמייהו.

תלמוד בבלי, שבת קיט,א

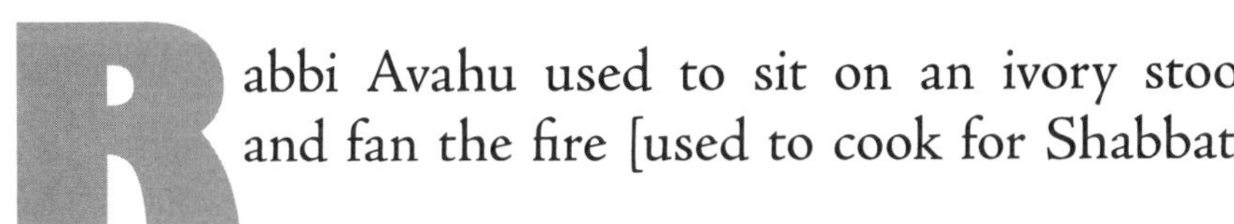

Rabbi Avahu used to sit on an ivory stool and fan the fire [used to cook for Shabbat].

Rav Anan would put on a black smock [while he did various chores in preparation for Shabbat] . . . .

Rav Safra would singe the head [of an animal being prepared for the Shabbat meal].

Rava salted *shibuta* [fish for the Shabbat meal].

Rav Huna would light lamps [in honor of Shabbat].

Rav Papa plaited the wicks [for the lamps].

Rav Chisda cut up the beetroots.

Rabah and Rav Yosef chopped wood.

Rav Zeira kindled the fire.

Rav Nachman bar Yitschak carried items [for Shabbat] into his home, and removed items from his home, saying, "If Rabbi Ami and Rabbi Asi visited me, would I not carry things in their honor?"

Talmud, Shabbat 119a

Text 4b

אף על פי שיהיה אדם חשוב ביותר ואין דרכו ליקח דברים מן השוק ולא להתעסק במלאכות שבבית חייב לעשות דברים שהן לצורך השבת בגופו שזה הוא כבודו . . . וכל המרבה בדבר זה הרי זה משובח.

רמב"ם, הלכות שבת ל,ו

Even a very important person who is unaccustomed to buying items at the marketplace or to doing housework is required to personally perform tasks to prepare for Shabbat. Doing so is one's personal honor. . . . The more one involves oneself in such activities, the more praiseworthy it is.

Maimonides, *Mishneh Torah*, Laws of Shabbat 30:6

Investing in Shabbat

Learning Activity 2

Your twenty-one-year-old daughter wants to spend the summer backpacking with a friend through South America. She tells you that the trip will cost X dollars. You think this is an exciting opportunity and know that she doesn't have much money at her disposal. You have the means to comfortably pay for the entire trip. Once you establish that the trip is safe, how do you respond to her plan?

A. You offer to foot the entire bill and to provide spending money for this trip of a lifetime.

B. You tell her that if she can save the money for half her trip, you will fund the other half.

C. Another option:

Explain your decision to your neighbor.

Text 5

נַחֲלָה מְבֹהֶלֶת בָּרִאשֹׁנָה וְאַחֲרִיתָהּ לֹא תְבֹרָךְ.

משלי כ,כא

An inheritance acquired hastily in the beginning, will not be blessed at the end.

Proverbs 20:21

Learning Activity 3

Reason for Preparing	Is Personal Involvement Necessary?
In order to eat	
In order to celebrate Shabbat with delight	
In order to show respect	
In order to truly appreciate Shabbat	

Transforming the Entire Week

Building Anticipation

Text 6

אמרו עליו על שמאי הזקן, כל ימיו היה אוכל לכבוד שבת. מצא בהמה נאה אומר: זו לשבת. מצא אחרת נאה הימנה מניח את השניה ואוכל את הראשונה.

תלמוד בבלי, ביצה טז,א

It was said about Shamai the Elder [that] all his life he ate in honor of Shabbat. If he found a robust animal, he would say, "Let this be for Shabbat." If [later] he found a superior one, he would reserve the second animal [for Shabbat] and eat the first.

Talmud, Beitsah 16a

Text 7a

זָכוֹר אֶת יוֹם הַשַּׁבָּת לְקַדְּשׁוֹ

שמות כ,ח

Remember the day of Shabbat to sanctify it.

Exodus 20:8

Text 7b

רבי יצחק אומר לא תהא מונה כדרך שאחרים מונין אלא תהא מונה לשם שבת.
מכילתא, פרשת בחדש, ז

Rabbi Yitschak said, "Do not count [the days of the week] as others count [them]; rather count with reference to Shabbat."

Mechilta, *Parashat Bachodesh* 7

Text 7c

Rabbi Moshe ben Nachman (1194–1270). Also known as Nachmanides, or by the acronym Ramban. Nachmanides authored a classic commentary on the Pentateuch that includes everything from critical examination of the text to kabbalistic insights. He also authored numerous other works, including a commentary on the Talmud. Born in Spain, he served as leader of Iberian Jewry. In 1263, he was summoned by King James of Aragon to a public disputation with Pablo Cristiani, a Jewish apostate. Though he was the clear victor of the debate, resulting persecution led to his expulsion from Spain. Settling in Israel, Nachmanides helped reestablish communal life in Jerusalem.

שהגוים מונין ימי השבוע . . . לכל יום שם בפני עצמו, או על שמות המשרתים . . . או שמות אחרים שיקראו להם, וישראל מונים כל הימים לשם שבת, אחד בשבת, שני בשבת, כי זו מן המצוה שנצטוינו בו לזכרו תמיד בכל יום.
רמב"ן, שמות כ,ח

The nations refer to the days of the week . . . by giving each day a name of its own, whether for the ministering planets . . . or other names.

However, Jews count all the weekdays with reference to Shabbat—Day One of Shabbat, Day Two of Shabbat—because this is part of the commandment to constantly remember Shabbat.

Nachmanides, Exodus 20:8

Figure 2.1

Day of the Week	Etymology	Hebrew Name
Sunday	Sun	יוֹם רִאשׁוֹן Day One
Monday	Moon	יוֹם שֵׁנִי Day Two
Tuesday	Mars	יוֹם שְׁלִישִׁי Day Three
Wednesday	Mercury	יוֹם רְבִיעִי Day Four
Thursday	Jupiter	יוֹם חֲמִישִׁי Day Five
Friday	Venus	יוֹם שִׁשִּׁי Day Six
Saturday	Saturn	שַׁבָּת **Shabbat**

Friday

Rabbi Yosef Caro (1488–1575). Born in Spain, fled the country with his family during the expulsion in 1492, and eventually settled in Safed, Israel. Also known as "the Beit Yosef," after the title of his commentary on the *Arba'ah Turim*, and Maran ("our master") for his status as a preeminent authority on Jewish law. Author of 10 works on Jewish law and the Torah, including the *Beit Yosef*, *Kesef Mishneh*, and a mystical work, *Magid Meisharim*. Rabbi Caro's magnum opus, the *Shulchan Aruch* (Code of Jewish Law), has been universally accepted as the basis for modern Jewish law.

Text 8a

ישכים בבוקר ביום ששי להכין צרכי שבת.

שולחן ערוך, אורח חיים רנ,א

One should arise early on Friday to prepare what is needed for Shabbat.

Rabbi Yosef Caro, *Shulchan Aruch, Orach Chayim* 250:1

Rabbi Yisrael Meir Hakohen Kagan (1839–1933). Prolific author on topics of Halachah and ethical behavior, and head of the illustrious yeshivah in Radin, Poland. His first work was *Chafets Chayim*, a comprehensive digest of laws pertaining to prohibited speech; Rabbi Yisrael Meir is hence often called "the Chafets Chayim." His *magnum opus*, on which he worked for 28 years, is *Mishnah Berurah*, a concise commentary of the first section of the *Shulchan Aruch*. He also authored *Bi'ur Halachah* on the *Shulchan Aruch* and numerous other works.

Text 8b

והוא יותר טוב משיקנה ביום ה' שהוא מינכר יותר שהוא לכבוד שבת.

משנה ברורה רנ,ב

Shopping on Friday is better than shopping on Thursday because it is more evident that [one is purchasing items] in honor of Shabbat.

Rabbi Yisrael Meir Hakohen Kagan, *Mishnah Berurah* 250:2

Text 8c

וַיְהִי בַּיּוֹם הַשִּׁשִּׁי לָקְטוּ לֶחֶם מִשְׁנֶה שְׁנֵי הָעֹמֶר לָאֶחָד וַיָּבֹאוּ כָּל נְשִׂיאֵי הָעֵדָה וַיַּגִּידוּ לְמֹשֶׁה.
וַיֹּאמֶר אֲלֵהֶם הוּא אֲשֶׁר דִּבֶּר ה׳ שַׁבָּתוֹן שַׁבַּת קֹדֶשׁ לַה׳ מָחָר אֵת אֲשֶׁר תֹּאפוּ אֵפוּ וְאֵת
אֲשֶׁר תְּבַשְּׁלוּ בַּשֵּׁלוּ וְאֵת כָּל הָעֹדֵף הַנִּיחוּ לָכֶם לְמִשְׁמֶרֶת עַד הַבֹּקֶר.
וַיַּנִּיחוּ אֹתוֹ עַד הַבֹּקֶר כַּאֲשֶׁר צִוָּה מֹשֶׁה וְלֹא הִבְאִישׁ וְרִמָּה לֹא הָיְתָה בּוֹ.
וַיֹּאמֶר מֹשֶׁה אִכְלֻהוּ הַיּוֹם כִּי שַׁבָּת הַיּוֹם לַה׳ הַיּוֹם לֹא תִמְצָאֻהוּ בַּשָּׂדֶה.

שמות טז,כב–כה

It came to pass on the sixth day that they gathered a double portion of bread, two *omers* for [each] person, and all the princes of the community came and reported [it] to Moses.

So he said to them, "This is what the Lord said, 'Tomorrow is a rest day, a holy Shabbat to the Lord.' Bake whatever you wish to bake, and cook whatever you wish to cook, and all the rest leave over for safekeeping until morning."

So they left it over until morning, as Moses had commanded, and it did not become putrid, and not a worm was in it.

And Moses said, "Eat it today, for today is a Shabbat to the Lord; today you will not find [manna] in the field."

Exodus, 16:22–25

Preparing the Inner Self
Making Shabbat

Text 9a

וְשָׁמְרוּ בְנֵי יִשְׂרָאֵל אֶת הַשַּׁבָּת לַעֲשׂוֹת אֶת הַשַּׁבָּת לְדֹרֹתָם בְּרִית עוֹלָם.
שמות לא,טז

The children of Israel shall observe the Shabbat, to make the Shabbat throughout their generations as an everlasting covenant.

Exodus 31:16

Text 9b

יש השראת קדושה לכל אדם בשבת . . . רק יש בני אדם אשר מרגישים כל כך רק מעט מן המעט, ויש שיש להם הרבה קדושה מאוד . . . והכל הוא לפי הכנת בני אדם, אשר מוכן מערב שבת לשבת, וכל שכן מחד בשבת לשבת אשר ממשיך על עצמו קדושת שבת בכל ששת ימי המעשה.
מאור ושמש, כי תשא

On Shabbat, holiness rests upon every person. . . . However, some people sense only the smallest amount [of holiness] while others experience much more. . . . It all depends upon the preparation of the person—how ready he is for Shabbat while it is still Friday, and more so, how ready he was from the first day of the week for Shabbat, bringing upon himself the holiness of Shabbat during all of the six days of the week.

Rabbi Kalonymos Kalman Halevi Epstein, *Ma'or Vashemesh, Ki Tisa*

Rabbi Kalonymos Kalman Halevi Epstein (1751–1823). A native of Cracow, Poland, he was a disciple of Rabbi Elimelech of Lizensk, the Seer of Lublin, and other great chasidic leaders. He authored a chasidic classic titled *Ma'or Vashemesh*, first published in 1842.

Learning Activity 4

Choose an activity that you might engage in as a preparation for Shabbat. Now, try to consider the spiritual significance of this act and how engaging in it mindfully can help make you more spiritually sensitive to the holiness of Shabbat.

Activity	Character Refinement

Spirit of Love

Text 10a

Rabbi Yeshayah Halevi Horowitz (1565–1630). Preeminent kabbalistic authority, also known as the "Shelah," the acronym of the title of his work, *Shenei Luchot Haberit*. Born in Prague, he studied under Rabbi Meir of Lublin and Rabbi Yehoshua Falk. He served as rabbi in several prominent Jewish communities, including Frankfurt am Main and his native Prague. After the passing of his wife in 1620, he moved to Israel. In Tiberias, he finished the *Shenei Luchot Haberit*, an encyclopedic compilation of kabbalistic ideas. He is buried in Tiberias, next to Maimonides.

כי יום השבת צריך להיות כולו בחן ובחסד ובשלום ובאהבה רבה . . . ועל כן עבירה כפולה היא מי שמראה כעס בשבת, וכבר נתנו סימנים לא תבערו אש בכל מושבותיכם ביום השבת (שמות לה,ג), והוא אש המחלוקת וחימום הכעס. ויהיה נזהר בזה בזהירות גדול מחצות ערב שבת ואילך.

שני לוחות הברית, שבת, נר מצוה לב

The entire day of Shabbat must be one of grace, kindness, peace, and extra love. . . . It is a double sin to exhibit anger on Shabbat. This is alluded to in the verse (Exodus 35:3), "A fire should not burn in your homes on Shabbat"—this refers to the fire of discord and the heat of anger. One must be very careful in this regard from Friday midday and on.

Rabbi Yeshayah Halevi Horowitz, *Shenei Luchot Haberit, Shabbat, Ner Mitzvah* 32

Text 10b

וצריך להזהירם קודם בין השמשות שידליקו את הנר ויפסקו מלעשות מלאכה וכשהוא שואלם ומזהירם על דברים אלו צריך שיאמר בלשון רכה כדי שיקבלו ממנו.

שולחן ערוך הרב, אורח חיים רס,ה

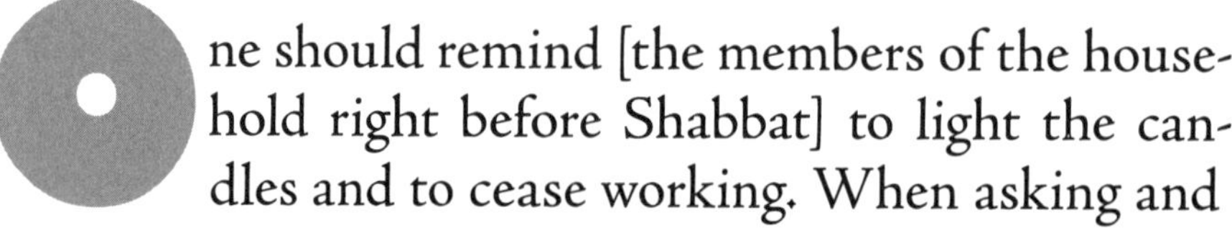

One should remind [the members of the household right before Shabbat] to light the candles and to cease working. When asking and reminding about these things, it must be said in a soft tone so that it will be accepted.

Rabbi Shne'ur Zalman of Liadi, *Shulchan Aruch HaRav, Orach Chayim* 260:5

Rabbi Shne'ur Zalman of Liadi (1745–1812). Chasidic rebbe and founder of the Chabad movement, also known as "the Alter Rebbe" and "the Rav." Born in Liozna, Belarus, he was among the principal students of the Magid of Mezeritch. His numerous works include the *Tanya*, an early classic containing the fundamentals of Chasidism; *Torah Or; Likutei Torah*; and *Shulchan Aruch HaRav*, a reworked and expanded code of Jewish law. He is interred in Hadiach, Ukraine, and was succeeded by his son, Rabbi Dovber of Lubavitch.

Anticipating Shabbat

Adding to Shabbat

Text 11

ואמר רבי יוסי: יהא חלקי ממכניסי שבת בטבריא וממוציאי שבת בצפורי.

תלמוד בבלי, שבת קיח,ב

Rabbi Yosei said, "Let my portion be with those that receive Shabbat in Tiberias and those that part with Shabbat in Sepphoris."

Talmud, Shabbat 118b

Welcoming Shabbat

Text 12a

רבי חנינא מיעטף וקאי אפניא דמעלי שבתא, אמר: בואו ונצא לקראת שבת המלכה.
רבי ינאי לביש מאניה מעלי שבת, ואמר: בואי כלה בואי כלה.
תלמוד בבלי, שבת קיט,א

Towards sunset on Friday, Rabbi Chanina would robe himself and stand. He exclaimed, "Come and let us go forth to greet the Shabbat queen."

Rabbi Yanai donned his robes on Friday and exclaimed, "Come in, O bride; come in, O bride!"

Talmud, Shabbat 119a

Figure 2.2

Who?	Does What?	To Whom?	With Whom?	How Is Shabbat Addressed?
Rabbi Chanina	Goes out to greet	The queen	Invites others to join in greeting	In third person (indirectly)
Rabbi Yannai	Stays inside to welcome	The bride	Welcomes by himself	In second person (directly)

Text 12b

השבת הוא השלמת העולם ומצד השלמה הזאת מתחבר העולם אל השם יתברך ולכך נקרא השבת כלה שיש לה חבור אל בעלה.

ונקראת עוד מלכתא והוא עוד יותר מדריגה שיש לעולם הזה מצד השבת מעלה נבדלת כי יום השבת נבדל משאר ימים כמו המלך שהוא נבדל מן העם והשבת הוא קודש כי כל דבר שהוא קודש נבדל מהכל.

חדושי אגדות מהר"ל, בבא קמא לב,ב

Shabbat completes the world. This completion allows the world to connect with God. Therefore, Shabbat is called a bride, for a bride is united with her husband.

But Shabbat is also called a queen. This refers to an additional dimension that the world has on Shabbat. Due to the exalted nature of Shabbat, it is elevated above the other days, as a king is elevated above the people. For Shabbat is holy; anything that is holy is exalted and distinguished from all else.

Rabbi Yehudah Loew, *Chidushei Agadot*, Bava Kama 32b

Rabbi Yehudah Loew (1525–1609). Talmudist and philosopher, also known as the Maharal of Prague. Descended from the Babylonian exilarchs; most likely born in Poznan, Poland, he initially served as rabbi in Mikulov, Moravia, and then rose to prominence as leader of the famed Jewish community of Prague. He is the author of more than a dozen works of original philosophic thought, most notably *Tiferet Yisrael* and *Netsach Yisrael*. He also authored *Gur Aryeh*, a super-commentary on Rashi's biblical commentary, and a commentary on the Talmud. He is buried in the Old Jewish Cemetery of Prague.

Text 13

סדר קבלת שבת הוא שתצא לשדה ותאמר בואו ונצא לקראת שבת מלכתא . . . ותעמוד מעומד במקום אחד בשדה ואם יהיה על גבי הר אחד גבוה הוא יותר טוב . . . ותחזור פניך כנגד רוח מערב ששם החמה שוקעת ובעת שקיעתה ממש אז תסגור עיניך ותשים ידך השמאלית על החזה ויד ימינך על גבי שמאל ותכוין באימה וביראה כעומד לפני המלך לקבל תוספות קדושת שבת ותתחיל ותאמר מזמור הבו לה׳ בני אלים כו׳ (תהלים כט) כולו בנעימה ואחר כך תאמר ג׳ פעמים באי כלה באי כלה באי כלה שבת מלכתא.

שער הכוונות, ענין קבלת שבת

Rabbi Chaim ben Yosef Vital (1542–1620). Born in Israel, lived in Safed, Jerusalem, and later Damascus. Vital was the principal disciple of Arizal, though he studied under him for less than two years. Before his passing, Arizal authorized Vital to record his teachings. Acting on this mandate, Vital began arranging his master's teachings in written form, and his many works constitute the foundation of the Lurianic school of Jewish mysticism, which was later universally adopted as the kabbalistic standard. Thus, Vital is one of the most important influences in the development of Kabbalah. Among his most famous works are *Ets Chayim*, and *Sha'ar Hakavanot*.

Welcome Shabbat in this way:

Go out to the field and say, "Come and let us go forth to welcome the Shabbat queen." . . .

Stand in a fixed place in the field. Even better, stand on a high hill. . . .

Turn your face west toward the setting sun.

Just as it sets, close your eyes, place your left hand on your chest and your right hand over your left. Mentally accept the added holiness of Shabbat with fear and awe, as one standing before a king.

Then say the psalm, "Render to the Lord, etc." (Psalms 29), reciting it in its entirety with a melody.

Then say three times, "Come O bride, come O bride, come O bride, Shabbat queen!"

Rabbi Chaim Vital, *Sha'ar Hakavanot, Inyan Kabalat Shabbat*

Text 14

לְכָה דוֹדִי לִקְרַאת כַּלָּה
פְּנֵי שַׁבָּת נְקַבְּלָה . . .

לִקְרַאת שַׁבָּת לְכוּ וְנֵלְכָה
כִּי הִיא מְקוֹר הַבְּרָכָה
מֵרֹאשׁ מִקֶּדֶם נְסוּכָה
סוֹף מַעֲשֶׂה בְּמַחֲשָׁבָה תְּחִלָּה . . .

בּוֹאִי בְשָׁלוֹם עֲטֶרֶת בַּעְלָהּ
גַּם בְּרִנָּה וּבְצָהֳלָה
תּוֹךְ אֱמוּנֵי עַם סְגֻלָּה
בּוֹאִי כַלָּה בּוֹאִי כַלָּה
בּוֹאִי כַלָּה שַׁבָּת מַלְכְּתָא.

לכה דודי, סידור תהלת ה׳

Come my beloved, to meet the bride,
Let us welcome the Shabbat. . . .

Come, let us go to welcome the Shabbat,
For it is the source of blessing;
From aforetime it was chosen;
Last in creation, first in [God's] thought. . . .

Come in peace, O crown of her husband,
Both with song and gladness;
Among the faithful, the beloved people,
Come, O bride, come O bride,
Come, O bride, O Shabbat queen.

Lechah Dodi, Sidur Tehilat Hashem

Rabbi Shlomoh Alkabets (ca 1500–1580). Born in Salonica, Greece. Kabbalist and poet; best known for his composition of the Shabbat hymn, *Lechah Dodi*. He married in 1529, and instead of giving his wife a more traditional wedding gift, he gave her his newly completed work, *Manot Halevi*, a commentary on the book of Esther. He eventually moved to Safed, Israel, where he was accepted into the circle of Rabbi Moshe Alshich, Rabbi Yosef Caro, and Rabbi Moshe Cordovero.

Key Points

1. We personally involve ourselves in the Shabbat preparations in order to honor Shabbat. The more work we do to prepare for Shabbat, the more we appreciate the value of this gift.

2. We anticipate and prepare for Shabbat all week. This is reflected in the names of the weekdays in Hebrew. But Friday is the optimal day for preparations because it is immediately evident that the preparations are being done in honor of Shabbat.

2. The spiritual experience of Shabbat depends on the spiritual experience one has during the week. Thus, we also prepare spiritually for Shabbat. The physical preparations themselves can teach us much about spiritual preparations.

4. We go out of our way to ensure that the hours and moments leading up to Shabbat are spent in love and respect.

5. Our anticipation for Shabbat motivates us to begin Shabbat earlier than the legally mandated time and to conclude it later than the legally mandated hour.

6. Shabbat is exalted above the other days of the week—a queen. At the same time, on Shabbat we are close and united with God like on no other day—as a bride with her groom.

7. We formally accept the Shabbat as queen and bride in the *Kabalat Shabbat* prayer. We welcome Shabbat into our action, speech, and thought, and into every fiber of our being.

Simply Shabbat: A Guide to Preparations

YOUR SHABBAT SHOPPING LIST

Your Shabbat shopping list will largely depend on the menu you create, depending on your particular taste. The traditional Friday night meal includes fish, soup, and a meat or chicken course. The Shabbat day meal is similar, with the main course including *cholent* or *chamin*, a warm stew that simmers overnight. All this, however, is contingent on one's personal palate.

The following are universal items that are needed in order to create the Shabbat experience:

Basic:

❑ Candles or tea lights (for Shabbat candles and *Havdalah*)
❑ Kosher wine or grape juice (for Kiddush and *Havdalah*)
❑ Three loaves of challah (or, for a small crowd, challah rolls)
❑ Salt (in which to dip the challah)
❑ Aromatic spices, such as whole cloves (for *Havdalah*)
❑ A prayer book or Shabbat table guide that contains the texts of the Kiddush and *Havdalah*, and the Shabbat meal liturgy.

And then enhance the experience:

❑ Fresh flowers
❑ Stylish candlesticks (Get creative! Anything from the traditional silver candlesticks to floating candles in a crystal dish with flower petals, marbles, and mirrors.)
❑ An elegant Kiddush cup
❑ A nice challah cover, cutting board, and knife
❑ A pressed white tablecloth
❑ Fine dishware, glassware, flatware, and napkins
❑ A braided *Havdalah* candle

YOUR PRE-SHABBAT CHECKLIST

Home-Related Tasks:

❑ Make beds.
❑ Wash dishes and counters, and tidy up kitchen.
❑ Sweep and mop floors.
❑ Vacuum carpets.
❑ Wash, fold, and put away laundry.
❑ Pick up Shabbat clothing from the dry cleaners.
❑ Polish shoes.
❑ Set the Shabbat table and arrange the Shabbat candles.

- ❑ Check the pockets of all clothing you will be wearing on Shabbat to ensure that they are empty.
- ❑ Set the lights, air conditioners, and heat the way you'd like them to remain for the duration of Shabbat.
- ❑ If your refrigerator or freezer has a light that goes on when the door is opened, unscrew the light bulb.

Note: You can use electronic timers to schedule lights and certain appliances (such as air conditioners) to go on and off on Shabbat at preset times.

Food-Related Preparations:

Before Shabbat, place all food that will be served warm—such as soup, chicken, or *cholent*—on the stovetop. A *blech* (thin sheet of metal, probably available at your local Judaica store) or a folded piece of aluminum foil should separate the food from the fire or heating element. If you are using an electric cooking pot, place a layer of foil between the outer cooker and the inner pot (this is not necessary if the electric cooking pot has only one setting, i.e., only an on/off switch).

Fill an urn with water and heat it until it is boiled (make sure that the urn's dispensing mechanism is not electronically operated); or boil a kettle of water and place it on the *blech*.

Self-Preparations:

- ❑ Bathe or shower.
- ❑ Groom hair and nails.
- ❑ Apply makeup and/or perfume.
- ❑ Get dressed in your Shabbat best.

Simply Shabbat: Baking Challah

When used in daily conversation, "challah" refers to the braided loaves of bread traditionally eaten at Shabbat and Jewish holiday meals. In talmudic and rabbinic literature, however, challah usually refers to the small portion of dough that we separate from the total dough before we bake any bread, in fulfillment of the biblical directive (Leviticus 15:21), "From the first portion of your dough, you shall give a gift to God."

Originally, this challah portion was given to a *kohen*, a priestly descendant of Aaron who served in the temple, a practice that will resume in the Messianic Era, with the rebuilding of the Holy Temple in Jerusalem. For various reasons, priests today are not permitted to eat challah—but neither are we. So, instead, we burn the small piece of challah.

Though today most people buy bread from bakeries (kosher bakeries also separate challah from the dough), Jewish women have traditionally embraced the custom of baking challah loaves in honor of Shabbat, allowing them the opportunity to perform the special mitzvah of separating challah on a weekly basis.

Why?

Separating challah reminds us that all we possess—our material possessions as well as our talents—are God-given. As such, we always designate part of what we were given and devote it to a Godly purpose—whether in the form of charity, volunteer work, or devoting time to studying Torah and doing *mitzvot*.

What?

We separate challah from batches of dough that are made from at least forty three ounces of wheat, rye, barley, oat, or spelt flour.

How?

1. After kneading the dough, before shaping it into loaves, place the dough in a single pan or bowl and say:[1]

בָּרוּךְ אַתָּה אֲדֹנָי, אֱלֹהֵינוּ מֶלֶךְ הָעוֹלָם, אֲשֶׁר קִדְּשָׁנוּ בְּמִצְוֹתָיו, וְצִוָּנוּ לְהַפְרִישׁ חַלָּה.

Baruch atah Adonai, Eloheinu melech ha'olam, asher kidishanu bimitsvotav, vitsivanu lihafrish challah.

Blessed are You, Lord our God, King of the Universe, Who has sanctified us with His commandments and commanded us to separate challah.

2. Separate a small piece (approximately one ounce) and say, "This is challah."

3. Wrap the challah in foil and burn it in a broiler, grill, or oven. (The charred bread may be discarded.)

[1] This blessing is only recited if there's at least fifty-nine ounces of flour in the batch. Otherwise, separate *challah*, but don't recite the blessing. Similarly, only recite the blessing if water comprises most of the liquid in the dough.

Additional Readings

Sephardic Shabbat

by **Rabbi Marc D. Angel**

On Friday afternoon, just before sunset, the mystics and pietists of 16th century Safed would go out to the fields and hills to greet the incoming Sabbath Queen. They would stand facing west as the sun receded from view. At the very moment when the sun set, they would close their eyes, clasp their hands together to their chests, and stand with fear and trembling as one stands before a king. At that moment, they received the additional holiness of the Sabbath. And as they felt this holiness enter them, they would sing Psalm 29, beginning the service of receiving the Sabbath. They recited phrases to welcome the Sabbath bride, the Sabbath Queen.

Those Jews of Safed, most of whom were Sephardim, lived Shabbat both as a cosmic and as a personal experience. Watching the sun set, the sky aglow with colors and shadows, they could sense in some vague way the greatness of God, the creator of the universe. At the very same sunset on the sixth day of Creation, God had created the holiness of Shabbat. But if, on the one hand, those Jews felt the mood of awe at God's greatness, they also felt the personal joy in feeling the holiness enter their own lives. They invested Shabbat with a special personality. She was a bride, she was a queen, she was the source for love, comfort, unthreatening royalty.

Few Jews nowadays go to the fields to greet the incoming Shabbat Queen, but all Jews who follow the traditional form of worship are influenced by the spirituality of that enigmatic and holy community of Sephardim of Safed. The universally chanted poem, *Lekha dodi,* was composed by a leading Sephardic figure of that period, Rabbi Shelomo Halevi Alkabets. "Come, my beloved, to greet the bride, let us receive the presence of Shabbat." Many Jews follow the custom of standing up during the singing of this hymn, while others rise at the end of it. As the phrase *Bo-i Kallah* is recited, most Jews bow, as if actually recognizing the presence of a royal visitor, while some turn around and face west at the recitation of these words. The spiritual insight developed in Safed thus continues in our synagogues today.

The perception of Shabbat as a bride received a special importance among the Sephardic Kabbalists, and certain customs which are prevalent in many Ashkenazic communities can be traced back to that perception. For example, it is common among many Sephardim to sing the "Song of Songs" on Friday just before the evening service. This beautiful love poem has been interpreted as a description of the love between God and Israel, and it is sung as part of the general marriage theme uniting God and Israel, Israel and Shabbat.

It should be noted that the influence of the Sephardic Kabbalists of Safed was spread not only though their own writings and works, but also through the teachings of Rabbi Isaac Luria, the famous Ari Hakadosh. Though not himself Sephardic, he lived within the Sephardic milieu and both influenced, and was influenced by, his Sephardic colleagues and students.

Throughout the generations and wherever Jews lived, the Shabbat has played a central role in the religious life of their community. Objectively, the twenty-four hours of Saturday are no different from the twenty-four hours of any other day of the week. To an observer who does not know Shabbat, Saturday is no different from any other day. But, subjectively, the Jew who observes Shabbat enters a new world, a new dimension of time. Those twenty-four hours are intrinsically different from all other periods of time. Shabbat is the special spiritual treasure of those who understand it and experience it; it is a sign of the private covenant between God and Israel. But it is invisible to everyone except those who keep the Shabbat.

Jewish law and custom prescribe that the Shabbat must be respected—by wearing nice clothes, by preparing special foods, by Torah study and prayer. Jews of all backgrounds have treated Shabbat as an extraordinary day. Whether they spoke Hebrew or Yiddish or Judeo-Spanish or Arabic; whether they ate *gefilte fish* or *cholent*, or *pescado con tomat* or *adafina* or whatever else; whether their Shabbat prayers and songs sounded Eastern European or Turkish or Arabic or whatever else—the central reality of Shabbat was true for all Jews.

Jews of all backgrounds who observe Shabbat have always been receptive to the spiritual insights and practices of Jews of communities other than their own. That is why the influence of the Sephardim of 16th century Safed has been so pervasive, and some of their less known contributions deserve to be more widely appreciated.

Sephardim have contributed notably to the poetic and musical dimension of the Shabbat observance. As Jews throughout the world sit around their Sabbath tables singing *zemirot,* they benefit—knowingly or not—from the creation of Sephardic poets. For example, *Yah Ribon Olam*, by Rabbi Israel Najara; *Bar Yohai,* by Shimon ibn Lavi; *Ki Eshmerah Shabbat,* by Rabbi Abraham ibn Ezra; *Dror Yikrah,* by Dunash ibn Labrat; *Yedid Nefesh*, by Rabbi Eliezer Azikri.

These poems—and many more like them—are significant for a number of reasons. They are evidence of the creativity which the Shabbat inspired. Moreover, they reflect the deep-seated need to enhance the observance of Shabbat with song. Not least significant are the recurrent themes which appear in almost all of them: the holiness of Shabbat, the spiritual freedom which comes with this holiness, the longing for Messiah and redemption. These ideas and feelings have spread from the Sephardic poets to the Jewish people everywhere, and have helped shape the religious mind of the Jewish people. Shabbat without the creative efforts of Sephardic poets would seem stark and empty.

It is well-known that we are supposed to eat three meals in honor of Shabbat: one on Friday evening, another on Shabbat morning, and the third on Shabbat afternoon. Rabbi Eliezer Azikri, in his volume, *Sefer Hareidim,* explains that these meals are tied to the three major themes of Shabbat. Friday night relates to the Shabbat of Creation, when God had finished the work of creating the Universe. Shabbat morning relates to the Shabbat when the Torah was revealed on Mt. Sinai to the children of Israel, and Shabbat afternoon relates to the "world that is all Shabbat," the future messianic period. Just as the synagogue services at these three times reflect the themes, so do the Shabbat meals relate to them. On Friday evening, the Kiddush recalls Creation; on Shabbat morning, people's minds are attuned to Torah study; on Shabbat afternoon, just before the sun sets, we already begin to feel the Sabbath slipping away from us and we long for a world that is all Sabbath. The Sephardic Kabbalists attached a great importance to yet a fourth meal, one that is served after the Shabbat has already left. This is known as the *Melaveh Malkah,* the escorting of the Queen. Just as the Shabbat Queen has been welcomed on Friday evening, so she is to be escorted on her departure.

The Sephardic observance of Shabbat included other elements, aside from those already discussed. A major factor was the communal nature of the day, and various practices popular among Sephardim tended to strengthen a person's tie to his family and to his particular community. For example, on Friday mornings, there would be collections of food to be distributed to the poor. Jews who had sufficient food for themselves and their families would invite others, who were less fortunate, to join them for the Shabbat meals, and officials in the synagogue would collect bread for the poor.

Shabbat was a special day for visiting relatives and neighbors. In closely knit Sephardic communities, all Jews might consider themselves to be part of one large extended family, and hospitality and social grace were highlighted on Shabbat.

Synagogue services were, of course, conducted in the custom of the particular Sephardic communities. Although the prayer ritual is quite similar among all Sephardim, there were some local variations in text, and more variation in the particular style of music used for the service. Among Sephardim in the Spanish and Portuguese communities of Western Europe, the music was more westernized and the services were more formal, while among the Jews in Turkey there was a notable influence of Turkish music. Among the Jews in the Middle East and North Africa, one could detect the musical influences from their native cultures.

Yet, for all the differences among the Sephardim, there are some universal features which deserve to be mentioned. Generally, the entire service is chanted aloud. Congregants read along with the Hazzan with enthusiasm. While Sephardic Hazzanim were expected to have pleasant voices, they were not seen to be primarily performers, since almost all of the service was chanted by the entire congregation. The Hazzan served, more or less, merely as the leader, but there were several points in the service where he could sing an elaborate passage by himself, and these sections were much enjoyed by the congregation. The Sephardic Hazzan was also expected to be an expert reader of the Sefer Torah and even if he had an excellent voice, he would not be excused for many mistakes in his reading. In Spanish and Portuguese congregations, the rabbis also were expected to read the Torah scroll expertly. Amateurs could not fulfill the obligation.

There were other customs in the synagogue services which reflected aspects of Sephardic personality. When a man was given an *aliyah*, his children and younger relatives stood in his honor and would remain standing until he finished his portion and returned to his seat. This custom imbued the younger family members with respect for their elders, and also had the effect of unifying the entire family. I recall when my grandfather, of blessed memory, was called to the Torah in our synagogue in Seattle, his children and grandchildren would all rise for him. There were quite a few of us and, as we stood up while the rest of the congregation remained seated, we could not help but feel the pride in our grandfather and our entire family. We all shared the glory of that moment and all felt the recognition of the community.

Another custom was that children and grandchildren would kiss the hands of their parents and grandparents in order to receive a blessing. This frequently would take place on Friday evening or during the day of Shabbat, although it also was done at other times, both in the synagogue and at home. When my grandfather, for example, would return to his seat after an *aliyah*, we would go to him and kiss his hand. He would then place his hand over our heads and give us each a blessing. This action had the effect of deepening our respect for him, of making us look to him for his blessing. It also gave him the satisfaction of blessing his children and grandchildren. The power of such a practice in strengthening the ties of members of a family is considerable.

An important word in the Sephardic vocabulary is the Hebrew term *kavod.* Literally, it means honor, but its significance goes beyond this simple translation. It includes ideas of self-respect, dignity, communal approval, a sense of one's own honor. *Kavod* was important to Sephardim on every day of the week, but on Shabbat it seemed to be even more important. Individuals would look forward to the opportunity of participating in the synagogue service in any way. They would take pride in their beautiful voices, or in the clear way in which they chanted. They were anxious to perform one of the honors of opening the Ark, or carrying the Sefer Torah, or placing the ornamental bells (*rimonim*) on the Torah. In many communities, these honors were actually auctioned off to the highest bidders, a practice which still takes place in some synagogues. The custom had a two-fold advantage. First, it provided revenue for the congregation. Second, and at least equally important, it diminished the possibility of disputes among congregants. Since so many wanted to perform one of the honors, it would be difficult to decide who should have the right. By auctioning off the honors, however, the problem was solved. Naturally, the solution also had its own problems, but, in most cases, congregations seemed to have managed this system very well. When a person won the auction for a particular honor, he would often give it to someone else to perform, in a significant gesture of goodwill, friendship and respect. When an individual went to perform one of these honors or was called to the Torah, congregants would call out to him: *Be-khavod,* with honor. The synagogue service, thus, reinforced a person's individual self-respect as well as enhancing family ties.

Rabbi Hayyim Ben Attar, in his famous Biblical commentary, *Or Hahayyim*, explains that Shabbat is the basis of the Creation. On each Shabbat, God decides whether to continue the Creation for the next six days. When Jews observe the Shabbat, they justify the continued existence of the world. If the Shabbat were not observed by anyone, the world would come to an end. Though this interpretation might be difficult to understand in a literal way, those who observe Shabbat can well understand it symbolically. Without the deep experience of Shabbat, it might just seem that the world as we know it had come to an end. Conversely, when we observe Shabbat, we feel ready to greet the next six days until the next Shabbat.

Judaism 31:1 (1982)
Reprinted by permission of the publisher

Making Shabbat Your Cornerstone

by **Yvette Alt Miller**

When I was newly married, I used to make large, elaborate Shabbat meals, clean the house, polish the silver, and get everything in order—all on Fridays. Consequently, when Friday evening rolled around, I was always stressed and grumpy. Sure, the house looked and smelled wonderful, but I was so miserable, it was no way to greet Shabbat. One weekend my mother (who is wise and very calm) visited and, observing my manic Friday, told me about the Shabbats of her childhood, when her Bubbe (Grandmother) Yitta would prepare everything each week.

My mother's Bubbe Yitta grew up in a shtetl (a small Jewish town) in Poland, and lived in a Yiddish-speaking environment for her entire life, even after she moved to London and raised her family. Many American Jews get nostalgic at thoughts of the rich Jewish life of our ancestors in Eastern Europe's shtetls; my mother was describing the real thing when she told me about her bubbe's strategies. Shabbat dominated Bubbe Yitta's week, my mother told me. She started preparing as early as Tuesday, and each day would cook and bake something to eat on the holiday. Once Friday rolled around, my Bubbe Yitta was busy, but never frenzied.

As the years have gone by, I've taken that advice, and added some of my own coping strategies. I soon realized that cooking new dishes each week was too time-consuming. Instead, I developed a limited menu that I make week after week. It is easy for me to cook the familiar dishes, and an added benefit is my children love our Shabbat menu: they now associate gefilte fish, chicken soup with matzah balls and other classic Jewish dishes with Shabbat's happiness.

More profoundly, observing Shabbat is easier once you get used to setting it aside as a special day, the best day of the week. Individuals and families who observe Shabbat routinely do this without thinking about it, and those who want to make the transition to observing Shabbat can ease their paths by designating Shabbat as the time to enjoy the best of what they have. Thus, in my home, for example, we rarely eat dessert after dinner during the week, but we always have lots of dessert after dinner on Friday night and lunch on Saturday. During the week, I insist on my kids eating healthy breakfasts, but on Shabbat we make special "surprise sandwiches" (which feature chocolate as a primary ingredient). During the week, my husband and I are often too busy to play games or read to the kids, but on Shabbat we spend hours playing board games and reading out loud. Try saving special things for Shabbat: by designating Shabbat your special day to enjoy the best material things your life has to offer, you guarantee their weekly use, as well as enhancing the special quality of your Shabbat. It isn't just children's activities that can be indulged on Shabbat. Once people begin integrating Shabbat into their lives, it becomes natural to reserve all the best things for that day. Here are two small examples that show how unconscious this reflex to honor Shabbat becomes. I once bought a book for my kids in a sale, and it quickly became a favorite: it is an amazing, magical, beautifully illustrated picture book about a child spending a summer with his grandmother exploring a river. The book is not Jewish or Shabbat-oriented in any way, but it is lovely, and my oldest son told me it really ought to be a "Shabbat book" that we take out only on Shabbat. Nobody ever told my son we had to restrict our book selections in this way, but to this boy who has grown up observing Shabbat, it seemed natural that beautiful, special things would be especially reserved for this special day.

When my son suggested this, I thought it was quaint. But then I unconsciously did the same thing some years later. When my grandmother, of blessed memory, died, I inherited her very large, very ornate engagement ring. The ring is too large and too grand to fit at all into my lifestyle. (My own husband proposed to me with a wrist watch, to give a sense of how unusual it would be for me to wear a large diamond ring.) I would never wear my grandmother's ring normally, but it was natural for me to start wearing it on Shabbat, my weekly time to become a subtly different person, and enjoy the finest things in my life.

To many people, the concept of keeping one's best things for Shabbat seems restrictive. Why shouldn't we enjoy our good clothes, our good china, our favorite foods any time we want? Why horde them all for one weekly 25-hour period? In many years of observing Shabbat, I've found that the answer to this question is deeply counterintuitive: by saving our best things for Shabbat, we actually use them more than we would otherwise. For instance, when was the last time you used your good china? Ate in your dining room? Wore your best jewelry? Invited over lots of guests? For many people I know, the answer is months or even years ago. Take one of my relatives: he and his family live in a house with a beautiful dining room—which they have used exactly once in five years of residence. I'm sure that when this relative and his wife bought their house, they looked in the pretty dining room and envisioned lovely family meals there. Yet busy life intervenes, and so often we never get out of "everyday" mode. My relatives mean to set aside time for special meals and other times, but like everybody else, they are very busy people, and that special time gets shunted aside. Shabbat might only come once a week, but it comes every week. It gives us a regular date when we are commanded to make everything in our homes and lives special.

This was brought home to me dramatically some years ago when a synagogue friend and I signed up for an activity that brought us together several times during the week. I had met my friend at synagogue, and for many years saw her almost exclusively on Shabbat. We chatted after services, and sometimes we would invite each other's families over for Shabbat and other holiday meals. And what was the impression I had of this friend? She was elegant. Gorgeous. Gracious and attractive and always beautifully turned out. Week after week I saw her wearing beautiful, feminine outfits with long skirts, high heels, and lovely jewelry. She always wore attractive hats that suited her face. She was a wonderful cook and presided over magnificent feasts in her lovely clean and tidy home. Her kids are well-behaved and would eat and play and help clean up after meals nicely and graciously.

Everything about my friend exudes beauty, refinement, and elegance. It was a shock, therefore, once our activity started, to see this friend during the week! She wore ordinary clothes that were completely utilitarian, if not downright dowdy. Boring shoes, dumpy handbags, flat hair. When I ran into her, she was often harried. I visited her house during the week and it was messy with clutter. Her kids were loud. I hardly recognized the majestic, elegant friend I still saw weekly at synagogue. No contrast could have been greater. For my friend is successful and competent during the ordinary work week, but on Shabbat she glows. I had become acquainted with a woman when she was accompanied by her extra Shabbat soul, and was startled to see the weekday woman, going about her business without the extra spark of Shabbat holiness that transforms her into a queen.

Angels at the Table (London: Continuum International Publishing Group, 2011), pp. 14–17
Reprinted by permission of the publisher

Lesson 3

Walking with Angels

Introduction

Rabbi Shimon ben Chalafta said, "God did not find a better vessel to contain blessings for Israel than peace" (Mishnah, Uktsin 3:12).

As Shabbat descends, we open ourselves to God's blessings by filling our homes with peace and love.

In this lesson, we will examine three approaches to building peace, all of which can be gleaned from our Shabbat experience.

Shabbat Shalom

Learning Activity 1

Think back on your interactions in the past few weeks—at home with family, at work, with friends, or even in your own inner dialogue or self-talk. Briefly jot down a situation or relationship that brings peace and harmony into your life, and a situation that lacks peace (or an area of conflict/stress). Now think about what makes the situation peaceful or stressful.

A Peaceful Situation	What Factors Make It Peaceful?
A Stressful Situation	What Factors Prevent Peace?

The Shabbat Candles
Embodiment of Holiness

Text 1

כל ימים שהיתה שרה קיימת היה נר דולק מלילי שבת ועד לילי שבת וכיון שמתה פסק אותו הנר, וכיון שבאת רבקה חזר.
בראשית רבה ס,טז

All the days of Sarah's life, a lamp burned from Shabbat eve to Shabbat eve. When she died, the lamp ceased. When Rebecca came, the lamp returned.

Midrash, *Bereishit Rabah* 60:16

Peace, Pleasure, and Honor

Rabbi Shlomoh Yitschaki (1040–1105). Better known by the acronym Rashi. Rabbi and famed author of comprehensive commentaries on the Talmud and Bible. Born in Troyes, France, Rashi studied in the famed *yeshivot* of Mainz and Worms. His commentaries, which focus on the simple understanding of the text, are considered the most fundamental of all the commentaries that preceded and followed. Since their initial printings, the commentaries have appeared in virtually every edition of the Talmud and Bible. Many of the famed authors of the *Tosafot* are among Rashi's descendants.

Text 2

ובמקום שאין נר אין שלום שהולך ונכשל והולך באפילה.

רש"י, שבת כה,ב

In a place where there is no lamp, there is no peace, for a person stumbles about and gropes in darkness.

Rashi, Shabbat 25b

Text 3

הדלקת נר בשבת חובה מדברי סופרים מפני שהיא ראש לכל עונג
שאין עונג בלא אורה.

בית הבחירה, שבת כה,ב

Rabbi Menachem Me'iri (ca. 1249–1310). Born in Provence, France. His monumental work, *Beit Habechirah,* summarizes in a lucid style the discussions of the Talmud along with the commentaries of the major subsequent rabbis. Despite its stature, the work was largely unknown for many generations, and thus has had less influence on subsequent halachic development than would have been expected given its stature.

Lighting Shabbat candles is a rabbinic obligation because it is a prerequisite for all pleasure. There can be no pleasure where there is no light.

Rabbi Menachem Me'iri, *Beit Habechirah,* Shabbat 25b

Text 4a

זָכַרְנוּ אֶת הַדָּגָה אֲשֶׁר נֹאכַל בְּמִצְרַיִם חִנָּם אֵת הַקִּשֻּׁאִים וְאֵת הָאֲבַטִּחִים וְאֶת הֶחָצִיר וְאֶת הַבְּצָלִים וְאֶת הַשּׁוּמִים. וְעַתָּה נַפְשֵׁנוּ יְבֵשָׁה אֵין כֹּל בִּלְתִּי אֶל הַמָּן עֵינֵינוּ.

במדבר יא,ה–ו

We remember the fish that we ate in Egypt free of charge, the cucumbers, the watermelons, the leeks, the onions, and the garlic. But now, our spirits are parched, for there is nothing at all; we have nothing but manna to look at.

Numbers 11:5–6

Text 4b

זכרנו את הדגה: מכאן שמדליקין נרות בשבת.

מדרש פליאה, בינת נבונים פא

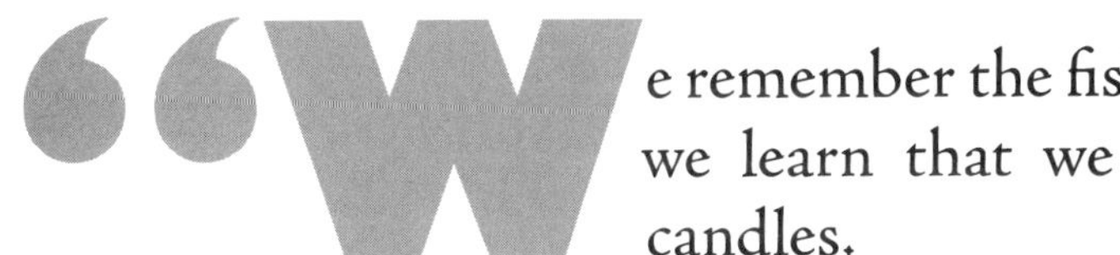

“We remember the fish”—from here we learn that we light Shabbat candles.

Midrash Peli'ah, Binat Nevonim 81

Rabbi Moshe ben Maimon (1135–1204). Better known as Maimonides or by the acronym Rambam; born in Cordoba, Spain. After the conquest of Cordoba by the Almohads, he fled Spain and eventually settled in Cairo, Egypt. There, he became the leader of the Jewish community and served as court physician to the vizier of Egypt. His rulings on Jewish law are considered integral to the formation of halachic consensus. He is most noted for authoring the *Mishneh Torah*, an encyclopedic arrangement of Jewish law, and for his philosophical work, *Guide for the Perplexed.*

Text 5

וצריך לתקן ביתו מבעוד יום מפני כבוד השבת, ויהיה נר דלוק ושולחן ערוך ומטה מוצעת שכל אלו לכבוד שבת הן.

רמב״ם, הלכות שבת ל,ה

One must clean the home before sunset in honor of Shabbat. A candle should be lit, a table set, and a bed prepared, all in honor of Shabbat.

Maimonides, *Mishneh Torah*, Laws of Shabbat 30:5

Peace by Distinction

Text 6

ויש לך לדעת, כי אין נקרא שלום רק האור בלבד, מפני שהוא נותן הבדל בין הדברים, וזהו השלום כאשר יש הבדל בין הדברים. כי כאשר נקרא החושך ערב, מפני שבחושך הדברים הם מעורבים, ואין נכר זה בפני זה . . . והאור נקרא בוקר שעל ידי האור יש ביקור בין הדברים בין זה לזה. וכאשר יש בקור בין דבר לדבר הוא השלום אשר הוא בין הדברים, ואין אחד נכנס ומתערב בחבירו רק כל אחד בפני עצמו.

ולפיכך נקרא נר שבת שלום.

חדושי אגדות מהר״ל, שבת כה,ב

Know that only light is referred to as "peace" because it provides distinction between different things. Peace requires distinction between things.

Darkness is called *erev*—mixture—because in darkness all items are jumbled together and one cannot be distinguished from another. . . . Light is called *boker*—examination—because in light one can examine things and distinguish between them.

When one can examine the difference between things, this brings peace between them, for one does not invade or mix into the domain of the other, but each remains within its own.

Thus, Shabbat light is called peace.

Rabbi Yehudah Loew, *Chidushei Agadot*, Shabbat 25b

Rabbi Yehudah Loew (1525–1609). Talmudist and philosopher, also known as the Maharal of Prague. Descended from the Babylonian exilarchs; most likely born in Poznan, Poland, he initially served as rabbi in Mikulov, Moravia, and then rose to prominence as leader of the famed Jewish community of Prague. He is the author of more than a dozen works of original philosophic thought, most notably *Tiferet Yisrael* and *Netsach Yisrael*. He also authored *Gur Aryeh*, a super-commentary on Rashi's biblical commentary, and a commentary on the Talmud. He is buried in the Old Jewish Cemetery of Prague.

Text 7

אי אפשר שיהיה אחד לגמרי מבלי הזדווגות בשום חבור אליו כלל שאם כן היה חסר . . . רק השם יתברך שהוא אחד שלם.

תפארת ישראל מ

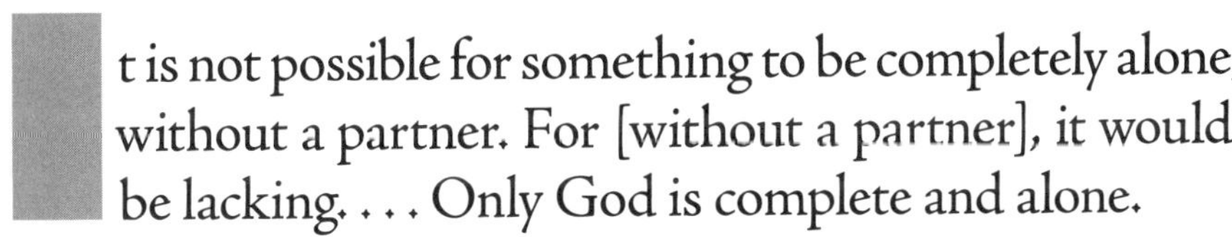

It is not possible for something to be completely alone, without a partner. For [without a partner], it would be lacking. . . . Only God is complete and alone.

Rabbi Yehudah Loew, *Tiferet Yisrael* 40

Text 8

אמרה שבת לפני הקדוש ברוך הוא, רבונו של עולם, לכולן יש בן זוג, ולי אין בן זוג. אמר לה הקדוש ברוך הוא כנסת ישראל היא בן זוגך. וכיון שעמדו ישראל לפני הר סיני אמר להם הקדוש ברוך הוא זכרו הדבר שאמרתי לשבת כנסת ישראל היא בן זוגך היינו דבור זכור את יום השבת לקדשו (שמות כ,ח).

בראשית רבה יא,ח

Shabbat pleaded before God, "Master of the Universe, all [of the days of the week] have a mate, while I have no mate!"

God responded to Shabbat, "The community of Israel is your mate."

When the Jewish people stood before Mount Sinai, God said to them, "Remember that I said to Shabbat, 'The community of Israel is your mate.'" That is the meaning of the verse (Exodus 20:8), "Remember the Shabbat day, to keep it holy (i.e., remember that I told Shabbat that you would consecrate it as a mate)."

Midrash, *Bereishit Rabah* 11:8

Learning Activity 2

Candle-lighting time presents a special opportunity to pause and pray for our lives and homes to be filled with peace and light. Based on what you have learned, write a short meditation for yourself for when you (or your wife) light(s) Shabbat candles.

(For example: May the light of these candles bring an atmosphere of calm and harmony into my home and a higher level of spirituality into my life. May I appreciate the members of my household for their uniqueness and differences, and may the light of these candles honor the Shabbat and welcome a holy presence into our midst.)

The Friday Night Angels

Greeting the Angels

Text 9

שָׁלוֹם עֲלֵיכֶם מַלְאֲכֵי הַשָּׁרֵת מַלְאֲכֵי עֶלְיוֹן מִמֶּלֶךְ מַלְכֵי הַמְּלָכִים הַקָּדוֹשׁ בָּרוּךְ הוּא.
בּוֹאֲכֶם לְשָׁלוֹם מַלְאֲכֵי הַשָּׁלוֹם מַלְאֲכֵי עֶלְיוֹן מִמֶּלֶךְ מַלְכֵי הַמְּלָכִים הַקָּדוֹשׁ בָּרוּךְ הוּא.
בָּרְכוּנִי לְשָׁלוֹם מַלְאֲכֵי הַשָּׁלוֹם מַלְאֲכֵי עֶלְיוֹן מִמֶּלֶךְ מַלְכֵי הַמְּלָכִים הַקָּדוֹשׁ בָּרוּךְ הוּא.
צֵאתְכֶם לְשָׁלוֹם מַלְאֲכֵי הַשָּׁלוֹם מַלְאֲכֵי עֶלְיוֹן מִמֶּלֶךְ מַלְכֵי הַמְּלָכִים הַקָּדוֹשׁ בָּרוּךְ הוּא.

שלום עליכם, סדור תהלת ה׳

Peace unto you, ministering angels, messengers of the Most High—of the supreme King of kings, the Holy One, blessed be He.

May your coming be in peace, angels of peace, messengers of the Most High—of the supreme King of kings, the Holy One, blessed be He.

Bless me with peace, angels of peace, messengers of the Most High—of the supreme King of kings, the Holy One, blessed be He.

May your departure be in peace, angels of peace, angels of the Most High—of the supreme King of kings, the Holy One, blessed be He.

Shalom Aleichem, Sidur Tehilat Hashem

Text 10

כד אתי בר נש מבי כנישתא יהכון עמיה מלאכין קדישין מהאי גיסא ומלאכין מהאי גיסא ושכינתא על כלהון . . . אם איניש יעיל לבייתיה בחדווא ויקבל אושפיזין בחדווא וכד אתי שכינתא ומלאכין ויחזו שרגא נהרא ופתורא מתתקנא ואיניש ואיתתיה בחדוה האי שעתא שכינתא אמרת זה שלי הוא ישראל אשר בך אתפאר.

זוהר חדש, אחרי מות פ,ב

When a person returns from the synagogue, holy angels accompany him on each side while the divine presence hovers over them all. . . . If the person enters his home with joy and receives guests with joy; and if upon arrival, the angels and the divine presence see the candles lit, the table set, and the husband and wife both joyous, at that moment the divine presence says, "This is mine—Israel in which I take pride" (Isaiah 49:3).

Zohar Chadash, Acharei Mot 80b

Text 11a

וַיַּרְא הָעָם וַיָּנֻעוּ וַיַּעַמְדוּ מֵרָחֹק.
שמות כ,טו

The people saw and they trembled and they stood from afar.

Exodus 20:15

Text 11b

היו נרתעין לאחוריהם . . . ומלאכי השרת באין ומסיעין אותן להחזירן.
רש"י, שם

The Jewish people drew back in awe. . . . The divine angels would come and assist them to return.

Rashi, ad loc.

Text 11c

חמו ישראל הכא מה דלא חמא יחזקאל בן בוזי וכלהו אתדבקו בחכמתא עלאה . . .
בישראל כתיב (דברים ה,ד) פנים בפנים דבר ה׳ וגו׳,
ביחזקאל כתיב כעין ודמות כמאן דחמי בתר כותלין סגיאין.
אמר רבי יהודה מה דחמו ישראל לא חמא נביאה אחרא.

זוהר ב, פב,א

The Jewish people saw [at Sinai] what the prophet Ezekiel ben Buzi did not see. All of Israel was united with the sublime wisdom. . . .

Regarding the Jewish people [at Sinai] it says, "Face to face, the Lord spoke with you" (Deuteronomy 5:4). However, Ezekiel used words like "similar" and "image"—like someone looking through many partitions.

Rabbi Yehudah said, "What the Jewish people saw [at Sinai] no other prophet ever saw."

Zohar 2:82a

Text 12

מיד ירד רבן יוחנן בן זכאי מעל החמור, ונתעטף וישב על האבן תחת הזית. אמר לו: רבי, מפני מה ירדת מעל החמור. אמר: אפשר אתה דורש במעשה מרכבה, ושכינה עמנו, ומלאכי השרת מלוין אותנו, ואני ארכב על החמור. מיד פתח רבי אלעזר בן ערך במעשה המרכבה ודרש . . .

וכשנאמרו הדברים לפני רבי יהושע היה הוא ורבי יוסי הכהן מהלכים בדרך, אמרו: אף אנו נדרוש במעשה מרכבה. פתח רבי יהושע ודרש . . . והיו מלאכי השרת מתקבצין ובאין לשמוע, כבני אדם שמתקבצין ובאין לראות במזמוטי חתן וכלה.

תלמוד בבלי, חגיגה יד,ב

Immediately, Raban Yochanan ben Zakai dismounted from his donkey, wrapped himself in a garment, and sat on a stone under an olive tree. Rabbi Elazar said to him, "Teacher, why did you dismount from your donkey?"

Rabban Yochanan replied, "Is it conceivable that you will expound on the esoteric teachings of the Torah with the divine presence among us and the angels accompanying us while I am riding on a donkey?"

At that point, Rabbi Elazar commenced expounding on the esoteric teachings of the Torah. . . .

When this was related to Rabbi Yehoshua, he and Rabbi Yosei Hakohen were walking on the road. They said, "Let us also expound on the esoteric teachings of the Torah."

Rabbi Yehoshua began expounding. . . . The angels gathered and came to hear [the teachings] the way people gather to see the merrymaking [performed before] the bride and groom.

Talmud, Chagigah 14b

Angelic Peace

Question for Discussion

Which of the following personalities do you think is hardest to get along with? Why?

1. An unintelligent person

2. A judgmental person

3. A negative person

4. An arrogant person

5. Other:

Text 13

An angel is a spiritual reality with its own unique content, qualities, and character. What distinguishes one angel from another is not the physical quality of spatial apartness but difference of level. . . . Angels are beings in the world that is the domain of emotion and feeling; and since this is the case, the substantial quality of an angel may be an impulse or a drive—say, an inclination in the direction of love or a seizure of fear, or pity, or the like. . . . Whereas among human beings emotions change and vary either as persons change or according to the circumstances of time and place, an angel is totally the manifestation of a single emotional essence. The essence of an angel, therefore, is defined by the limits of a particular emotion. . . .

The real difference between man and angel is not the fact that man has a body, because the essential comparison is between the human *soul* and the angel. The soul of man is most complex and includes a whole world of different existential elements of all kinds, while the angel is a being of single essence and therefore in a sense one-dimensional. . . . From the point of view of its essence, the angel is eternally the same; it is static, an unchanging existence, whether temporary or eternal, fixed within the rigid limits of quality given at its very creation.

Rabbi Adin Steinsaltz, *The Thirteen Petalled Rose* [Jerusalem: Koren Publishers, 2010], pp. 4–5

Rabbi Adin Steinsaltz (Even-Yisrael) (1937–). Born in Jerusalem, Steinsaltz is considered one of the foremost Jewish thinkers of the 20th century. Praised by *Time Magazine* as a "once-in-a-millennium scholar," he has been awarded the Israel Prize for his contributions to Jewish study. He is the founder of the Israel Institute for Talmudic Publications, a society dedicated to the translation and elucidation of the Talmud.

Text 14a

עוֹשֶׂה שָׁלוֹם בִּמְרוֹמָיו הוּא יַעֲשֶׂה שָׁלוֹם עָלֵינוּ וְעַל כָּל יִשְׂרָאֵל וְאִמְרוּ אָמֵן.

קדיש, סידור תהלת ה׳

e Who makes peace in His heavens, may He make peace for us and for all Israel; and let us say, Amen.

Kaddish, Sidur Tehilat Hashem

Text 14b

וזהו דבר פלא גדול איך אפשר שיוכללו ב׳ הפכים בעצם כאחד ממש . . . והוא מפני שנמשך והאיר עליהם מאור העליון האלקי . . . שגבוה מאד נעלה מכל עיקר ומקור התהוות מציאות המלאכים על כן יבואו בהתכללות יחד בתכלית כי נתבטלו לגבי האור העליון הזה מכל עיקר ומהות מציאות שלהם לגמרי מכל וכל.

כמו על דרך משל ממה שאנו רואים בשרי המלוכה למטה דגם ב׳ שרים גדולים מנגדים זה עם זה בתכלית וכל אחד הוא יש גדול בפני עצמו וכאשר יבואו יחד לפני המלך המרומם שמובדל ומרומם בערך נבדל מכל עיקר גדולתם אזי יתבטלו שניהם לגמרי מכל וכל לגמרי עד שלא ירגישו את עצמם בשום דבר יש כו׳ ואז יתחברו ויתכללו יחד בתכלית השלום לאחדים יחדיו וישכנו כאלו לא יש בהם שום פירוד כלל וכלל כו׳.

וכמו כן אנו רואים בב׳ תלמידים היפוכים בתכלית . . . כאשר יבואו יחד לפני רבם שנעלה בערך כח חכמתו עליהם בהפלגות הערך אזי יתבטלו שניהם ואינם ב׳ הפכים כלל ויחדיו יקבלו כאחד מאור חכמת רבם.

מאמרי אדמו״ר האמצעי, במדבר א,רעב

It is an astonishing thing: how can two intrinsic opposites unite as one entity? . . .

The answer is that a lofty divine light shines upon the angels . . . one that is much greater than the [divine] source that brings them into being. [This light] causes them to completely lose all sense of selfhood and identity, which then allows them to fuse.

Rabbi Dovber of Lubavitch (1773–1827). The eldest son of and successor to Rabbi Shne'ur Zalman of Liadi, also known as "the Miteler Rebbe"; he greatly expanded upon and developed his father's groundbreaking teachings. He was the first Chabad rebbe to live in the village of Lubavitch. Dedicated to the welfare of Russian Jewry, at that time confined to the "pale of settlement," he established Jewish agricultural colonies. He was arrested on libelous charges in 1826; however, he was released shortly thereafter. His most notable works on chasidic thought include *Sha'ar Hayichud*, *Torat Chayim*, and *Imrei Binah*.

An analogy can be drawn from our observation of terrestrial royal ministers. When two arrogant ministers who are the nemeses of one another together approach the king—whose exaltedness far exceeds their own—both totally surrender to the extent that they are not aware of themselves at all. In this state, the two can cooperate in total harmony, as if there is no divide between them.

Similarly, we sometimes see two students who think in diametrically different ways. . . . When they come together before their teacher whose intellectual prowess is greatly superior to theirs, both surrender [their individual identities, in the interest of absorbing the teacher's wisdom]. Together and united as one, they receive their master's wisdom and cease to be opposites.

Rabbi Dovber of Lubavitch, *Ma'amarei Admur Ha'emtsa'i*, Bamidbar 1:272

Text 15

שִׁוִּיתִי ה׳ לְנֶגְדִּי תָמִיד.

תהלים טז,ח

I have placed the Lord before me constantly.

Psalms 16:8

A Soul Guest

Extra Soul

Text 16

אמר רבי שמעון בן לקיש: נשמה יתירה נותן הקדוש ברוך הוא באדם ערב שבת,
ולמוצאי שבת נוטלין אותה הימנו.

תלמוד בבלי, ביצה טז,א

Rabbi Shimon ben Lakish said, "On the eve of Shabbat, God gives a person extra soul; at the close of Shabbat it is withdrawn from the person."

Talmud, Beitsah 16a

Learning Activity 3

A. Circle the correct definition(s) of "soul."

1. That which makes an inanimate body come alive
2. That which allows the inner workings of the body to function (i.e., to grow, to digest, to breathe, and to otherwise operate as a healthy organism)
3. The emotions of a human being
4. The intelligence of the human being
5. The essence of a created existence
6. The purpose of a created existence
7. A drive to be connected with God
8. A piece of God
9. All of the above
10. Other: ______________________________

B. Read the following two texts from Rashi and Nachmanides regarding the extra soul of Shabbat and determine which definition of the soul they are referring to:

Rashi:

רוחב לב למנוחה ולשמחה, ולהיות פתוח לרוחה, ויאכל וישתה ואין נפשו קצה עליו.

רש״י, ביצה טז,א

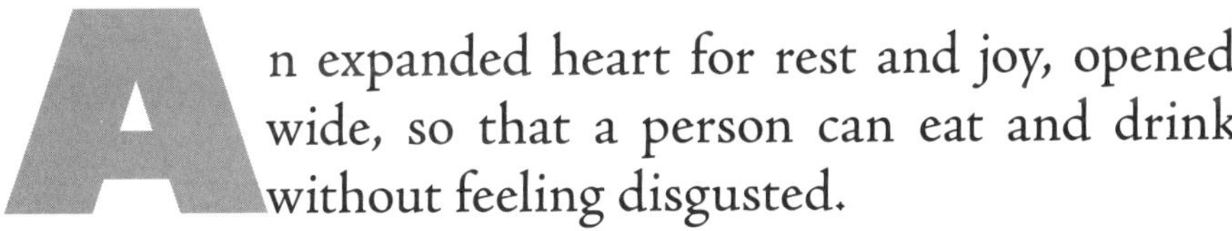

An expanded heart for rest and joy, opened wide, so that a person can eat and drink without feeling disgusted.

Rashi, Beitsah 16a

What is Rashi's definition of soul in this context? ______________

____

Rabbi Avraham ibn Ezra:

ורבי אברהם אמר . . . שזימן אותו לקבל בו הנפש תוספת חכמה יותר מכל הימים.

רמב״ן, שמות כ,יא

Rabbi Avraham [ibn Ezra] said, ". . . God designated [the day of Shabbat] to allow the soul to receive more wisdom than on all other days."

Nachmanides, Exodus 20:11

What is Ibn Ezra's definition of soul in this context? ______________

____

Text 17

בשבת נתוסף בכל אחד נשמה יתירה . . .
והיינו בחינת אהבה ורצון לה׳ שלמעלה מן השכל וההתבוננות.
כי הנה אית רצון ואית רצון פי׳ אית רצון שנולד מהשכל וההתבוננות . . . אבל אית
בחינת רצון העליון שלמעלה מעלה מהחכמה . . . שזהו בחינת יחידה . . .
וכמו על דרך משל כאשר יחפוץ האדם בחפץ ורצון לאיזה דבר הנוגע לעצם הנפש
ממש וגורם לו לעשות דברים שלא על פי הדעת והשכל כלל כי רצון זה עמוק עמוק
מהשכל . . . ובחינת אהבה ורצון זה לה׳ מתגלה בנפש אדם ביום השבת דוקא.
תורה אור, ויקהל פז,ד

Rabbi Shne'ur Zalman of Liadi (1745–1812). Chasidic rebbe and founder of the Chabad movement, also known as "the Alter Rebbe" and "the Rav." Born in Liozna, Belarus, he was among the principal students of the Magid of Mezeritch. His numerous works include the *Tanya*, an early classic containing the fundamentals of Chasidism; *Torah Or; Likutei Torah*; and *Shulchan Aruch HaRav*, a reworked and expanded code of Jewish law. He is interred in Hadiach, Ukraine, and was succeeded by his son, Rabbi Dovber of Lubavitch.

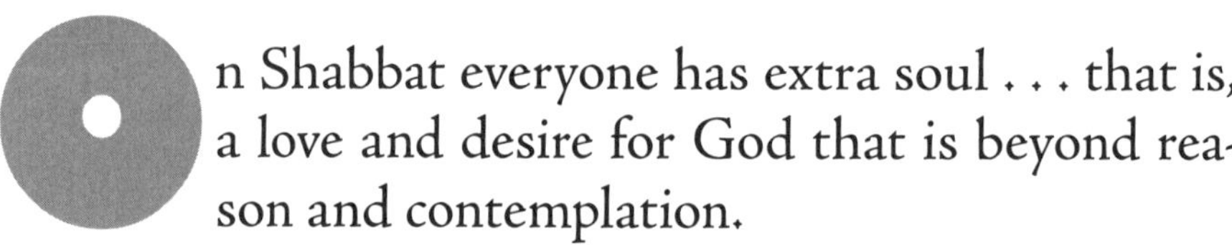

On Shabbat everyone has extra soul . . . that is, a love and desire for God that is beyond reason and contemplation.

There are two levels of desire. There is the desire that results from reason and contemplation . . . but there is also a level of desire that is far beyond reason. . . . This is the level called *yechidah*—oneness. . . .

By way of illustration, when a person wants something that affects his very essence, it causes the person to do things that are not based on rational reflection, because the desire is much deeper than reason. . . . It is this level of love and desire for God that is revealed in the soul of a person on Shabbat.

Rabbi Shne'ur Zalman of Liadi, *Torah Or, Vayakhel* 87d

Peace of Unity

Text 18

כתיב לא תקום ולא תטור את בני עמך היך עביד הוה מקטע קופד ומחת סכינא לידוי תחזור ותמחי לידיה.

תלמוד ירושלמי, נדרים ט,ד

It says, "You shall neither take revenge from nor bear a grudge against the members of your people" (Leviticus 19:18). How can this be? [Consider this example:] If while cutting meat a person [accidentally] cut his hand, would he retaliate and cut the hand [that was holding the knife]?

Jerusalem Talmud, Nedarim 9:4

Lesson Conclusion
Processing Exercise

Learning Activity 4

A. In this lesson we have surveyed three fundamental elements of Shabbat. The first two were physical actions or practices—lighting candles and singing *Shalom Aleichem*—and the third, the mystical concept of *neshamah yeteirah*. In turn, each of these sections taught us a lesson about achieving peace in our lives and relationships. To summarize:

1. Candle lighting: We recognize the uniqueness of each individual and respect their distinctive role. Moreover, when we have a relationship with another person, we gain something that we were missing and become more complete.

2. *Shalom Aleichem*: We put aside our differences when we become conscious of something greater than ourselves.

3. *Neshamah yeteirah*: We realize that we are really all part of one entity. As we love ourselves, we ought to love the other.

Together with your neighbor, review the methods of achieving peace discussed in this lesson by answering the questions in the chart on the next page.

B. After completing the chart, take a moment to think of a relationship or situation in your life where you can actively apply at least one of these approaches in order to bring more peace, love, and light into your life.

	Candle Lighting: Respect differences and distinctiveness	***Shalom Aleichem:*** Unite under a greater cause	***Neshamah Yeteirah:*** Appreciate your essential oneness
Do I see the other person's positive qualities or is that irrelevant?			
Do I need to overlook my own distinctive qualities or not?			
Does peace come from within the two parties or is it superimposed from without?			

Key Points

1. The Shabbat candles symbolize and embody the holiness of Shabbat.

2. We light Shabbat candles in order to avoid the chaos of darkness, to take pleasure in the food we eat, and to respect the Shabbat. We endeavor to have a special and unique light just for Shabbat.

3. Shabbat lights symbolize the recognition that everybody has a unique contribution that is needed by others. As a result, we respect differences among individuals.

4. The angels come to our home in order to help us overcome our hesitation to greet Shabbat and to witness the divine presence uniting with the Jewish people. They then depart, leaving us alone to be united with God.

5. When the house is prepared for the Shabbat meal and the people are in a joyous mood, the divine presence proclaims, "This is mine—the Jewish people in which I take pride."

6. Angels teach us that peace is achieved by surrendering to something greater that automatically dwarfs the significance of petty differences.

7. On Shabbat we have extra soul. This reflects itself in appetite and intellect but ultimately is the revelation of the innate connection of the soul with God.

8. The extra soul teaches us that we can achieve peace by focusing on the fact that we are really all part of one entity.

9. The highest levels of holiness, whether in time, place, or personhood, can only be achieved through a people united in heart as one.

Simply Shabbat: Lighting the Candles

"And God blessed the seventh day" (Genesis 2:2).

With what did He bless it? With the Shabbat candles (Midrash, *Bereishit Rabah* 11:2).

Why Shabbat Candles?

Having light on Shabbat honors the Shabbat and contributes to its pleasurable ambiance. It's no fun to eat in the dark. Furthermore, trying to navigate one's way through a dark house certainly doesn't make for a peaceful Shabbat. Because it is forbidden to light a candle on Shabbat, the sages instituted that candles should be kindled beforehand in every room of the house that requires illumination. Bedrooms, for example, generally don't require light.

Candles vs. Electric Lighting

Today, when homes are equipped with electric lighting, keeping the house well lit on Friday night is not a problem. Before Shabbat, check the electric lighting for all the rooms of the home that will require lighting—such as the kitchen, corridors, and bathroom. However, the most beautiful way to honor Shabbat is to light Shabbat candles. Thus, before Shabbat, we light candles in the room where the Shabbat meal will be held.

Who?

The mitzvah of lighting Shabbat candles applies to men and women equally. Nevertheless, if there is a woman (over the age of bat mitzvah) in the house, she lights the candles for the entire household. As the mainstay of the home, it is the woman's privilege and responsibility to ensure that light, peace, and harmony prevail. If there is no woman in the house, the candles are kindled by a man.

Girls start lighting Shabbat candles as soon as they start speaking and can recite the candle-lighting blessing, around the age of three. By lighting Shabbat candles, a person marks personal acceptance of Shabbat and may no longer do any of the activities forbidden on Shabbat, which includes striking a match or lighting a candle. Therefore, young girls light before their mother so that she can assist them.

In many households, it is customary for the husband to participate in the mitzvah by setting up and preparing the candles for lighting. Some char the wicks, making it easier later for the candles to be lit.

How Many Candles?

The custom for married women is to light at least two candles, corresponding to the two biblical commands regarding Shabbat: "Remember the day of Shabbat to sanctify it" (Exodus 20:8), and "Observe the day of Shabbat to sanctify it" (Deuteronomy 5:12).

Until marriage, the custom is for women and girls to light one candle.

What Kind of Candles?

Wax candles or oil and wicks are both fine. Colored candles are also fine. The only specification that the Shabbat candles must meet is that they emit a clear smooth flame; as such, virtually all candles and oils manufactured today are kosher for use as Shabbat candles, even if they contain ingredients that are non-kosher for eating. The candles should be long enough to burn until nightfall, and ideally, until after the meal.

When?

Shabbat candles must be lit before sunset. Because it is never wise to wait until the last moment, it is customary to light the candles at least eighteen minutes before sunset. The candles should be lit no earlier than approximately 1¼ hours before sunset (a bit longer than that in the summer, a bit shorter in the winter).

It is very important not to light candles after sunset; doing so would constitute a desecration of the holiness of Shabbat.

For the proper candle-lighting time for any date and location, go to: **www.chabad.org/candlelighting.**

How?

The Zohar extols the greatness of lighting the candles with joy and good feeling. This has a broader implication as well: We must illuminate our environment with the light of Torah and *mitzvot* with great joy, recognizing the tremendous privilege inherent in being God's "ambassador of light" to the world.

1. Safety first. Set the candles on a metal tray in a location that is out of the reach of young children and clear of flammable objects.

2. Set the candles on or near the table on which the Shabbat meal will be eaten.

3. It is customary to light the Shabbat candles while dressed in Shabbat clothing.

4. It is appropriate to place some money in a charity box before lighting the Shabbat candles.

5. Light the candle(s).

6. Do not extinguish the match, but let it burn down on the metal tray upon which the candles are standing.

7. Extend your hands and draw them inward in a circular motion three times.

8. Cover your eyes with your hands, and recite the following blessing:

בָּרוּךְ אַתָּה אֲדֹנָי, אֱלֹהֵינוּ מֶלֶךְ הָעוֹלָם, אֲשֶׁר קִדְּשָׁנוּ בְּמִצְוֹתָיו, וְצִוָּנוּ לְהַדְלִיק נֵר שֶׁל שַׁבָּת קוֹדֶשׁ.

Baruch atah Adonai, Eloheinu melech ha'olam, asher kidishanu bemitsvotav, vetsivanu lehadlik ner shel Shabbat kodesh.

Blessed are You, Lord our God, King of the Universe, Who has sanctified us with His commandments, and commanded us to kindle the light of the holy Shabbat.

9. While your eyes are still covered, take a moment to silently pray for whatever your heart desires. It is customary to use this special time to beseech God for children who will be illuminated by the radiance of the Torah, and to ask God to illuminate the world with the light of redemption.

10. Open your eyes and say "Shabbat Shalom," or "Good Shabbos" to all who are present.

Shabbat Shalom!

Additional Readings

What Are Angels?

by **Rabbi Adin Steinsaltz**

The world of formation may be said to be, in its essence, a world of feeling. It is a world whose main substance, or type of experience, is emotion of one kind or another, and in which such emotions are the elements that determine its patterns. The living beings in it are conscious manifestations of particular impulses—impulses to perform one or another act or responding one or another way—or of the power to carry through an incentive, to realize, to fulfill the tendency of an inclination or an inspiration. The living creatures of the world of formation, the beings who function in it as we function in the world of action, are called, in a general way, "angels."

An angel is a spiritual reality with its own unique content, qualities, and character. What distinguishes one angel from another is not the physical quality of spatial apartness but difference of level—one being above or below another—with respect to fundamental causality in terms of some difference in essence. Now as we have said, angels are beings in the world that is the domain of emotion and feeling; and since this is the case, the substantial quality of an angel may be an impulse or a drive—say, an inclination in the direction of love or a seizure of fear, or pity, or the like. To express a larger totality of being, something more comprehensive, we may refer to "a camp of angels." In the general camp of love, for example, there are many subdivisions, virtually innumerable shades and gradations of tender feeling. No two loves are alike in emotion, just as no two ideas are alike. Thus, any general and inclusive drive or impulse is a whole camp, perhaps even a mansion, and is not consistently the same at every level. Whereas among human beings emotions change and vary either as persons change or according to the circumstances of time and place, an angel is totally the manifestation of a single emotional essence. The essence of an angel, therefore, is defined by the limits of a particular emotion, in terms of itself, just as personality and inwardness define the self of each person in our world. An angel, however, is not merely a fragment of existence doing nothing more than just manifesting an emotion; it is a whole and integral being, conscious of itself and its surroundings and able to act and create and do things within the framework of the world of formation. The nature of the angel is to be, to a degree, as its name in Hebrew signifies, a messenger, to constitute a permanent contact between our world of action and the higher worlds. The angel is the one who effects transfers of the vital plenty between worlds. An angel's missions go in two directions: it may serve as an emissary of God downward, to other angels and to worlds and creatures below the world of formation; and it may also serve as the one who carries things upward from below, from our world to the higher worlds.

The real difference between man and angel is not the fact that man has a body, because the essential comparison is between the human *soul* and the angel. The soul of man is the most complex and includes a whole world of different existential elements of all kinds, while the angel is a being of single essence and therefore in a sense one-dimensional. In addition, man—because of his many-sidedness, his capacity to contain contradictions, and his gift of an inner power of soul, that divine spark that makes him man—has the capacity to distinguish between one thing and another, especially between good and evil. It is this capacity which makes it possible for him to rise to great heights, and by the same token creates the possibility for his failure and backsliding, neither of which is true for the angel. From the point of the view of its essence, the angel is eternally the same; it is static, an unchanging existence, whether temporary or eternal, fixed within the rigid limits of quality given at its very creation.

Among the many thousands of angels to be found in the various worlds are those that have existed from the very beginning of time, for they are an unaltering part of the Eternal Being and the fixed order of the universe. These angels in a sense constitute the channels of plenty through which the divine grace rises and descends in the worlds.

But there are also angels that are continuously being created anew, in all the worlds, and especially in the world of action where thoughts, deeds and experiences give rise to angels of different kinds. Every *mitzva* that a man does is not only an act of transformation in the material world; it is also a spiritual act, sacred in itself. And this aspect of concentrated spirituality and holiness in the *mitzva* is the chief component of that which becomes an angel. In other words, the emotion, the intention, the essential holiness of the act combine to become the essence of the *mitzva* as an existence in itself, as something that has objective reality. And this separate existence of the *mitzva*, by being unique and holy, creates the angel, a new spiritual reality that belongs to the world of formation. So it is that the act of performing a *mitzva* extends beyond its effect in the material world and, by the power of the spiritual holiness within it—holiness in direct communion with all the upper worlds—causes a primary and significant transformation.

More precisely, the person who performs a *mitzva*, who prays or directs his mind toward the Divine, in so doing creates an angel, which is a sort of reaching on the part of man to the higher worlds. Such an angel, however, connected in its essence to the man who created it, still lives, on the whole, in a different dimension of being, namely in the world of formation. And it is in this world of formation that the *mitzva* acquires substance. This is the process by which the specific message or offering to God that is intrinsic in the *mitzva* rises upward and introduces changes in the system of the higher worlds—foremost in the world of formation. From here, in turn, they influence the worlds above them. So we see that a supreme act is performed when what is done below becomes detached from a particular physical place, time, and person and becomes an angel.

Conversely, an angel is sometimes sent downward from a higher world to a lower. For what we call the mission of the angel can be manifested in many different ways. The angel cannot reveal its true form to man, whose being, senses, and instruments of perception belong only to the world of action: in the world of action there are no means of grasping the angel. It continues to belong to a different dimension even when apprehended in one form or another. This may be compared with those frequencies of an electromagnetic field that are beyond the limited range ordinarily perceived by our senses. We know that human vision assimilates only a small fragment of the spectrum; as far as our senses are concerned, the rest of it does not exist. That which is ordinarily invisible is "seen" only through appropriate instruments of transmutation, or interpretation, when, in the language of the Kabbala, they are dressed in clothes or vessels that make it possible for us to apprehend them—as, for example, radio or television waves have to be transmitted through appropriate vessels to be revealed to our senses. In the same way, there are aspects of the reality of the spiritual world of which we are only vaguely conscious. Even animals can sometimes be sensitive, if to a limited degree, to the presence of such a spiritual essence. The ass of Balaam, for instance, who "saw" an angel, did not of course actually see the angel: probably the animal had some obscure sensation of being confronted or threatened by something.

Angels have been revealed to human beings in either of two ways: one is though the vision of the prophet, the seer, or the holy man—that is, an experience by a person on the highest level; the other is through an isolated act of apprehension by an ordinary person suddenly privileged to receive a revelation of things from higher levels. And even so, when such a person or prophet does in some way experience the reality of an angel, his perception, limited by his senses, remains bound to material structures, and his language inevitably tends to expressions of actual or imagined physical forms. Thus, when the prophet tries to describe or to explain to others his experience of seeing an angel, the description verges on the eerie and fantastic. Terms like "winged creature of heaven" or "eyes of the supreme chariot" can be only a pale and inadequate representation of the experience because this experience belongs to another realm with another system of imagery. The description will of necessity tend to be anthropomorphic. Or when, as we know, the angel whom the prophet describes as having the face of an ox does not have any face at all—and certainly not that of an ox—its inner essence, seeking elucidation and reflection within material reality, may express itself in a way that shows a certain likeness between the face of an angel and the face of an ox as the expression of a known spiritual quality.

Thus, all the articulated visions of prophecy are nothing more than ways of representing an abstract formless spiritual reality in the vocabulary of human language; although, to be sure, there may also be a revelation of an angel in quite ordinary form, clothed in some familiar vessel and manifested as a "normal" phenomenon in nature. The difficulty is that the one who sees an angel in this way does not always know that it is an apparition, that the pillar of fire or the image of a man does not belong entirely to the realm of natural cause and effect. And at the same time, the angel—that is to say, the force sent from a higher world—makes its appearance and to a certain extent acts in the material world, being either entirely subject to the laws of our world or operating in a sort of vacuum between the worlds which physical nature is no more than a kind of garment for some higher substance. In the Bible, Manoah, the father of Samson, sees the angel in the image of a prophet; yet he senses in some inexplicable way that it is not a man he sees, that he is witnessing a phenomenon of a different order. Only when the angel changes form completely and becomes a pillar of fire does Manoah recognize that this being, this marvel which he has seen and with whom he has conversed, was not a man, not a prophet, but a being from another dimension of reality—that is to say, an angel.

The creation of an angel in our world and the immediate relegation of this angel to another world is, in itself, not at all a supernatural phenomenon; it is a part of a familiar realm of experience, an integral piece of life, which may even seem ordinary and commonplace because of its traditional rootedness in the system of *mitzvot*, or the order of sanctity. When we are in the act of creating the angel, we have no perception of the angel being created, and this act seems to be a part of the whole structure of the practical material world in which we live. Similarly, the angel who is sent to us from another world does not always have a significance or impact beyond the normal laws of physical nature. Indeed, it often happens that the angel precisely reveals itself in nature, in the ordinary common-sense world of causality, and only a prophetic insight or divination can show when, and to what extent, it is the work of higher forces. For man by his very nature is bound to the system of higher worlds, even though ordinarily this system is not revealed and known to him. As a result, the system of higher worlds seems to him to be natural, just as the whole of his two-sided existence, including both matter and spirit, seems self-evident to him. Man does not wonder at all about those passages he goes through all the time in the world of action, from the realm of material existence to the realm of spiritual existence. What is more, the rest of the other worlds that also penetrate our world may appear to us as part of something quite natural. It may be said that the realities of the angel and of the world of formation are part of a system of "natural" being which is as bound by law as that aspect of existence we are able to observe directly. Therefore neither the existence of the angel nor his "mission," taking him from world to world, need break through the reality of nature in the broadest sense of the word.

The domain of angels, the world of formation, is a general system of nonphysical essences, most of them quite simple and consistent in their being. Each angel has a well-defined character which is manifested in the way it functions in our world. This is why it is said that an angel can carry out only one mission, for the essence of an angel is beyond the existing many-sidedness of man. The particular essence of an angel can be evinced in terms of different things and separate forms, but it remains a single thing in itself, like a simple force of nature. Because even though the angel is a being that possesses divine consciousness, its specific essence and function are not altered by it, just as physical forces in the world are specific and single in their mode of functioning and do not keep changing their essences. It follows, then, that just as there are holy angels, built into and created by the sacred system, there are also destructive angels, called "devils" or "demons," who are the emanations of the connection of man with those aspects of reality which are the opposite of holiness. Here, too, the actions of man and his modes of existence, in all their forms, create angels, but angels of another sort, from another level and a different reality. These are hostile angels that may be part of a lower world or even a higher, more spiritual world—this last because even though they do not belong to the realm of holiness, as in all worlds and systems of being, there is a mutual interpenetration and influence between the holy and the not–holy.

The Thirteen Petalled Rose,
(Jerusalem: Koren Publishers, 2010),
excerpt from ch. 1, "Worlds," pp. 3–9
Reprinted with permission of Maggid Books, an imprint of Koren Publishers, Jerusalem Ltd.

Shabbat Candles

by **Carol Kasser**

"The dimly burning wick shall he not quench." (Isaiah 42:3)

It was Friday afternoon, and the Jewish nursing home residents filled the activity room for Shabbat services. I lit the Shabbat candles—two tapers of the same size, lit from the same match. Yet one candle burned with a large orange flame and the other produced a minute, barely visible flicker of blue. "That one isn't lit," called out several of the residents. I looked again and saw that the blue flicker was still barely visible. I said the blessings, and as always I felt the spirit of Shabbat fill the room as the residents joined me in singing *Shalom Aleichem, Peace to You*.

But my eyes kept going back to those two candles, the one blazing; the other just flickering. When it came time for my sermon, I threw out what I had prepared, and talked instead about those candles. It occurred to me that those candles were a metaphor for humanity. All of us were given the same spark of Divinity from the same Source. Yet some let that spark shine forth and brighten the world; others squelch the soul-light until it is almost extinguished. They show nothing of their soul-light to the world.

After flickering through most of the service, the little light suddenly burst into full flame. And that too was a metaphor for humanity. No matter how dark our lives have been, no matter how hard we have tried to extinguish our soul-light, it never goes out completely. And with repentance and change of heart, it is never too late to let G-d's light within us shine and brighten the world.

I think the metaphor of the candles is particularly appropriate for the nursing home residents. For some of them, in pain, frail, forgetful, life must seem like that flickering blue candle, but for a moment, during Shabbat, when they join in prayer, the life and the soul blaze forth brightly again.

I think again of Dr. Fishman, the silent man in the end state of Alzheimer's, who broke his silence to say, "Good Shabbos." I realize that for that one brief moment, I had seen a flicker again become a flame. And that is why life, even when it is reduced to a flicker, is so precious. . . . I am sometimes given the blessing of seeing the Divine spark shine forth from "the dimly burning wick."

Cast Me Not Off When I Am Old: A Sourcebook for the Aging, Their Families, and Caretakers. (Lincoln, NE: iUniverse, 2004), p. 39
Reprinted by permission of the publisher

Shabbat Poems

by **Zelda Schneersohn Mishkovsky**

My Mother's Room Was Lit

The pale painter mixed in the wet paint
the faintest of pinks
the glory of apple blossom, a babe's smile.
Silver clusters he put, and brass crowns engraved
in the candlesticks of inheritance,
glittering on the chest,
reflected in a round mirror,
(orchards of love from generation
to generation and the crowns of
lineage and tears).
And on the table, through the tales of
the righteous, the golden tales,
(that Rabbi Zevin gathered, collected),
a mountain breeze leafs slowly slowly,
mixing snowy landscapes with an arid landscape.
My mother is praying—on her head, silken checkers.
The big inner room is as dark
as Rabbi Shim'on bar Yochai's cave.
In it, a sea's silence—
in it, Sabbath, as if it were the world to come.
The entire flat is still.
My husband went to his office.
My mother is in the palace of her
prayers.
I'm in the kitchen.
And in the tin can, a geranium overflows like blood.
In the paved courtyard, by the plants,
a cat is pacing like a landlady from the old generation.
Slowly slowly
the door opens
to milk, to bread, to candles,
to taxes, to a letter.
Friday is the day of a laughing eye painted blue,
and the day of the sad mouth.
Friday is the day of the poor.
So pass the days,
so pass the years.
Faint light shall cover pain, helplessness,
mistakes.
So pass the days and the roaring life,
abounding with desires, buds, babes, seas and forests,
stealthily deserting my limbs, spilling like blood.
When I die,
God shall unravel my embroidery
thread by thread,
and to the sea throw my paints,
to His warehouses in the abyss.
And perhaps He shall turn them to a
flower and perhaps He shall turn
them to a butterfly,
dark-nocturnal-soft; dark-nocturnal-alive.

The Silver Candlesticks

The silver candlesticks, the radiance of inheritance,
turned my room to an ancient castle,
to a heavenly castle, to a lofty abode
on a starry nothingness.
The silver candlesticks are songs of glory,
crowns scoured by tears,
which gladden the heart
with their engravings,
brighten the darkness
with wreaths of forged roses.

They are vessels of sensitive
greatness, which absorbed
bitter pain,
a weeping uprooting
the voice of praise and hope.
To silver flowers I likened them,
to ancient silver flowers,
whose calyxes hold the light of peace,

the joy of babes
and a candle of blessing to the Eternal One.
Their living flames
kissed my soul,
and my thoughts became a river of rose-colored flowers,
became fowls from the wild forests,
became lightning.

And all of me is a burning being
free, happy in God,
who has thrown off herself the tatters of conventions,
and my heart is again wide as a white cascade.
Where is the winsome one who fashioned
this diadem to rest,
who cast rejoicing and trembling like ornaments
for the Sabbath?
In metal he set down yearning for ancient holiness,
his desire for a living God,
I will hold in my hand.
These silver stems
are a prayer, a confession.

Bring forth wine, pour to the hidden!
I will beseech him, I will atone,
for I've forgotten that he is a silent crescent
in Death's forests,
that his name is buried in snow and his memory,
the storm blotted out,
only his tear is still warm,
and from my eye is spilling
at night, this evening,
with the flickering of the candles.

A Sabbath Candle

My heart asked the evening,
my deep and compassionate companion:
How can fire
sprout golden wings
and embark on a magical flight.
What is its secret?
A lonely flower replied to the heart:
Love is the root of fire.
The sea breeze
answered my thoughts:
The lily of all freedom in the universe,
this is the fire of wondrous light.

My blood hearkens—
and weeps bitterly.
Woe, a flame—even an auto-da-fe.
It was also said—
fire is a wondrous mockery of dust.

Is it proper for a mortal woman,
soft of heart,
to roam and wander
in the garden of fire.
How dare she
in the smoke of waste conjure
the ember of peace,
an ember with which Sarah Bat Tovim would light
a Sabbath candle in the gloom of pain.
Between the walls of nightmare
it would bloom, burning slowly
in the crumbling house, in the pit.
Facing it, the woman of sorrowful depths
shut her eyes,
to worry, to mourning, to shame, to the mundane.

The candle's sparks are palaces,
and in the midst of the palaces
mothers sing to the heavens

to endless generations.
And she wanders in their midst
toward God, with a barefoot baby
and with the murdered.
Hurrah!
The soft of heart comes in dance
in the golden Holy of Holies, inside a spark.

Sabbath and Weekdays

To light candles in all the worlds
this is Sabbath.
To light Sabbath candles
is the leap of a soul pregnant with secrets,
mysterious with the fire of sunset,
to a magnificent sea.
As I light the candles, my room
turns to a River of Fire,
my heart sinks in emerald waterfalls.

But on the first day of the week
my soul is thrown
from the ocean's heart to a land's shore
long, narrow, and desolate.
When I come to the store
the grocer immediately senses
that I've come from another planet, and with dismay
surveys my looks, foreign to him, the
remnant of the abyss—
and in his cold pupils, as if in a black mirror,
I see my crumpled scarf, my embarrassed smile.
And in the store stands another woman, a round lady,
slowly selecting golden fruit,
a creature of a distant world.
I wake up from a daydream
when the tone of the air, the rhythm of
voices change, for the short one discovered
that her money was gone ... Woe to me!
The dark grocer pours dung of suspicion
on my disheveled, neglected looks. Before his gaze
my future wilts like a flower, my past withers.
My dreams are dying.
Woe to me for I'm alone in the thick of the forest,
in the darkness, a roaring lion answers
my weeping, and mute trees
set on me from all sides . . .
The door is open, but I cannot get out
from the store's trap.
Now I see with cruel clarity
how little a person knows about one's fellows—
even your household
members, even your dear ones, may
in a moment of eclipse
find in you any wicked fault.
I drown in the darkness . . .

Suddenly, in the very heart of blindness,
I heard a voice:
Truth will not die with the grocer,
Truth will not die with the short lady,
Truth will not die with your death.
My soul awakened, and trembling
sensed that the King of Glory was with her
in the foul store.

I always said:
The voice of God is over the mighty waters,
The voice of God is in the song of the morning stars,
The voice of God is in the whirlwind.
And here
in the heart of the tumult, the Lord
of Winds gathered me,
on the waves of hatred as on a viscous stone
I came in dance before Him,
I raised my voice in song
to truth, whose footstool are sun, moon, and stars.
I almost kissed the grocer,

for behind his worried back was revealed to me
the view of shining freedom,
the freedom of the lands of the Sabbath
which burns in the songs of the palace dwellers.

I did not lose favor with the butterfly
in paradise and with the winds
that roar above the sea.
I did not bow before the glance that sees
in my cheeks the wrinkles of defeat
but doesn't see my soul that roams
in the fullness of the universe, doesn't know
that my soul is a ray of the sun
and will not be caught in the palm.

Selected poems from "Seven Poems by Zelda,"
Trans. Varda Koch Ocker, *Judaism*, 54:1–2 (2005)
Reprinted by permission of the publisher

Lesson 4
Pure Pleasure

עונג שבת

Introduction

The Talmud (Shabbat 119a) tells the story of an emperor who asked Rabbi Yehoshua ben Chananyah, "Why does the Shabbat food have such a fragrant smell?"

"We have a certain seasoning called Shabbat that we add to our food that gives it this wonderful smell."

"Give me some of it," said the emperor.

Rabbi Yehoshua responded, "For one who observes Shabbat, it is effective, but for one who does not observe Shabbat, it is of no use."

In this lesson, we will discuss the special foods of Shabbat and why they provide such delight.

Necessary Pleasures

Learning Activity 1

How does Judaism view pleasure?

1. Totally evil
2. Somewhat negative or dangerous
3. Neutral: neither good nor evil
4. Somewhat positive or life-enhancing
5. Totally good

Share your answer with your neighbors. Do they agree with your assessment? Why or why not?

Text 1

אין למעלה מעונג.
ספר יצירה ב,ד

There is nothing higher than pleasure.

Sefer Yetsirah 2:4

The Pleasures of Shabbat

The Shabbat Meals

Text 2a

חייב אדם לאכול שלש סעודות בשבת אחת ערבית ואחת שחרית ואחת במנחה, וצריך להזהר בשלש סעודות אלו שלא יפחות מהן כלל, ואפילו עני המתפרנס מן הצדקה סועד שלש סעודות . . . וצריך לקבוע כל סעודה משלשתן על היין ולבצוע על שתי ככרות.
רמב"ם, הלכות שבת ל,ט

A person is obligated to eat three meals on Shabbat: one [Friday] evening, one [Shabbat] morning, and one [Shabbat] afternoon. One should be extremely careful not to skip any of these three meals. Even a poor person who derives his livelihood from charity should eat these three meals. . . . All three meals must be significant ones at which

Rabbi Moshe ben Maimon (1135–1204). Better known as Maimonides or by the acronym Rambam; born in Cordoba, Spain. After the conquest of Cordoba by the Almohads, he fled Spain and eventually settled in Cairo, Egypt. There, he became the leader of the Jewish community and served as court physician to the vizier of Egypt. His rulings on Jewish law are considered integral to the formation of halachic consensus. He is most noted for authoring the *Mishneh Torah,* an encyclopedic arrangement of Jewish law, and for his philosophical work, *Guide for the Perplexed.*

wine is served; at each, one must break bread on two complete loaves.

Maimonides, *Mishneh Torah*, Laws of Shabbat 30:9

Text 2b

איזה הוא עונג . . . שצריך לתקן תבשיל שמן ביותר ומשקה מבושם לשבת הכל לפי ממונו של אדם, וכל המרבה בהוצאת שבת ובתיקון מאכלים רבים וטובים הרי זה משובח.

רמב״ם, הלכות שבת ל,ז

What is meant by delight? . . . A person must prepare a particularly sumptuous dish and a pleasantly flavored beverage for Shabbat—commensurate with one's financial status. The more one spends for Shabbat and the more good food one prepares, the more praiseworthy it is.

Maimonides, *Mishneh Torah*, Laws of Shabbat 30:7

Text 2c

כל המענג את השבת נותנין לו משאלות לבו.

תלמוד בבלי, שבת קיח,ב

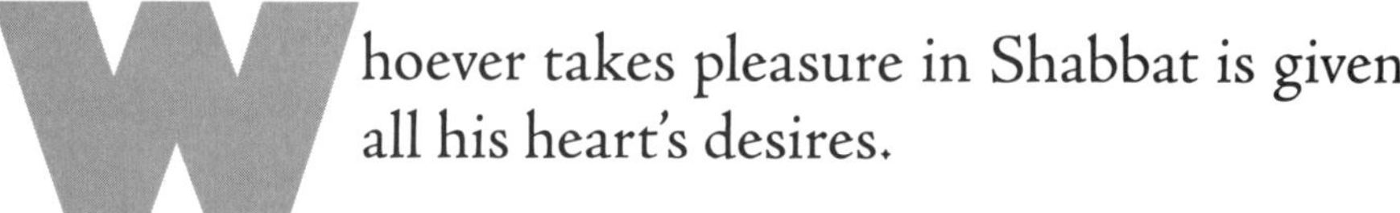

Whoever takes pleasure in Shabbat is given all his heart's desires.

Talmud, Shabbat 118b

Kiddush

Text 3a

זָכוֹר אֶת יוֹם הַשַּׁבָּת לְקַדְּשׁוֹ.
שמות כ,ח

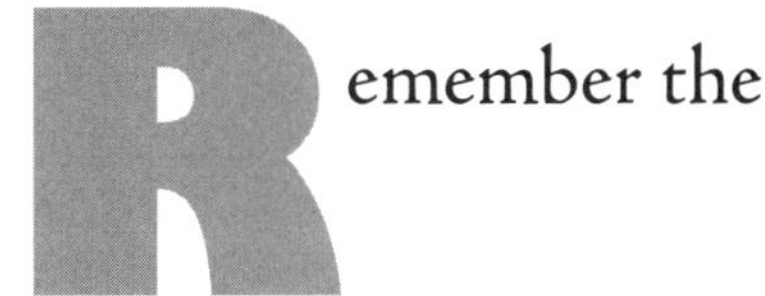

Remember the day of Shabbat to sanctify it.

Exodus 20:8

Text 3b

יוֹם הַשִּׁשִּׁי. וַיְכֻלּוּ הַשָּׁמַיִם וְהָאָרֶץ וְכָל צְבָאָם. וַיְכַל אֱלֹקִים בַּיּוֹם הַשְּׁבִיעִי מְלַאכְתּוֹ אֲשֶׁר עָשָׂה. וַיִּשְׁבֹּת בַּיּוֹם הַשְּׁבִיעִי מִכָּל מְלַאכְתּוֹ אֲשֶׁר עָשָׂה. וַיְבָרֶךְ אֱלֹקִים אֶת יוֹם הַשְּׁבִיעִי וַיְקַדֵּשׁ אֹתוֹ כִּי בוֹ שָׁבַת מִכָּל מְלַאכְתּוֹ אֲשֶׁר בָּרָא אֱלֹקִים לַעֲשׂוֹת.
קידוש ליל שבת, סדור תהלת ה׳

The sixth day. And the heavens and the earth and all their hosts were completed. And God finished by the seventh day His work which He had done, and He rested on the seventh day from all His work which He had done. And God blessed the seventh day and made it holy, for on it God rested from all His work that He created and fashioned.

Friday Night Kiddush, *Sidur Tehilat Hashem*

Question for Discussion

Look at the text of Kiddush (Text 3b). Can you find a phrase that does not fit?

Text 4a

וַיְהִי עֶרֶב וַיְהִי בֹקֶר יוֹם חֲמִישִׁי.

בראשית א,כג

nd it was evening, and it was morning, a fifth day.

Genesis 1:23

Text 4b

וַיְהִי עֶרֶב וַיְהִי בֹקֶר יוֹם הַשִּׁשִּׁי.

בראשית א,לא

nd it was evening and it was morning, the sixth day.

Genesis 1:31

Text 4c

The definite article "the" which precedes a noun presents the thing (or person or entity) as something expected; we are prepared for it, and expect it, due to what was stated before. "Here is *a* man" presents "man" as a new idea, without any preparation, whereas "Here is *the* man" presents "man" as something expected, something we have a right to expect in light of the preceding.

Thus, had Scripture said *yom shishi*, "a sixth day," there would have been no relation to the preceding days, except for the ordinal relation; there would have been no indication that this day was prepared for by all those days that preceded it, and was awaited by all that came before it.

Scripture, however, says, "And it was evening and it was morning, *the* sixth day." The clear implication is that this is the day for which all the preceding days served as preliminaries; all of creation led up to the sixth day which gave creation its goal and culmination. . . . All the preceding days are mentioned without the definite article "*the*." . . . But in our verse Scripture says: "*the* sixth day"—i.e., the day for which all the preceding days served as preliminaries, the day to which they all led, the day that bestowed upon them their purpose and culmination.

Now the sixth day brought man to earth. On this day the earth was given its master and governor, who would rule it in God's stead. . . . All of creation hinges

Rabbi Samson Raphael Hirsch (1808–1888). Born in Hamburg, Germany; rabbi and educator; intellectual founder of the *Torah Im Derech Eretz* school of Orthodox Judaism, which advocates combining Torah with secular education. Beginning in 1830, Hirsch served as chief rabbi in several prominent German cities. During this period he wrote his *Nineteen Letters on Judaism*, under the pseudonym of Ben Uziel. His work helped preserve traditional Judaism during the era of the German Enlightenment. He is buried in Frankfurt am Main.

on whether this creature—man—will accept and fulfill his exalted mission. . . .

Thus the sixth day became the crowning seal of creation, and thus it, too, was elevated into the sphere of the Shabbat. For the seventh day . . . was assigned the following task: to remind man, who was created on the sixth day, of the exaltedness of his position and of the dependence of his position—and of the duties that devolve upon him as a result. Accordingly, the seventh day hinges on the sixth day, which preceded it; the seventh day flows from the sixth day and completes it. The task of the seventh day is to ensure the realization of man's mission in creation. . . .

The sixth day caps the concrete world and is essential to its existence, whereas the seventh day is essential to the noblest creation of the sixth. The seventh day brings to the noblest of the physical creations the consciousness of the eternity of the metaphysical world. It is with good reason, then, that we begin the Kiddush with "The sixth day, and God completed," etc.

Rabbi Samson Raphael Hirsch, Genesis 1:31

Text 5

דאמר רב המנונא: כל המתפלל בערב שבת ואומר ויכלו מעלה עליו הכתוב כאילו נעשה שותף להקדוש ברוך הוא במעשה בראשית.

תלמוד בבלי, שבת קיט,ב

Rav Hamenuna said, "One who prays on Friday night and says *'vayechulu'* is considered by Scripture as if he were a partner with God in Creation."

Talmud, Shabbat 119b

Text 6

נכנס יין יצא סוד.

תלמוד בבלי, סנהדרין לח,א

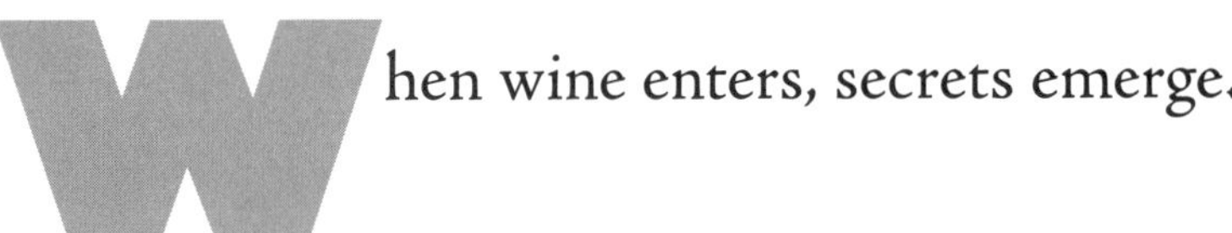

When wine enters, secrets emerge.

Talmud, Sanhedrin 38a

Text 7

בָּרוּךְ אַתָּה ה׳ אֱלֹקֵינוּ מֶלֶךְ הָעוֹלָם, אֲשֶׁר קִדְּשָׁנוּ בְּמִצְוֹתָיו וְרָצָה בָנוּ, וְשַׁבַּת קָדְשׁוֹ בְּאַהֲבָה וּבְרָצוֹן הִנְחִילָנוּ, זִכָּרוֹן לְמַעֲשֵׂה בְרֵאשִׁית, תְּחִלָּה לְמִקְרָאֵי קֹדֶשׁ, זֵכֶר לִיצִיאַת מִצְרָיִם . . .

קידוש ליל שבת, סדור תהלת ה׳

Blessed are You, Lord our God, King of the Universe, Who has hallowed us with His commandments, has desired us, and has given us, in love and goodwill, His holy Shabbat as a heritage, in remembrance of the work of Creation; the first of the holy festivals, commemorating the Exodus from Egypt. . . .

Friday Night Kiddush, *Sidur Tehilat Hashem*

Challah

Text 8

ואני שמעתי טעם לעשות זכר למן שהיה מונח כמו בקופסא טל למעלה וטל למטה וזכר לזה נותנין מפה תחת הפת ואחרת על גביו.

טור, אורח חיים רעא

I have heard that one reason [for covering the bread on Shabbat] is in order to commemorate the manna, which would appear as if it were in a chest, with dew on bottom and dew on top. To commemorate this, we put one cloth under the bread and another above it.

Rabbi Ya'akov ben Asher, *Tur, Orach Chayim* 271

Rabbi Ya'akov ben Asher (ca. 1269–1343). Spanish rabbi and halachic codifier. Originally from Germany, in the beginning of the 14th century he (with his father, the Rosh) fled persecution and settled in Toledo, Spain. He earned fame as one of the greatest halachists in history by authoring the *Arba'ah Turim*, an ingeniously organized and highly influential code of Jewish law. He also wrote a commentary on the Pentateuch which, as an introduction to each section, included interesting terse explanations, often using the method of *gematria*. Many printed Bibles include just this section of his work.

Text 9a

כִּי ה׳ אֱלֹקֶיךָ מְבִיאֲךָ אֶל אֶרֶץ טוֹבָה . . . אֶרֶץ חִטָּה וּשְׂעֹרָה וְגֶפֶן וּתְאֵנָה וְרִמּוֹן אֶרֶץ זֵית שֶׁמֶן וּדְבָשׁ.

דברים ח,ז–ח

For the Lord your God is bringing you to a good land . . . a land of wheat and barley, vines and figs and pomegranates, a land of oil-producing olives, and honey.

Deuteronomy 8:7–8

Text 9b

בירושלמי קאמר שלא יראה הפת בושתו פירוש שהוא מוקדם בפסוק והיה ראוי להקדימו בברכה ומקדימין בברכת היין.

טור, אורח חיים רעא

In the Jerusalem Talmud it states [that we cover the bread] so that it will not see its own humiliation. The explanation of this is: grain is mentioned first in the verse. Thus, it would be proper to make the blessing first [on bread which is made from grain], yet we make the blessing on the wine first.

Rabbi Ya'akov ben Asher, *Tur, Orach Chayim* 271

Text 9c

These values [of love and kindness] are so imbedded in our national psyche that they are intertwined with all our commandments. . . .

Obviously, challah does not have feelings, but our sages wanted to impart a lesson to us. If bread, which is inanimate, must be treated with such care and consideration, how much more so must we be on guard not to embarrass or hurt a person.

Rebbetzin Esther Jungreis, *The Committed Life* [New York: Cliff Street Books, 1999], p. 19

Rebbetzin Esther Jungreis (1936–). Born in Szeged, Hungary. She came to the U.S. after surviving the Bergen-Belsen concentration camp. Determined to devote her life to strengthening Judaism in the U.S. and around the world, she founded Hineni, an organization which provides Torah classes and other programs for the Jewish community. Noted lecturer and author of numerous books, including *The Jewish Soul on Fire* and *The Committed Marriage*.

Fish and Meat

Text 10

במה מענגו. רב יהודה בריה דרב שמואל בר שילת משמיה דרב אמר: בתבשיל של תרדין, ודגים גדולים, וראשי שומין. רב חייא בר אשי אמר רב: אפילו דבר מועט, ולכבוד שבת עשאו, הרי זה עונג. מאי היא. אמר רב פפא: כסא דהרסנא.

תלמוד בבלי, שבת קיח,ב

How should one have pleasure on Shabbat?

Rav Yehudah, son of Rav Shmuel bar Shilat, said in Rav's name, "With a dish of beets, large fish, and heads of garlic."

Rav Chiya bar Ashi said in Rav's name, "Even something small, if it is prepared in honor of the Shabbat, is a delight."

What is [something small]? Rav Papa said, "A pie of fish-hash."

Talmud, Shabbat 118b

Text 11

Cholent . . . [is a] stew, traditionally prepared on Friday and placed in the oven before the Sabbath begins, to cook overnight and be eaten at Saturday lunch. Since cooking or heating food is forbidden by the *halakhah* on the Sabbath, such a process is necessary in order to have something hot to eat for the Sabbath morning meal, and thus the dish is common to Jewish communities throughout the world, but is known under various names. Among Ashkenazim it is called *cholent* or *shulent* (possibly from the French *chaud lent* [meaning "hot" and "slow"] or from the Yiddish *shul ende,* i.e., end of the Saturday synagogue service) and in parts of North Africa, *dafina* and also *shahine*. The Hebrew name *hamin* means "hot."

Encyclopedia Judaica, 2nd edition (Detroit: Macmillan Reference USA, 2007), 4:664

Text 12

לֹא תְבַעֲרוּ אֵשׁ בְּכֹל מֹשְׁבֹתֵיכֶם בְּיוֹם הַשַּׁבָּת.
שמות לה,ג

You shall not cause fire to burn in any of your dwelling places on the day of Shabbat.

Exodus 35:3

Text 13

במה מענגו בימי חכמי הגמרא היו מענגין בדגים גדולים ובתבשיל של תרדין שמאכלים אלו היו חשובים ענג בימיהם וכל מקום ומקום לפי מנהגו יענגוהו במאכלים ומשקים החשובים להם ענג.
ואין חיוב לאכול בשר ולשתות יין בשבת אלא לפי שמן הסתם יש לרוב בני אדם ענג באכילת בשר יותר מבשאר מאכלים ובשתיית יין יותר מבשאר משקים לכך יש להם להרבות בבשר ויין כפי יכלתם והשגת ידם.
שולחן ערוך הרב, אורח חיים רמב,ב

How does one have pleasure on Shabbat? In the days of the talmudic sages they would have pleasure with large fish and a dish of beets. These foods were considered to be delightful in those days. In every place, one should have delight in the food and drink that are considered delightful in that location.

There is no obligation to eat meat and drink wine on Shabbat. But because most people enjoy eating meat more than other foods and in drinking wine more than

Rabbi Shne'ur Zalman of Liadi (1745–1812). Chasidic rebbe and founder of the Chabad movement, also known as "the Alter Rebbe" and "the Rav." Born in Liozna, Belarus, he was among the principal students of the Magid of Mezeritch. His numerous works include the *Tanya*, an early classic containing the fundamentals of Chasidism; *Torah Or; Likutei Torah*; and *Shulchan Aruch HaRav*, a reworked and expanded code of Jewish law. He is interred in Hadiach, Ukraine, and was succeeded by his son, Rabbi Dovber of Lubavitch.

other drinks, these people should have as much meat and wine as they can enjoy and afford.

Rabbi Shne'ur Zalman of Liadi, *Shulchan Aruch HaRav, Orach Chayim* 242:2

Why Pleasure?

Text 14a

וביאר על פי משל למלך שנשבה בנו יחידו בשבי הקשה מכולם, ועברו זמני זמנים ותוחלתו נמשכה מלפדותו ולהשיבו אל אביו. וברוב עתים ושנים הגיעוהו מכתב אביו המלך, לבל יתייאש שמה ושלא לשכוח נמוסי המלכות בין זאבי ערב, כי עוד ידו נטויה להחזירו אל אביו, על ידי כמה וכמה טצדקאות במלחמה או בשלום וכו׳.

ומיד שמח בן המלך שמחה גדולה, אפס שהיה מגילת סתרים, ואי אפשר היה לו לשמוח בגלוי. מה עשה, הלך עם בני עירו אל בית היין או שאר דבר המשכר, והם שמחו ביין שמחה גשמיות, והוא שמח באגרת אביו וכו׳.

וככל החזיון הזה הוא ממש מצות עונג שבת אל הגוף שהוא החומר, במאכל ומשתה, כדי שיהיה פנאי להצדיק לשמוח שמחה ב׳ שהוא שמחת הנשמה בדביקות השם יתברך כל היום, לבל יסיח דעתו מקדושת ומורא השבת.

תולדות יעקב יוסף, קדושים א

Rabbi Ya'akov Yosef of Polnoye (d. ca. 1783). One of the most dedicated disciples of the Ba'al Shem Tov, Ya'akov Yosef is credited with taking a leading role in the dissemination of Chasidic philosophy in its nascent years. He authored *Toladot Ya'akov Yosef*, the first printed work of Chasidic philosophy, in which he quotes the Ba'al Shem Tov more than 250 times. Until today, this work is cherished in chasidic circles.

Rabbi Menachem Mendel of Baer explained this with a parable of a king whose only son was trapped in harsh captivity. Much time passed, yet there was longing that one day the prince might be redeemed and returned to his father. After many years, the prince received a letter from his father exhorting him not to lose hope nor to forget the court etiquette while among the savages, for his father was still actively pursuing the possibility of his rescue, whether through battle or peaceful means.

Upon receipt of this letter the prince was overjoyed but could not celebrate openly since the matter was secret. He took the townspeople to a tavern. They were joyous due to the wine, while he was joyous because of his father's letter.

This parable represents the mitzvah of *oneg Shabbat* in which the coarse body eats and drinks so that the righteous [soul] can rejoice on another plane: namely, the joy of the soul as it clings to God throughout Shabbat, without turning away from its sanctity and awe.

Rabbi Ya'akov Yosef of Polnoye, *Toladot Ya'akov Yosef, Kedoshim* 1

Learning Activity 2

In the left-hand column are the elements of the parable. Together with a neighbor, decide what these elements represent with regard to the dilemma of the body's taking pleasure on Shabbat, and write them in the right-hand column.

Elements of the Parable	Symbolism
King	
Prince	
Trapped in a harsh captivity	
The prince longs to be redeemed.	
The prince receives a letter.	
The prince is given hope that his father will yet come to rescue him.	
The prince is happy but cannot openly celebrate this secret matter.	
The prince takes the townspeople to a tavern.	
The townspeople are joyous due to the wine.	
The prince is joyous because of his father's letter.	
The peasants rejoice, thereby allowing the prince to celebrate undisturbed.	

Question for Discussion

Based on the above parable, what is the role of the body in appreciating Shabbat?

Text 14b

העולה מזה דאין מקום לגוף לשמוח בשבת ויום טוב, כי אם כדי שיהיה אז פנאי לבן מלך שהיא הנשמה לשמוח בשמחת אביו שבשמים.

תולדות יעקב יוסף, כי תבא א

We may conclude that there is no reason for the body to rejoice on Shabbat and the holidays other than to allow the prince—the soul—to take joy in his Father in Heaven.

Rabbi Ya'akov Yosef of Polnoye, *Toladot Ya'akov Yosef, Ki Tavo* 1

Rabbi Chaim ben Yosef Vital (1542–1620). Born in Israel, lived in Safed, Jerusalem, and later Damascus. Vital was the principal disciple of Arizal, though he studied under him for less than two years. Before his passing, Arizal authorized Vital to record his teachings. Acting on this mandate, Vital began arranging his master's teachings in written form, and his many works constitute the foundation of the Lurianic school of Jewish mysticism, which was later universally adopted as the kabbalistic standard. Thus, Vital is one of the most important influences in the development of Kabbalah. Among his most famous works are *Ets Chayim*, and *Sha'ar Hakavanot*.

Text 15

ואמנם ידעת גם כן כי כל המצות אינם אלא לצרף ולברר הצלם והחומר אך הצורה אינה צריכה תיקון כלל ולא הוצרכה להתלבש בצלם וחומר רק להמשיך בהם אור לתקנם והבן זה מאד. כי זה טעם ירידת הנשמה בעולם הזה לתקן ולברר.

עץ חיים, שער כו, א,מב

Know as well that all of the *mitzvot* are only there to purify the physical [body], but the spiritual [soul] does not need any rectification. It did not need to enclothe itself into the body for any other reason than to illuminate the body and to rectify it. Understand this well: The reason the soul descended to this world was to fix, [not to be fixed].

Rabbi Chaim Vital, *Ets Chayim*, *Sha'ar* 26, 1:42

Question for Discussion

Based on this explanation, what is the body's role in life?

Text 16

The Torah command that Shabbat (and holidays) must be a time of pleasure for the Jewish people . . . does not mean that only the soul should derive (spiritual) pleasure from Shabbat (or the holiday). The body must (also) derive pleasure from Shabbat (or the holiday). Moreover, the primary objective of the mitzvah [of *oneg*] is specifically (to refine) the body.

Rabbi Menachem Mendel Schneerson (1902–1994). Known as "the Lubavitcher Rebbe," or simply as "the Rebbe." Born in southern Ukraine. Rabbi Schneerson escaped from the Nazis, arriving in the U.S. in June 1941. The towering Jewish leader of the 20th century, the Rebbe inspired and guided the revival of traditional Judaism after the European devastation, and often emphasized that the performance of just one additional good deed could usher in the era of Mashiach.

Because the natural pleasure of the body is in eating and drinking, the Torah says that the obligation to take pleasure [on Shabbat] is through eating. It is only in this way that the pleasure of Shabbat can truly permeate and refine the body.

On the other hand, fasting in order to repent (and so forth) brings no pleasure to the body (although it brings spiritual pleasure to the soul). Even if someone has refined himself to the point that fasting does not cause his body pain, and even provides his body with some satisfaction because his soul is having pleasure . . . still, this is not a natural pleasure for the body. . . . Rather it is a result of the soul forcing the body . . . to deny its basic nature, even if is a holy and refined body.

Rabbi Menachem Mendel Schneerson, *Likutei Sichot* 23:28–29

Text 17

אמר להו רב ענן בר תחליפא זימנין סגיאין הוה קאימנא קמיה דשמואל ונחית מאיגרא לארעא והדר מקדש.

תלמוד בבלי, פסחים קא,א

Rav Anan bar Tachlifa said to them, "Many times I would stand before Shmuel and he would go down from the roof to the ground floor and only then recite Kiddush."

Talmud, Pesachim 101a

Figure 4.1

	Why does the soul descend into the body?	Why is there a mitzvah to have pleasure on Shabbat?	Which pleasure is an important and fundamental part of life?
Soul-Oriented	So the body can challenge the soul	So that the body won't hinder the soul's experience of Shabbat	Spiritual pleasure
Body-Oriented	So the soul can infuse the body with holiness and thus transform it	To permeate the body with the holiness of Shabbat	Physical pleasure guided by spiritual goals

Key Points

1. The highest faculty of the soul is pleasure—the purpose to which everything is directed. One way we experience pleasure on Shabbat is through eating special foods.

2. When we recite Kiddush, thereby testifying that God is the Creator and the essence of everything, we become partners with God in creation.

3. Recalling the Creation underscores that each of us is imbued with the ability to fulfill a unique part of the global purpose. Recalling the Exodus reminds us that we need to free ourselves from inner spiritual slavery.

4. The Shabbat challah reminds us of the manna and the fact that, ultimately, our sustenance comes from God.

5. Eating fish on Shabbat reminds us of a spiritual state in which there is no possibility for spiritual pitfall, for we are submerged in awareness of God, just as fish are submerged in water.

6. By eating hot food on Shabbat, we not only have more pleasure and joy, but we also demonstrate our allegiance to the authenticity of the oral tradition.

7. While physical pleasure can be seen as ensuring that the body does not distract the soul from its spiritual delights, a deeper approach is to view the physical pleasure of Shabbat as a way of allowing the body to share the spiritual pleasures of Shabbat.

8. Physical pleasure is integral to human life, but to be truly satisfying it must be exercised in conjunction with a spiritual vision.

Simply Shabbat:
Kiddush

Soon after the day of rest descends upon the world, we take a few moments to acknowledge its entry. We do so over a cup of wine—a royal beverage that befits the guest of honor, the Shabbat Queen. This brief ceremony is called "Kiddush."

The Friday night Kiddush, which serves as the opening of the first Shabbat meal, is preceded by the *Shalom Aleichem,* in which we greet the Shabbat angels, and the *Eishet Chayil* ("Woman of Valor") ode, which extols the virtues of the Jewish woman.

The Shabbat day meal also begins with Kiddush, though the text is a different one. The Kiddush texts can be found in any prayer book, or print them out before Shabbat from: **www.chabad.org/258650**

How?

Here are the Kiddush basics:

1. The Kiddush cup should hold at least 3 fluid ounces. Fill the cup with kosher wine (or grape juice), and then pour a bit more so that it overflows the brim—symbolizing your cup overflowing with God's blessings.

2. Rise and hold the cup in your right (or dominant) hand. On Friday night, glance at the Shabbat candles and take in the Shabbat light as you start saying the Kiddush.

3. Glance at the wine in the cup when you say the wine (*hagafen*) blessing.

4. After concluding the Kiddush, drink at least 1.5 ounces from the cup.

If there are other family members or if guests are joining you for your Shabbat meal, you can recite the Kiddush aloud, and all who wish to be included in your recitation of Kiddush should answer "Amen" after the blessings are said. After Kiddush, it is then customary to share a sip of the Kiddush wine with all present.

Simply Shabbat:
Two Challah Loaves

At the Shabbat meals, the *hamotsi* blessing is recited on two loaves, commemorating the double portion of manna that fell in the desert every Friday—in honor of Shabbat. Here's how to serve the challah loaves at the Shabbat meal:

1. Before the Kiddush, place two whole and uncut loaves of challah on the table. (Whole rolls, matzah slices, or pita breads can also be used.)

2. Then cover the challah loaves until after the Kiddush is recited. Beautiful "challah covers" are available at Judaica stores and online for reasonable prices, but a cloth napkin does the job as well.

3. "Unveil" the challah loaves only after the Kiddush, demonstrating that they—as well as the entire meal—are in honor of the Shabbat whose presence and holiness you just acknowledged.

4. After the Kiddush, ritually wash your hands before eating challah.

5. Lightly score the top of one of the challah loaves with a knife, and then hold them both and say:

בָּרוּךְ אַתָּה אַדֹנָ‑י, אֱלֹהֵינוּ מֶלֶךְ הָעוֹלָם, הַמּוֹצִיא לֶחֶם מִן הָאָרֶץ.

Baruch attah Adonai, Eloheinu melech ha'olam, hamotsi lechem min ha'arets.

Blessed are You, Lord our God, King of the Universe, Who brings forth bread from the earth.

6. Slice the loaf that you scored, dip a piece of the bread in salt, and enjoy! Salt, which never spoils or decays, is symbolic of our eternal covenant with God.

7. After you take a piece for yourself, slice pieces of challah for all present.

8. It is not necessary to eat both challah loaves; if only one is consumed, you can put the second one away for the next meal.

Additional Readings

An Additional Note on the *Kiddush* Ritual

by **Rabbi Adin Steinsaltz**

The eve of the Sabbath does not only usher in the day of rest; it has its own particular aspect and significance. Every hour of the preceding afternoon marks another level of an emotionally peaked transition from the six working days of the week to the Sabbath day. The evening before the holy day is therefore itself a climax and a final stage of the transition, to all that the day means, both as a conclusion of the week and as a higher level of existence, beyond the six days of action, beyond time.

This higher level of the Sabbath is bound up with the divine manifestation in the *Sefirah* of *Malkhut* ("kingdom"), which represents the *Shekhinah* and also the totality, the receptacle that absorbs all that occurs, and is also connected with the first *Sefirah*, the Crown. Therefore the quality of Sabbath Eve, which is the summing up of work and events in time, can also be a preparation for the manifestation of the Sabbath as the crown and beginning of time. The *Sefirah* of *Malkhut*, or the *Shekhinah*, represents the divine power as manifested in reality, operating in an infinite variety of ways and means. It has seventy names, each expressing another aspect, another face of this all inclusive *Sefirah*. For *Malkhut* is the seventh of the lower *Sefirot* and, as the last, also includes in itself the entire ten; in other words, it expresses all of the *Sefirot*, each in seven different forms; so that seventy is the key number to the unfolding of the ritual of the evening devoted to *Malkhut* and to the *Shekhinah* which *Malkhut* represents.

What is equivalent in all the manifestations of the *Shekhinah* is that each represents a certain aspect of the feminine. Consequently the symbols and the contents of Sabbath Eve are always oriented to the female, with emphasis on the woman in her universal aspect as well as in terms of the Jewish family.

On entering a home on the eve of the Sabbath, one may see how a dwelling is made into a sanctuary. The table on which are set the white loaves of Sabbath bread and the burning candles recall the Holy Temple with its menorah and its shew bread. The table itself is, as always, a reminder of the altar in the Temple, for eating could and should become an act of sacrifice. In other words, the relation between man and the food he consumes, as expressed in the intention behind the eating of the food, corresponds to the cosmic connection between the material and the spiritual as expressed by every sacrifice on an altar. Especially is this true on the Sabbath, when the Sabbath feast takes on the character of a sacramental act. A sort of communion, in the performance of the *mitzvah* of union of the soul, the body, the food, and the essence of holiness. Therefore at mealtimes the table always has on it a salt container, just as salt had to be on the holy altar as a sign of the covenant of salt. The candles lit by the woman of the house emphasize the light of the Sabbath, the sanctification of the day, and the special task of the woman as representative of *Shekhinah* of *Malkhut*. There are two loaves of special white bread, called *challah* (some houses have twelve *challot*), covered with a cloth; these also recall the bread from heaven, the manna, which on the Sabbath day came down in double portions covered with a layer of dew.

As part of the preparations for the *Kiddush* ("consecration") ceremony, the members of the household sing or recite the song of praise for the "woman of valor" (Proverbs 31:10-31). The song, with its appreciation for the woman, the mother, the housekeeper, has on this Sabbath Eve a double connotation, as praise for the lady of the house and as glorification of the *Shekhinah of Malkhut* who is, in a sense, the mother, the housekeeper of the real world. Following this is the Twenty-third Psalm, expressing the calm trust in God. And one is ready for the *Kiddush* ceremony itself.

In terms of *Halakhah*, the *Kiddush* is the carrying out of the fourth of the Ten Commandments: "Remember the Sabbath Day to keep it holy." At the very beginning of the Sabbath there has to be some act of separation, of consecration, emphasizing the difference between the work days of the week and the holy day and enabling the soul to move into a state of inner tranquility and spiritual receptiveness. To be sure, the words of the consecration are also said at the time of evening prayer and on other occasions; but in Judaism there is a general principle that, to as great an extent as possible, abstract events or processes and all that pertain to them are bound up with specifics and definite actions. Thus the *Kiddush* consecration is connected with the drinking of wine, which, in turn, becomes part of a ceremony and, in turn, is associated with the Sabbath wine sacrifices of the Holy Temple.

The *Kiddush* cup symbolizes the vessel through which, and into which, the blessing comes. The numerical weight of the letters in the word for drinking cup (*kos*) is the same as that of the letters in that name of God expressing the divine revelation in the world, in nature, in law. And into the cup is poured the bounty, the wine that represents the power of the blessing of the word "wine," whose numerical equivalent is seventy, which is also the number of Sabbath Eve. Wine then evokes the bounty, the great plentitude and power; and red wine especially expresses a certain aspect of the *Sefirah* of *Gevurah*, which also has an aspect of severity and justice. Thus after one has poured most of the wine into the cup, a little water, symbol of grace and love, is added to create the right mixture, or harmony, between *Hesed* and *Gevurah*. After the filling of the cup, which is now the vessel of consecration containing the divine plenty, one places it on the palm of the right hand in such a way that the cup, supported by the upturned fingers, resembles or recalls a rose of five petals. For one of the symbols of *Malkhut* is the rose. And the cup of wine, thus expressing also the *Shekhinah*, stands in the center of the palm and is held by the petal fingers of the rose. The time has come for the recitation of the Kiddush prayer itself.

The Kiddush is composed of two parts. It begins with that part of the Torah (Genesis 2:1-3) where the Sabbath is first mentioned, and then proceeds to the second half which is a prayer composed by the sages especially for the *Kiddush* and in which the various meanings of the Sabbath are poetically and precisely stated. Between the two parts there is the blessing of the vine, or fruit of the grape. In each of these two parts there are exactly thirty-five words, together making seventy, the number of the Eve of the Sabbath. Before reciting the first words from the Torah, two words are added—the last words of the preceding verse: "the sixth day"—because they fit in with the recitation, "Thus the heavens and the earth were finished . . . " and because the first letters of these words form the abbreviation of the Holy Name. In this first section the Sabbath is treated as the day of the summation and cessation of Creation, as God's day of rest.

The second section, selected and determined by the sages, expresses the other side of the Sabbath, the imitation of God by Israel. Before the blessing of the wine, there are two words in Aramaic telling those present to get ready for the blessing. The following words of the *Kiddush* express the primary elements of the Sabbath and the special relation between Sabbath and the nation. There is first the declaration "Blessed art Thou . . . by whose commandments we are sanctified," which is to say that the *mitzvah* is a way of reaching a level of holiness, a way to God. After this the prayer speaks of the chosenness of Israel, as a consequence of which Israel, more than all other nations, has to assume the task of carrying on the act of Creation and its aftermath of rest and holiness. Mention is then made of the exodus from Egypt, as in the version of the Ten Commandments in Deuteronomy (5:15), where the Sabbath, proclaimed as the day of rest from work, recollects the time of slavery in Egypt and likens the Sabbath to the divine act of release from bondage and bestowal of salvation. So that Sabbath is also the weekly day of freedom, celebrating the release and the exodus from Egypt, as well as the concept of salvation which, as the ultimate in time, is the Sabbath of the world.

And out of this emphasis on divine choice and love and out of the need to understand man's obligation to God to continue and to create and to be able to rise above and beyond creation unto the Sabbath rest, the *Kiddush* prayer concludes with the relation of the Jewish people to the Sabbath and thus closes the circle of the relation between God and man. After the recital of the *Kiddush* the one who has performed the ceremony himself drinks from the cup, thereby participating in that communion of the physical with the spiritual which is the essence of all ritual. And from the same cup drink all those gathered at the table. In this way everyone participates in the meaningful act of introducing the Sabbath, represented by the flowering of the rose, which is the cup of redemption of the individual and of the nation and of the world as a whole.

The Thirteen Petalled Rose,
(Jerusalem: Koren Publishers, 2010), ch. 12, pp. 115–119
Reprinted with permission of Maggid Books,
an imprint of Koren Publishers, Jerusalem Ltd.

Sabbath Fish

by **Eric G. Freudenstein**

> "Your approach," I said, "is too body-oriented. Try to imagine a meta-dinner, not so much a filling occasion as a fulfilling one."
>
> From "When an Invitation Isn't . . . " by Anatole Broyard,
>
> *The New York Times,* May 10, 1979.

Introduction

When I arrived in the States as a young immigrant, just after the end of World War II, I heard stories of "our boys" in the service who had been stationed in the far corners of the world, cut off from any contact with their families. When the Jewish chaplain was able to get them *gefilte fish* on Friday night or a Jewish holiday, tears would come to their eyes as memories of home were aroused by the sight and taste of the fish. In the smugness and conceit typical of youth and ignorance, I smiled inwardly at these stories. How vulgar, I thought, to associate the love for Judaism with a piece of food. How ignorant, furthermore, to attribute religious significance to *gefilte fish*, something that, to the best of my knowledge, was not even mentioned in the *Shulhan Arukh*, the authoritative book on Jewish laws. As a matter of fact, I had never even heard of *gefilte fish* before my arrival in this country. But fate is often strange and, as Providence would have it, I came to love *gefilte fish*, to develop recipes suitable for mass production and, as Director of Production for the largest manufacturers of kosher fish products for over thirty years, I was probably responsible for serving more servings of *gefilte fish* than anyone else in history.

I decided to take a new look at this custom of fish eating. Leafing through the pages of Jewish lore and history, laws and customs, I became aware of the fact that while *gefilte fish*, as we know it today, may be relatively new (by the standards of our four-thousand-year-old history), the custom of eating fish on the Sabbath and on special occasions goes back to the very origins of our history as a people.

According to an ancient midrash, Miriam's well, stocked with fish, accompanied the Israelites during the forty years of their wanderings in the desert. As if this were an omen, the custom of a fish meal on the eve of the Sabbath accompanied the Jewish people in their wanderings through the millennia and across all continents.

In Ancient Egypt

The Bible records for us that the Israelites complained to Moses about the lack of variety in the food available to them in the desert:

> In Egypt we had fish for the asking, cucumbers and water-melons, leeks and onions and garlic. Now our throats are parched; there is nothing wherever we look except this manna (Numbers 11:5, 6).

Modern archeological evidence bears out the fact that fish was available for enslaved laborers like the children of Israel in Egypt. There is an Egyptian document concerning a petition addressed to the royal authorities in the 29th year of Ramses III (about 1150-1200 B.C.E.) by the Union of Gravediggers who, as part of their payment, received large amounts of fish four times monthly. The petitioners requested a pay increase, pointing out that they came to the authorities without clothes and ointments, and even without fish, that indispensable food. We know that the ancient Egyptians were able to preserve large quantities of fish for long periods of time by a process of drying and salting, and a warehouse of dried fish was discovered near the Sun Temple of Amarna.

But to the Israelites wandering in the desert, fish meant even more than the free ration handed out to the slaves. There was a beautifully romantic aspect, as told us by the midrash.

> Under the apple-trees I roused thee (Song of Songs 8:5). Rabbi Avira expounded: It was by the merit of the pious women in the generation of the oppression that our ancestors were redeemed from Egypt. The women were determined that the heritage of Abraham, Isaac and Jacob not perish from the earth. When they went to draw water, the Holy One, blessed be He, summoned little fishes into their pitchers. They drew half water and half fish. They came home and placed two kettles on the stove, one to prepare hot water and the other for cooking fish. Then they carried the kettles out to the fields to their husbands and washed them, anointed them, fed them and gave them to drink and lay with them between the kettles.[1]

What species were these little fishes which our ancestors found so delectable during their sojourn in the land of Egypt? To our amazement, the evidence that has been preserved permits us to identify them and to conclude that some of the varieties that are used in the preparation of *gefilte fish* today are the very same species that were present in the Nile delta thousands of years ago. Thus, the Egyptologist Ingrid Gamer-Wallert reaches the following conclusion:

> It appears that the composition of the fish population of Egypt did not substantially change in the last five millennia. More than 30 species can be proven for Ancient Egypt and these still exist today in the waters of the Nile.[2]

These varieties include carp, pike and mullet, and while these carp and pike families are not of the genus used in the Sabbath meal, the mullet (genus Mullet *Mugilidae cephalus)* is exactly the same fish that we use in the preparation of our present-day *gefilte fish* blend. A truly remarkable phenomenon.

[1] *Sotah*, 11b.

[2] Aegyptologische Abhandlungen (Wiesbaden, 1970), Vol. 21.

The Mishnah records "Egyptian Fish" as an article of commerce,[3] and, according to the commentary of Maimonides, this was a variety of small fish imported from Egypt to Palestine in metal containers and still well-known in his own day. We can only speculate whether the popularity of this fish in Palestine[4] was based on ancient traditions.

The starting point of our investigation of the fish meal in ancient Egypt is that passage in Numbers cited above: "In Egypt we had fish, cucumbers, water-melons, and leeks, onions and garlic." Don Isaac Abarbanel, the Jewish Minister of Finance to the Portuguese Court, in his Bible commentary written in the early 16th century, takes the Hebrew word *eth* in the context of our verse to signify "with." The Israelites in Egypt, writes Abarbanel, cooked fish with cucumbers, melons (or better, squash), leeks, onions and garlic in order to improve the poor taste of their ration. In other words, the Bible here gives us the first recorded recipe for fish cookery.

In The Era Of The Talmud

Once we come to the period of the Mishnah and Talmud we find a wealth of information about the fishing industry and about the marketing and consumption of fish and fishery products. The main center of fishing was Lake Tiberias, but the Mediterranean and the Jordan river were also known for the bounty of their resources, and their waters were exploited commercially. The coastal town of Acco was the trading center for the commerce in fish, so that "bringing fish to Acco" had the same connotation as "carrying coals to Newcastle." Generally, the fish for sale were attractively spread on leaves and reeds, and they were also served this way at the table,[5] much as the labels on American cans of *gefilte fish* suggest that the portions be served on lettuce leaves. Smaller varieties of fish were sold in metal containers and baskets. Fish were eaten pickled, boiled or fried, and served with vegetables and milk. A popular dish was fish prepared with flour in a type of pie

[3] Mahshirin 6:3.

[4] There was a *Shaar Hadagim*, a fish-gate, in Jerusalem, where the fishermen brought their wares. (See Zeph. 1:10; Neh. 3:3 and 12:39; 2 Chron. 33:14).

[5] *Tosefta Shabbat* 13, 16.

and fish with good, aged wine was considered a meal fit for a king.

The Jews—like the Greeks—loved fish food and were connoisseurs. Said Rabbi Yose ben Halafta (quoted in the famous Bible commentary of Rashi, on Genesis 1:10): "The taste of fish that comes up in Acco cannot be compared to the taste of fish that is caught in neighboring Sidon, and the taste of fish from Sidon does not compare to the taste of fish from neighboring Aspamia." Because of this predilection of the Jews for fish it was the custom to honor the Sabbath with a fish meal on Friday night, at the beginning of the Sabbath.[6]

> Rav Yehudah said in the name of Rav: He who delights in the Sabbath will be granted his heart's desire, as it has been said: "Delight in God and He will grant your heart's desire" (Psalms 37:4). This delight in God shall be understood by reference to the prophet Isaiah: "You shall call the Sabbath a delight," and it concerns, therefore, the delight in the Sabbath. How does one delight in the Sabbath? Rav Yehudah, son of Rav Samuel bar Shilat said in the name of Rav: With a course [of] spinach-beets, large fish and garlic cloves. Rav Hiyya bar Ashi said in the name of Rav: Even a modest meal, if prepared in honor of the Sabbath, is a delight. What might this be? Said Rav Papa: A pie of fish-hash (small fish prepared with flour and fish jelly) (*Shabbat* 118b).

Even the poorest of the poor were entitled to the Friday night fish-meal from the public kitchen: "When may those who possess less than fifty shekels have the dish of vegetables and fish? Every Friday night of the Sabbath."[7]

Talmudic laws regulating the relations of employer and worker take into consideration the need to prepare the Sabbath meal. In general, the worker who is hired for a full day must travel on his own time, so that he can start at his day-break. However, it is understood by both parties that the employer must let him leave *every day* in order to reach his home by night-fall. What about Fridays?

> Rabbi Ammi said in the name of Resh Lakish: On Friday afternoon the employer has to let his workers off in time so that they can draw a barrel of water and fry a fish, before lighting the Sabbath candles (Genesis *Rabba* 72, 3).

No one is to consider himself exempt from the obligation of preparation for the Sabbath. The Talmud records that even the great masters did menial labor to prepare the home in honor of the Sabbath: "Rava (the famous Head of Academy in Mehosa) salted the turbot (he seasoned the fish in honor of the Sabbath)."[8] The custom of honoring the Sabbath with fish is also stressed in the Aggadah, the moral tales of the Sages where we see that people were regarded as especially praiseworthy in the eyes of God if, at any cost, they got fish for sacred occasions. The story of "Joseph, Who Honored the Sabbath."[9] Tells us how a rich pagan was warned that his neighbor, Joseph, would someday eat up all his possessions. To safeguard himself, the pagan sold all that he had and bought a single pearl. Unfortunately he then lost the pearl in a lake where it was swallowed by a fish which was later caught and sold to Joseph. Joseph found the pearl and sold it for a fortune. The moral of the story is pointed out: "He who lends to the Sabbath is repaid by the Sabbath."

A second story[10] brings out the same moral:

> A pious man in Rome held the Sabbaths and festal days much in honor. On the eve of the Day of Atonement he went shopping in the market but found only a fish, which the servant of the Prefect also wanted to buy. They bid against each other, until finally the Jew got the fish, but at a gold denarius per pound. When, at dinner, the Prefect heard why no fish came to the table he had the Jew who, he presumed, was wealthy, called for him. The Jew came, and represented himself as a tailor.
>
> "And a tailor eats fish at a gold denarius per pound?"
>
> "My lord, permit me to speak!"
>
> "Speak," said the Prefect.

6 The oldest reference linking fish and the Sabbath is in Neh. 13:16, where we are told that the Tyrians sold fish in Jerusalem on that day until the practice was stopped by Nehemiah.

7 *Tosefta,* end of tractate *Peah*, and Maimonidies, *Laws of Charity* 7, 8.

8 *Shabbat* 119a.

9 Ibid.

10 Genesis *Rabba*, Chapter II also quoted by *Tosafot Ketubot* 5 a; V. *ela me-atah.*

"We have a day which is more precious to us than all days of the year. All the sins which we have committed during the whole year are forgiven us on this day. Therefore we honor this day more than all the days of the year."

Then said the Prefect: "You have justified yourself and are free."

How did God repay the man who thus honored the festival? He had him find a valuable pearl in the fish, from the sale of which he supported himself for the rest of his life.[11]

We know that the Jewish custom of eating fish on the Sabbath eve was noted by the Romans, for it is alluded to in a rather obscure anti-Semitic stanza in a long poem by Perisus:

> But when Herod's birthday is come, and the lamps (like on every Sabbath and Holiday—E. F.), put in the greasy windows along with violets, emit their unctuous clouds of smoke and when the tail of a tunny floats curled round a red dish, and the white jar is bulging with wine, you move your lips in silences and turn pale at the circumcised Sabbath.[12]

Even though Persius' statement is confused, all scholars have connected the passage with the traditional Friday night meal of the Jews. Pliny the Elder, the Roman historian and naturalist who called Jerusalem "the most illustrious city in the East" also comments, in his *Natural History,* on the fish-eating customs of the Jews. In ancient Jewish liturgy, the wish for resurrection in the company of the Just is a frequent motif. It is also found on a tomb inscription, touching in its simplicity, for the nine-year-old daughter of Rabban Gamliel in Bet Shearim: "May she rise again with the Just" (*Tehi amidatah im kesherim*). The desire to be with the saints at the Feast of the Leviathan is the explanation offered to account for the presence of a fish symbol on some Jewish graves in Roman catacombs. The fish meal, fundamentally a festive meal to do honor to the holy days of the year, here becomes a symbol of the good life in the world to come, when legendary Leviathan becomes part of the menu for the ultimate feast in Paradise.[13]

On a more earthy level, fish also served as an aphrodisiac and, especially in later periods, as a symbol of fertility, a protection against the evil eye and as an omen for bringing good luck. All of these ancillary meanings are based on ideas already present in Talmudic literature.

The Age of Mysticism: Kabbalah

In the imagery of the Bible and the Talmud, the Royal Table is one of the trappings of kinghood, much as crown and scepter are the insignia of monarchy in the Western tradition. When, in the famous twenty-third psalm, King David sang

> Thou preparest a table before me
> In the presence of mine enemies

the Rabbis comment[14] that this table is the symbol of royalty, parallel to the line that follows, "Thou has anointed my head with oil," which refers to that other symbol of kinghood, the consecration of the king by divine authority. The Royal Table of the ancients was not necessarily one long table, but, rather, a series of small ones: one for the king, with others in the same hall for favorites, friends and the more important servants of the land or of the royal household. In a more general sense, to eat at the king's table came to mean to be supported by the king, regardless of where the meals were physically eaten. The Zohar, the holy book of the Kabbalah, in a lesson extolling the Sabbath meal, opens the passage by calling Israel "sons of the royal palace."[15] They are guests, as it were, at the Sabbath table, the mystic table of God, the King, and of the Sabbath Queen. In this sense we must understand the severe reprimand and punishment for those who, as *lès majesté,* slight the Sabbath table, and the happiness and reward that, according to the Zohar, await those who honor the Sabbath table.

The Holy Shelah,[16] a famous authority among the Kabbalists, prefaces his thoughts on the Sabbath meals with a quotation from Maimonides to the effect

11 These two stories are rendered here largely as translated by Goodenough, *Jewish Symbols in the Greco-Roman Period,* Vol. 5, p. 44.

12 Persius, *Satire,* V. 180-184.

13 *Baba Batra,* 74b.

14 Midrash *Shohar Tov* to Psalm 23.

15 *Zohar* II, 252.

16 Isaiah ben Abraham haLevi Horowitz, *Shnei Luhot haBrit,* (Jerusalem, 1963), Part I, pp. 97-98.

that the Sabbath table should be honored with proper good food, including fish. He proceeds to quote an anonymous authority who recommends that fish be included in each of the three obligatory Sabbath meals. The Shelah then develops a *gematria*, a play on the numerical value of Hebrew letters, to indicate that wine, meat and fish at the three Sabbath meals are a desideratum. What follows is a frequently quoted but often neglected call for moderation in food and drink, to which we will refer later.

The *Book of Delight of the Days, (Sepher Hemdat HaYamim)* which has been called the most beautiful book in Lurianic Kabbalah,[17] is a treasury of lore and ethical exhortation concerning the *mitzvot* of Friday night. In the first chapter the author writes:

> The custom is to eat fish on the Sabbath because then there is a proliferation of (mystical) sparks that must be channeled and elevated by the power of the holiness of the Sabbath.

This is a reference to the transmigration of souls in fish. The Holy Or ha-Hayyim, a Sephardic kabbalistic Bible commentator, is also of the view (in his commentary on Genesis 1:26) that the souls of the pious transmigrate into fish. An opposite school of thought, among the believers in the doctrine of transmigration of souls (*gilgul*), prefers to eat fish rather than meat, precisely because souls that have been condemned to be reincarnated in lower forms of life will never enter the body of a fish, but only the bodies of warm-blooded animals. Hence, fish are preferred for the Sabbath meal.

An excerpt from the previously mentioned writing of the Holy Shelah will serve to conclude this brief review of kabbalistic thought on the Sabbath meal:

> Those who thoughtlessly fill their bellies, going for the pleasant taste and the intoxicating drink, and then because of the excess of eating fall into a stupor and their mind gets confused—they do not delight *in* the Sabbath, rather they delight *themselves on* the Sabbath. Therefore, one should measure one's actions wisely. A person can eat and drink properly without filling up one's belly, because the latter is not called Rest and Delight, but waste of food and destruction of one's health. It is also harmful to the soul because one is unable to study the Law and perform the commandments after overeating. The idea is to eat and to drink, in good spirit and with joy, food that is wholesome, properly prepared and seasoned and easily digestible—small quantities but good quality, as long as one does not stuff oneself. One may even drink two or three cups of wine to cheer the heart—everything depends on the individual's ability to hold his drink—and then one gets up, with the satisfaction of a good meal, to start an arranged program of study, or to nap briefly in order to rest one's head and limbs a little and then one sits down to study. Abudraham wrote, in the name of a scholar, that one of the reasons for the traditional three Sabbath meals is to avoid stuffing oneself at any one meal. For, by knowing that there will be three meals during the day, there is no need to overindulge at any one of them. It is the holy Sabbath and it shall be used to cling to holiness.[18]

The Hasidic masters, steeped in love for the Jewish people and for every Jewish tradition elaborated on the meaning of the fish course on the Sabbath. Thus it is related by the disciples of the *Zaddik*, Rabbi Simha Bunem of Przysucha:

> Our master—may his merit protect us—said that the custom to eat fish as the first food on the holy Sabbath is based on the fact that fish were the first created living beings, and the holiness of the Sabbath, too, is the root of life; for this reason Israel has the tradition to start delighting in the Sabbath with fish food.[19]

The *Zaddik*, Abraham Joshua Heschel of Apta, adds another thought.[20] The midrash, he says, tell us that the manna of the desert had every conceivable taste that one could wish for, except for the taste of fish. That is why the people murmured: "We remember the fish we ate in Egypt." This lack of fish became the focus of their dissatisfaction with their lot. Israel now has the custom to eat this very fishfood to demonstrate that we are thankful to God and that our delight in the Sabbath is complete. The symbol of grievance has become the symbol of gratitude.

17 Gershom G. Scholem, *Major Trends in Jewish Mysticism* (New York: Schocken Books, 1961), p. 285.

18 Shelah *loc, cit.*

19 M. Nirenberg, ed., *Likutei Kol Simhah* (New York, 1955). p. 30.

20 *Sefer Torat Emet,* section *Aykeb.*

Rabbi Zevi Elimelekh of Dynow, known as "the *B'nei Yisoskher"* (the title of his best-known work), refers repeatedly to the custom of serving fish on the Sabbath table.

> We find in the Biblical story of the creation that three things were blessed on three successive days. The fishes were blessed on the fifth day, mankind was blessed on the sixth, and the Sabbath-day was blessed on the seventh day. This is "the three-fold cord that is not quickly broken" (Ecclesiastes). That is why man eats fish on the Sabbath, so that he may be blessed with the triple blessing. This is also alluded to in the twenty-third psalm: "He maketh me to lie down in green pastures," since the Hebrew word for green pastures—*deshe*—consists of three letters that are the initial letters for the words fish, Sabbath and man in Hebrew, and these are joined on the day of rest; hence the verse concludes: "He leadeth me beside the still waters."[21]

Elsewhere, we encounter a more moralistic interpretation of the custom. The Sabbath day shall be devoted to the study of Torah, an act symbolized by the fish meal:

> The element of the fishes is water and the element of Israel is the Torah that has been compared to water. "Ho, everyone that thirsteth, go ye to the water" (Isaiah 55:1). The parable of a fox and the fishes is well-known from the Talmud.[22] And just as the fishes, even though they swim constantly in water, when a drop of rain falls they open their mouths to snap up the drops as if they never tasted water in their life, so Israel—even though their element is Torah all the days of the week—when they hear new interpretations of the Torah on the Sabbath they bend their ears to hear it well. It is written in the *Zohar* that the Sabbath is the day of the Torah par excellence, and the day of the soul—for it was on a Sabbath that the Torah was given to Israel on Sinai.[23]

The custom of eating a piece of *hallah* (white bread) with the fish is a topic of discussion in hasidic literature. Some authors attribute the practice to the requirements of healthy nutrition, while others cite the fact that the Hebrew letters for fish and for grain (*dagim* and *dagan*) have the same numerical value, this making them compatible foods. In conclusion, let us quote the *Bnei Yisoskhor* on this topic:

> The saintly Rabbi Menahem Asariah DeFano (famous Kabbalist and contemporary of the Ari and of Rabbi Moses Cardovero) wrote that, in the world to come, at the banquet of the Leviathan—since there cannot be a religious banquet without breaking bread—they will bring out the flask of manna that had been hidden (Exodus 16:33). Note that Scripture says "for your generations" and that refers to the time when all the generations will gather. This manna is called "bread," and it is written "this is the bread that God has given you."[24]

The author adds that the blessing to be pronounced over the manna will be "Blessed art Thou Who bringest forth bread from Heaven," in contrast to our regular benediction, "Blessed art Thou who bringest forth bread from the earth."

The commentators on the *Shulhan Arukh* cite the custom, introduced by the Kabbalists, that after the breaking of the *hallah*-bread at the Friday night meal, the children kiss their mother's hand. It is she who baked and provided the festive meal, fulfilling the task expected of the mistress of the household. In our time, a New York rabbi remembers the custom from his home in Transylvania, a beautiful memory from a world that is no more but that shall not be forgotten.

The Age of Enlightenment: Old Vienna

When the age of emancipation dawned in Western and Central Europe, the hold of the Jewish religion weakened considerably and some of the intellectuals went so far as to forswear the faith of their ancestors, in order to buy "an admission ticket to European culture." Having spent childhood years in an intensely Jewish milieu, these apostates penned bitter-sweet reminiscences of the Sabbaths of their youth, including meals. Heinrich Heine, the famous German poet, in his *Hebrew Melodies*, describes nostalgically how the simple Jew, with the arrival of the Sabbath, is miraculously transformed from a peddle into a prince who

21 *Bnei Yisoskhor, Maamarei Hashabbatot* (New York: Chaim Ubracha Pub., 1975) 1:11. 3:16. 8:20.

22 *Berakhot* 61b.

23 *B'nei Yisoskhor*, 1:21.

24 Ibid., 3:13.

welcomes the Princess Sabbath. Several times, in the *Hebrew Melodies*, he characteristically lapses from lyrical heights to ironical self-ridicule, and after rhapsodizing about the quasi-magical transformation of the lowly work-a-day Jew into the radiant bridegroom of Princess Sabbath, he makes us chuckle about the traditional meals: "Kugel, the beautiful spark of the gods, heavenly ambrosia."

Moritz Gottlieb Saphir was a contemporary of Heine. Born into a Yiddish-speaking, Orthodox family in a small town near Budapest, and having attended *yeshivot* in Pressburg and Prague, he later abandoned traditional Judaism and eventually was baptized as a Lutheran. He settled in Vienna, where he wrote humorous and satirical poems, essays, literary criticism, theater reviews, comedies and short stories. Saphir's popularity and influence were widespread and his witticisms and satirical sketches were frequently reprinted and often quoted. In a nostalgic autobiography he devotes several pages to "Jewish fish." Here follows a slightly condensed English translation:

> Lucullus, (he muses), got quite far in gastronomy. Pompey was no slouch either and he paid to M. Aufidius Lucro, who had invented a technique for fattening peacocks, the sum of 60,000 sesterces; Apicius invented the art of fattening pigs with figs, Vitellius was the first to dine on pies made with nightingale tongues; he paid 2,000 sesterces for a single Swedish nightingale . . . however, none of these virtuosos of culinary art and gluttony had any idea of the *hautgout,* the peculiar charm of the Jewish cuisine. Lord Protector Cromwell once dined with the famous Manasseh Ben Israel and he admitted that he had never eaten so delightful a meal.
>
> Delightful indeed! That must have contained garlic! Whether you call them Brown Carp with Jew-sauce, or Jew-fish, the sweet-sour Jewish fish are world-famous. Once upon a time I tendered a "sweet-sour Jew-fish dinner" to my Gentile literary friends in Munich. I placed a platter of "sour Jew-fish heads" in front of them and I made a little speech:
>
> "Gentlemen! I have invited you all to join me for 'sour Jew-fish heads.' You met here for this *tête-a-tête* and, before we dig in, permit me a few words. Jews and fish have great sympathy for one another. Jews like to eat fish and fish like to eat Jews, as we know from the famous fish that swallowed a whole Jew, from head to toe, for a snack. Of course, he returned him unharmed . . . But the Jews love fish so much because, when they wanted to cross the Red Sea, the fish suddenly started to swallow so much water, that the Jews were able to cross dry land, and when Pharaoh arrived, the fish gave all the water off again, drowning the pursuers.
>
> "For this reason the Jews, out of gratitude, invite the fish on every Sabbath and holiday. But the Jews themselves have so often been invited guests, only to be fleeced and cleaned out, that they do the same to their own guests, the fish! They remove the scales, they clean them out, and then they finish them off. Look here, gentlemen, these are extraordinarily good fish-heads! For, what is characteristic of a good head? To make life sweet for oneself, even in a sour mess. So one has to sweeten the sour sauce with raisins, almonds, nuts, a little celery and spices to remove some of the bitterness. And then the fish-heads become tasty and inviting!"[25]

The famous satirist ends on a whimsical note: "In order to understand the Jewish national dishes," he writes, "one has to be a scholar; to describe them, one must be a genius; to enjoy them in a mood of sanctity, one must be a Jew; but in order to truly appreciate them, one must be a *meshumed* (an apostate)!"

The Fish Meal in Hebrew and Yiddish Song, in Art and Literature

A complete traditional Friday evening table requires Sabbath candles to set the festive mood, the presence of guests (often needy people whom the head of the household would pick up after the synagogue prayer service to join the family circle at the table) and the singing of happy Sabbath songs, the *zemirot.* The lyrics of several of these songs which date back to the early Middle Ages allude to the fish course served on the Sabbath:

> How beloved is your tranquility,
>
> Oh, Queen Sabbath,
>
> How do we hasten to receive you.
>
> Come, Crowned Princess,

[25] M. Saphir, *Meine Memoiren und Anderes* (Leipzig: Phillip Reclam jun.).

We welcome you in festive dress,

The candles are lit,

All work and labor has ceased.

We delight in your honor

With all kinds of fowl and fish.

Every manner of delicacy

Has been prepared well ahead . . .

A foretaste of paradise

Is the rest of the Sabbath day.

Oh, let our redemption come quickly,

May lament and suffering disappear.

Leaping across several centuries, we find what may be called a Yiddish song of social protest. The ancient Sabbath hymn just cited glorifies the Sabbath food. But the words of the song have a different meaning for the poor than for the wealthy. For the rich, the words of the song conjure up a sumptuous fish course, but for us

Kaptsonechlech,

Oi, kaptsonechlech

the poor, oh the despised poor people, the tail of a herring is all that can be anticipated.

Parallel with the dissatisfaction of the impoverished masses with their lot, there is a nostalgic anticipation of Israel's ultimate redemption. The joys of paradise are described in a folk-song that takes the form of a dialogue between a questioning child and the father who must satisfy his offspring's curiosity about all the details of the fascinating *Gan Eden.*

Tatenyu, father dear

What is going to be served at the banquet that the Messiah has in store for us?

My child,

The Leviathan is going to be served

At the great banquet for the righteous people of Israel

In Jewish pictorial art, fish often represents this same longing for redemption. On an old pewter Passover Seder-plate (in the Rheinisches Museum, Cologne, Germany) we can see the star of David surrounded by fishes. The combination is an appropriate messianic symbol because on the night of the Seder the Messiah and the prophet Elijah, who will announce his coming, will arise to prepare the redemption. Again, this time on a pewter Purim-plate dating from 1787 in Bamberg, Germany we find three fishes, the symbol of the zodiac sign for the month of Adar, Pisces. Here the fishes, in addition to the redemption theme, are a sign of good luck. Representations of fish are widespread in the orient as amulets, and in Eastern Europe some boys were named Fishl as a good omen against the evil eye.

Representations of fish in ancient Bible manuscripts have been reproduced in the Encyclopaedia Judaica (Volume 4, pages 908, 962, 965). These include the Leviathan as the food of the righteous in paradise (the last page of a giant 3-volume Ambrosian Bible written in Ulm, South Germany, in 1236–38), a floral and fish motif in a beautiful Yemenite Bible from the year 1469, and a picture of Jonah and the whale in an Ashkenazi Bible now in the British Museum.

The Jewish Museum in New York has in its collection several paintings on our subject matter. Mention should be made of Hermann Junker's "The Buying of the Fish for Sabbath" (oil on canvas, 1880) which depicts the hustle and bustle of the fish market in a quaint inner city street of old Frankfurt am Main, as Jewish burghers and their womenfolk, dressed in the costume of early eighteen hundreds, go about the business of purchasing food for the Sabbath table. Nahum Tschacbasov's "Family at the Sabbath Table" (oil on canvas, New York, 1946) is an example of modern art. It shows a family partaking of the Sabbath fish course. The Jewish Museum also has a fine specimen of a fish-shaped box (made somewhere in western Europe in the 18th century) which holds the spices for *havdalah.* Until our own time, the fish has been a favorite form for these spice-boxes. It symbolizes fertility, protection from the evil eye, and good luck for the week to come.

As might be expected, the Sabbath fish-meal finds a place in the descriptions of Jewish life in the literature of the 20th century. Scholem Asch, in his trilogy, *Three Cities*, portrays a traditional Sabbath eve family supper of fish in the home of a *maskil* school teacher at a time of political, social and intellectual ferment of Poland's Jewish masses. Isaac Bashevis Singer, the Nobel laureate, in his masterful short story, "Short

Friday," describes an idyllic Sabbath meal complete with a course of *gefilte fish.*

Thus, the old custom of fish eating on the Sabbath has found its reflection in hymn and folk song, in art and literature. What about the cook-books? Starting with a recipe in a Yiddish cook-book, *Di Yiddishe Kúch* by B. Shafran (Warsaw, 1930), there has been a veritable explosion of Jewish cook-books in English that teach the making of traditional Sabbath-fish, whether American, European or Israeli style, as well as such exotic varieties as French, Italian and Chinese-style *gefilte fish*. But how did we make the transition from fish to *gefilte fish*?

Gefilte Fish

In the last two hundred years or so the custom has taken over to eat the Sabbath fish as *gefilte fish*. That phrase is, of course, the Yiddish for stuffed fish. In the original version of this delicacy, the fish was chopped, mixed with flour and condiments, and this filling was used to stuff the skin of the fish. The whole was then cooked, cut into slices and served. In the modern version, in which the dish has reached this country, the skin is discarded, and *gefilte fish* is the end result of the blending of several varieties of sweetwater fish with onions, eggs, matzo meal and condiments, simmered in a broth of fish trimmings, vegetables and spices. While there are several varieties of the basic recipe, depending on the origin of the cook and his or her skill, there are two main schools of *gefilte fish* cooking: the *litvishe*, the way the Jews from Lithuania or *litvacks* like it, which is unsweetened, but well seasoned with salt and pepper, and the *galitsianer* version, preferred by Jews originating in Austria or Galicia, who like theirs generously sweetened with a heavy dose of sugar.

An important reason why fish, rather than meat, became the preferred Sabbath fish dish was economics. Impoverished Jewish communities could hardly have afforded meat on every ordinary Sabbath, but some kind of fish was usually available at prices that were within reach. The utilization of every morsel was important for a poor community, and in the making of *gefilte fish* the housewife could use every ounce. Moreover, *gefilte fish* was good whether served hot or cold, and since cooking was not permitted on the Sabbath, such a dish could be served either hot on Friday night or for a cold luncheon or supper on the following Sabbath day. We are reminded somehow, of the baked beans of the New England Puritans. The early American settlers, not permitting themselves to cook on the Christian Sabbath, developed a dish that could be put on the stove the previous day and allowed to simmer until Sunday dinner. Religious requirements and Yankee ingenuity combined to give New England baked beans, just as East European Jews developed *gefilte fish.*

Religious law entered into the picture in yet another way. The Sabbath laws specify the preferred manner in which the edible part of the food shall be separated from the inedible portion, and even the manner in which the residue of the meal, such as the peelings and pits of fruit or the bones and skin of fish, can be removed from the table is laid down in the rules. To do so according to the strictures of *halakhah* requires a learning which not everyone possessed and which could not be expected from the indigent guests who were often invited to the Sabbath table. All of these problems were eliminated by serving the fish in boneless and skinless portions.

"Come and let us give credit to Israel, the holy people," writes a halakhic authority in the name of the Brisker Rav, "for establishing the custom of eating fish on the Sabbath in the form of stuffed fish, thereby eliminating all manner of religious scruples and doubts."[26] During the past thirty years, commercially prepared *gefilte fish* has increasingly filled this demand.

Conclusion

And so the saga of our Jewish national dish, *gefilte fish*, continues. It started with the story of the pious women of the land of Egypt, and ever since then the Sabbath fish meal has been a symbol of our will to national self-preservation, the perpetuation of the race, of Jewish identity, and of the love we feel towards our heritage.

Judaism 29:4 (1980)
Reprinted by permission of the publisher

---

26 Neuwirth, *Shemirat Shabbat Kehilkhatah* (Jerusalem: Feldheim, 1965), 2. 24.

Down to Earth

by **David B. Green**

In his surviving diary entries from space, Ilan Ramon unintentionally authenticated his public persona as sensitive, large-hearted and smart—but only after extensive conservation work made them legible.

Rona Ramon was still living in Houston, Texas, when the people at NASA told her that searchers in a rural part of the state had turned up some documents in Hebrew that had fallen out of the sky. It had been two months since the orbiter of Space Shuttle Columbia had been destroyed on its re-entry to earth's atmosphere, on February 1, 2003, killing all seven astronauts aboard, including Israeli Ilan Ramon, Rona's husband.

"They thought it was technical material, but they sent it to my house," Rona Ramon recalled recently, in a phone conversation. "I was the only one there at the time who read Hebrew. And it wasn't technical material," she adds, flatly. Rather, the pages, some 18 of them, contained entries from Ilan's handwritten astronaut's log. They had survived an explosion that enveloped the spaceship when, hitting the atmosphere at a speed of 17,000 miles per hour, it was exposed to heat in excess of 5,000 degrees Fahrenheit, after its heat-resistant tiles had been damaged during liftoff. Once the spaceship broke up, the diary underwent a free fall to earth of some 65 kms (40 miles) in a temperature as low as minus 700F, and then spent two months exposed to a rainy Texas winter as it waited for a search team to find it. Eventually, over 80,000 pieces, amounting to some 38 percent of the orbiter and its contents, were collected by the 25,000 searchers, and the remains of all seven astronauts were found and brought to burial.

A lengthy investigation by NASA concluded later that year that, on the technical level, the protective tiles had been damaged only seconds into the flight, when they were hit by plastic foam that broke off from the shuttle's large, orange liquid-fuel tank. But a final report also referred to institutional problems within NASA that prevented open discussion of the problem within the organization as soon as it was discovered, on day two of the flight.

As she looked at the few legible pages, Rona Ramon recalls, she began to cry. "It was a very, very emotional moment."

Ilan Ramon, who was 48 when he died, had begun writing diaries in 1981, the year he participated, as the pilot of one of eight F-16s, in an Israel Air Force mission over Iraq that ended with the destruction of the Osirak nuclear reactor then under construction outside Baghdad. Although each of the seven astronauts aboard Columbia had a simple crew notebook, which hung, together with a pen, by a chain from his or her waist, only the pages from Ramon's survived the disaster. "There are parts where he speaks to me and to the children," says Rona (the couple had four). "He writes as if the reader is with him. It still moves me."

Miraculous as the survival of the pages might have been, most of them were not in a state that allowed for them to be read. One group of six pages were largely intact, but most of the writing on them had faded into unrecognizability. Another eight pages were basically blank, both the writing and the blue lines on them having been washed away. A third set might have been legible if they hadn't been found either in tatters or folded in and curled up on themselves.

It is thanks to Sharon Brown and Michael Maggen that some of the final words written by Ilan Ramon in space, as well as material he wrote beforehand and took with him, have been deciphered. Brown is a chemist, with the rank of superintendent, who works at the Israel Police headquarters examining and identifying "questioned documents." Together with Maggen, who heads the Israel Museum's paper conservation lab, working over a period of eight months, she restored large sections of the pages that were found.

Perhaps because he was writing for himself, rather than with posterity in mind, Ramon unintentionally authenticates in his words the persona that his death left to the public memory: a highly intelligent, feeling and large-hearted individual, who was no less moved by his role as emissary of Israel and the Jewish people than he was exhilarated by being in space.

The first page that was deciphered was in the category of unreadable, even when placed in a Video Spectral Comparator (VSC), a high-tech imaging device that can enhance ink and other markings on damaged documents. Only when the police photo lab digitized the smudges on the sheet, and manipulated the wavelengths of the light reflected from those marks, was it possible to make out the fact that there was writing on it. Even then, says Sharon Brown, it took her several weeks before she understood that Ramon had taken the unusual and tedious step of adding vowels to the text he had written. Generally, only poetry and liturgical texts are printed with vocalization, and indeed, when Brown saw that Ramon had written out the full name of God in Hebrew, and made out the word "hinhaltanu" (literally, "bestowed upon us"), she realized that she was looking at the text of the Kiddush, the blessing said over wine on Sabbath eve—apparently copied out before he embarked so he could recite it on Friday night.

Ramon was a self-described "secular Jew" (otherwise, he likely would have known the full Kiddush by heart), but it was important for him not only to carry out this Jewish ritual before a global audience, but to do it correctly. To that end, he also brought with him into space a Kiddush cup and grape juice. He had even consulted with a rabbi about just when Sabbath should be observed when in orbit.

The first step in treating the pages was a prosaic one: disinfection. "The microorganisms they picked up during two months outdoors could have destroyed them quickly," says Maggen, who put the sheets and fragments, some of which already bore smudges from mold, in a fumigation chamber at the museum for 10 days. From there they went back to police headquarters for deciphering, a stage that included the painstaking piecing-together of fragments. After Brown figured out where the pieces of the puzzle went, Maggen did the actual gluing, using a translucent paper produced in Japan to fill in any lacunae that remained.

Maggen had convened a consultative team of the country's leading paper conservators—from the Tel Aviv Museum of Art, the Bahai World Center, and the National and University Library—and they agreed that their goal was "minimal intervention." He explains, "We just wanted the materials to be able to last."

Another sheet had a text that materialized with the help of the VSC, but still remained hard for Brown to interpret, because it contained many technical terms, part of a set of six pages of notes Ramon had prepared for himself before the mission. Those pages included notes on medicines to be carried into orbit, and on emergency procedures. Some of the terminology became comprehensible only when Brown consulted with another astronaut, sent by NASA to Israel on the first-year anniversary of the explosion.

The page in question contained a list of 12 things Ramon wanted to mention or explain when he was interviewed from space. He apparently intended to describe to listeners the effects of weightlessness on astronauts, and wanted to explain each of the various other symbolic items he carried with him into orbit, including a copy of Israel's Declaration of Independence, a drawing that had been made by Peter Ginz, a Jewish child who died at Auschwitz, and the personal patch he designed for his uniform.

Speaking with those involved in the restoration work, it is clear that they too appreciated both the deeply personal and the public aspects of the diary's presentation. Israel Museum director James Snyder says he would be happy for the museum to exhibit some of the diary, since "we were pleased, when Rona Ramon approached us, that we had the hands-on experience and the technology, which we use on such materials as the Dead Sea Scrolls, to be effective on these pages," but adds that "we're deferential to the wishes of Rona and the family, as we felt we were doing it for them."

Michael Maggen explains that when he was repairing pages whose content seemed unusually personal, "I worked with the pages upside down. I didn't want to be in a peep show." Brown, on the other hand, whose job it was to make sense of the text, says that method didn't work for her. "I couldn't work on it upside down. I needed to try and get into his head." Still when she shows me the page containing Ramon's list of subjects to be covered, and I ask if he noted the names of former air force commander Eitan Ben-Eliyahu and Avi Har-Even, who heads

Israel's space agency, because he intended to mention them, she first says yes, and then corrects herself, saying: "We can guess that that may have been his intention, but we have no right to assume anything."

Indeed, Ilan Ramon could often surprise. In his first e-mail to his family from orbit (as quoted in the film "Columbia: The Tragic Loss," directed by Naftaly Gliksberg), Ramon described the vision of earth's atmosphere at night as "a beautiful halo, a green light emanating from the atmosphere ... as if another planet enveloped the planet Earth. And how thin it is!" And, in a broadcast from space, he and fellow crew member William McCool explained, in English and Hebrew, their identification with John Lennon's song "Imagine," as they urged earthlings to "imagine the world as borderless, as we see it, and to try to live as one, in peace," fairly subversive imagery for a representative of the Zionist national endeavor.

Rona Ramon isn't sure yet what will happen with the diary. She is hopeful there will be an exhibition at the museum, but also says she looks forward to publishing in book form a selection of Ilan's two decades of diaries. "Over the years, he opened up, and could express himself about what he was experiencing inside," adding that Ilan "was thinking about writing a book as early as 1981. It will happen, but I'm not ready yet to publish them."

In the meantime, Rona Ramon is involved in several projects meant to perpetuate Ilan's memory as a "role model" for young Israelis. One is a government project to create a center for astronomy and space near the Negev town of Mitzpeh Ramon, where there is already an observatory operated by TAU. Another is a project to promote "leadership and excellence" in education, and there are two other museum shows now in the planning, one at Haifa's national science museum, the other at the air force museum.

When I mention to her that it's hard not to read Ilan's words, or to see pictures of him, and not be taken by his genuine, down-to-earth quality, she says that she still feels as if "it was my good fortune to live with him. He was a loving husband, a friend and a partner, and a wonderful father. He was optimistic, modest, and he spoke to people at their own level. I could talk with him about everything. He always had time for others."

The Jerusalem Report, June 13, 2005
Reprinted with permission by publisher

Asader L'se'udata— I Shall Prepare the Feast

Rabbi Yitschak Luria, (1534–1572), also known as the "Ari," "Arizal," or "Ari HaKadosh," is one of the greatest Kabbalists of all time. He lived in Safed, where he established a following of illustrious students. He composed three songs for Shabbat, one for each meal. The Friday night song is "*Azamer Bishvachin*"; the one for Shabbat afternoon *is* "*Benei Haichala*." "*Asader L'se'udata*" is his composition for the Shabbat day meal. All three songs reflect his deep immersion in Kabbalah and contain many allusions to mystical concepts. An acrostic of the stanzas spells out "*Ani Yitschak Luria*—I am Yitschak Luria."

I shall offer praise at the Shabbat morning meal,
and shall herewith invite the holy Ancient One.

May the supernal light shine thereon through the
great Kiddush and good wine that gladdens the soul.

May He send to us its resplendence
and we shall behold its glory;
May He reveal to us His hidden things
that are said in secret.

May He disclose to us the reason
for the twelve breads,
which symbolize a letter of His Name—
both in the combined and the single form.

May we be united with the Supreme One
in Whom is the life of all things.
May our strength be increased,
and may [our prayer] ascend
and become [a diadem] upon His head.

Field laborers [Torah scholars],
rejoice with speech and voice,
and speak the words [of the Torah]
and deliver new insights [in it];

To adorn the table
with the precious secrets [of the Torah],
profound and hidden,
which are ordinarily not revealed.

And these words will become firmaments. Who will abide therein?
None other than the [Shechina,
which is allegorically called the] sun.

He will ascend to a more lofty level;
and He will take to Himself His mate, [Israel,]
from whom He was separated [during the week].

Siddur Tehillat Hashem with English Translation, Annotated Edition (Brooklyn, NY: Merkos L'Inyonei Chinuch, 2002), p. 250

Dror Yikra— God Proclaims Freedom

This song was composed by Rabbi Dunash Halevi ben Levrat (920–990) of Baghdad. He was a nephew and student of Rabbi Saadia Gaon and a contemporary of Rabbi Chasdai ibn Shaprut and Rabbi Menachem ibn Saruk. In addition to his poetry, ben Levrat served as a judge in a Jewish court and was a noted grammarian. The author's name appears in an acrostic four times in stanzas 1, 2, 3, and 6. His song is a plea to God to protect the Jewish people, destroy its oppressors, and redeem it with peace and salvation.

God proclaims freedom for all His children
And will protect you like the apple of His eye.
Pleasant is your name, and rest and repose
will not be destroyed on the Sabbath day.

Seek My Temple and My Sanctuary;
Show me a sign of deliverance.
Plant a branch within my vineyard;
Turn to the cry of my people!

Tread the wine-press in Botzrah,
And in Babylon, that overpowered.
Crush my enemies in wrath and fury.
Hear my voice on the day I call!

O God, plant in the desert mountain
Myrtle, acacia, cypress, and elm.
Grant to those who teach care
and those who learn care
Abundant peace like a river.

Repel my enemies, O jealous God,
With melting heart and despair.
Then shall we open our mouth and fill it;
Our tongue will be entirely praise to You.

Let your soul know wisdom
And it shall be a crown for your head.
Keep watch over the mitzvot of your Holy One,
Guard your holy Sabbath.

Adapted from "*Zemiros and Bircas Hamazon*," Rabbi Nosson Scherman, Ed. (Brooklyn, NY: ArtScroll Series—Mesorah Publications, 1990) with permission of the copyright holders, ArtScroll / Mesorah Publications, Ltd.

Tzamah Nafshi— My Soul Thirsts

This song was composed by the great medieval Spanish scholar and poet, Rabbi Abraham ibn Ezra (1089–1164), whose name is spelled out by an acrostic of the initial letters of each stanza. Ibn Ezra endured a difficult life of poverty, wandering, and the death of his wife. The composition speaks of longing for God's closeness, and deep devotion to Him. It ends with a plea for redemption.

My soul thirsts for the Almighty for the God of life,
My heart and flesh will sing joyously to the living God.

The One God created me and said, "I swear as I live,
That no man will see Me and remain alive!"
My heart and flesh will sing joyously to the living God.

With wisdom He created everything,
with understanding and forethought;
How deeply hidden it is
from the eyes of every living thing.
My heart and flesh will sing joyously to the living God.

Exalted above all is His Glory
and so every mouth should express His majesty.
Blessed is He in Whose hand
is the soul of every living thing.
My heart and flesh will sing joyously to the living God.

He divided the grandchildren of the
wholesome one [Jacob] to teach them laws
That each person should fulfill them and thereby live!
My heart and flesh will sing joyously to the living God.

Which person can justify himself
knowing that he is compared to fine dust?
In truth, before You, no living thing can.
My heart and flesh will sing joyously to the living God.

Within the heart, desire lies as if the poison of a viper,
And, thus, how can one return to G-d
and become whole and healthy?
My heart and flesh will sing joyously to the living God.

Those who went astray, if only they had
desired, and from their way repented
Before they would rest in that place
appointed for all [the grave].
My heart and flesh will sing joyously to the living God.

For everything and all, I shall glorify You.
Every mouth shall acknowledge Your Oneness.
You open Your hand and satisfy every living thing.
My heart and flesh will sing joyously to the living God.

Remember the love of the ancient ones [forefathers]
and revive the slumbering ones
And bring close the days
when Yishai's son shall live [the Messiah].
My heart and flesh will sing joyously to the living God.

See and recognize the true woman.
The maidservant proclaims,
"No! It is your son who is dead, and my son who lives!"
My heart and flesh will sing joyously to the living God.

I will prostrate unto my face
and spread out my hands to You.
At the moment I open my mouth
when saying *Nishmat kol chai* (soul of all living).
My heart and flesh will sing joyously to the living God.

Lesson 5

Working Definitions

Introduction

It is hard to imagine learning chemistry without the periodic table, or studying history without a good map. Often, the right organizational paradigm can instantly clarify a jumble of information in a way that makes the underlying structure clear and aids comprehension and recall.

This lesson will introduce you to the key concepts and patterns of logic that underlie the "science" of Shabbat observance.

The Thirty-Nine *Melachot*

Creativity Defined

Text 1

אֲבוֹת מְלָאכוֹת אַרְבָּעִים חָסֵר אֶחָת: הַזּוֹרֵעַ, וְהַחוֹרֵשׁ, וְהַקּוֹצֵר, וְהַמְעַמֵּר, הַדָּשׁ, וְהַזּוֹרֶה, הַבּוֹרֵר, הַטּוֹחֵן, וְהַמְרַקֵּד, וְהַלָּשׁ, וְהָאוֹפֶה, הַגּוֹזֵז אֶת הַצֶּמֶר, הַמְלַבְּנוֹ, וְהַמְנַפְּצוֹ, וְהַצּוֹבְעוֹ, וְהַטּוֹוֶה, וְהַמֵּסֵךְ, וְהָעוֹשֶׂה שְׁנֵי בָתֵּי נִירִין, וְהָאוֹרֵג שְׁנֵי חוּטִין, וְהַפּוֹצֵעַ שְׁנֵי חוּטִין, הַקּוֹשֵׁר, וְהַמַּתִּיר, וְהַתּוֹפֵר שְׁתֵּי תְפִירוֹת, הַקּוֹרֵעַ עַל מְנָת לִתְפֹּר שְׁתֵּי תְפִירוֹת, הַצָּד צְבִי, הַשּׁוֹחֲטוֹ, וְהַמַּפְשִׁיטוֹ, הַמּוֹלְחוֹ, וְהַמְעַבֵּד אֶת עוֹרוֹ, וְהַמּוֹחֲקוֹ, וְהַמְחַתְּכוֹ, הַכּוֹתֵב שְׁתֵּי אוֹתִיּוֹת, וְהַמּוֹחֵק עַל מְנָת לִכְתֹּב שְׁתֵּי אוֹתִיּוֹת, הַבּוֹנֶה, וְהַסּוֹתֵר, הַמְכַבֶּה, וְהַמַּבְעִיר, הַמַּכֶּה בַפַּטִּישׁ, הַמּוֹצִיא מֵרְשׁוּת לִרְשׁוּת, הֲרֵי אֵלּוּ אֲבוֹת מְלָאכוֹת אַרְבָּעִים חָסֵר אֶחָת.

משנה, שבת ז,ב

There are thirty-nine primary *melachot*:

Sowing, plowing, reaping, binding sheaves, threshing, winnowing, selecting, grinding, sifting, kneading, baking;

Shearing wool, washing it, combing it, dyeing it, spinning, stretching [threads], making two loops, weaving two threads, separating two threads, tying, untying, sewing two stitches, tearing in order to sew two stitches;

Capturing a deer, slaughtering it, skinning it, salting it, curing its hide, scraping it [of hair], cutting it up;

Writing two letters, erasing in order to write two letters, building, demolishing, extinguishing, kindling, striking with a hammer, carrying from one domain to another;

These are the thirty-nine *melachot*.

Mishnah, Shabbat 7:2

Learning Activity 1

Quickly peruse Text 1. You should readily be able to identify four patterns, or strings of related activities. What are they?

1. ______________________________

2. ______________________________

3. ______________________________

4. ______________________________

Figure 5.1
The *Melachot*

Baking	Producing Cloth	Producing Hides	Constructing
1. Sowing	12. Shearing	25. Trapping	32. Writing
2. Plowing	13. Washing	26. Slaughtering	33. Erasing
3. Reaping	14. Combing	27. Skinning	34. Building
4. Binding Sheaves	15. Dyeing	28. Tanning	35. Demolishing
5. Threshing	16. Spinning	29. Smoothing	36. Striking the Final Hammer's Blow
6. Winnowing	17. Stretching the Threads	30. Scoring	37. Extinguishing a Fire
7. Selecting	18. Making Loops	31. Cutting	38. Kindling a Fire
8. Grinding	19. Weaving		
9. Sifting	20. Separating the Threads		
10. Kneading	21. Tying a Knot		
11. Baking	22. Untying a Knot		
	23. Sewing		
	24. Tearing		

Text 2a

וַיַּקְהֵל מֹשֶׁה אֶת כָּל עֲדַת בְּנֵי יִשְׂרָאֵל וַיֹּאמֶר אֲלֵהֶם אֵלֶּה הַדְּבָרִים אֲשֶׁר צִוָּה ה׳ לַעֲשֹׂת אֹתָם.
שֵׁשֶׁת יָמִים תֵּעָשֶׂה מְלָאכָה וּבַיּוֹם הַשְּׁבִיעִי יִהְיֶה לָכֶם קֹדֶשׁ שַׁבַּת שַׁבָּתוֹן . . .
וַיֹּאמֶר מֹשֶׁה אֶל כָּל עֲדַת בְּנֵי יִשְׂרָאֵל לֵאמֹר זֶה הַדָּבָר אֲשֶׁר צִוָּה ה׳ לֵאמֹר.
קְחוּ מֵאִתְּכֶם תְּרוּמָה לַה׳ כֹּל נְדִיב לִבּוֹ יְבִיאֶהָ אֵת תְּרוּמַת ה׳ זָהָב וָכֶסֶף וּנְחֹשֶׁת . . . וְכָל
חֲכַם לֵב בָּכֶם יָבֹאוּ וְיַעֲשׂוּ אֵת כָּל אֲשֶׁר צִוָּה ה׳.

שמות לה,א–י

Moses called the whole community of the children of Israel to assemble, and he said to them, "These are the things that God commanded to make:

"Six days work may be done, but the seventh day shall be holy for you, a day of complete rest. . . ."

And Moses spoke to the entire community of the children of Israel, saying, "This is the matter that God has commanded to say:

"Take from yourselves an offering for God; every person of generous heart shall bring God's offering: gold, silver, and copper. . . . And every person of wise heart among you shall come and make everything that God has commanded [for the construction of the Tabernacle]."

Exodus 35:1–10

Rabbi Shlomoh Yitschaki (1040–1105). Better known by the acronym Rashi. Rabbi and famed author of comprehensive commentaries on the Talmud and Bible. Born in Troyes, France, Rashi studied in the famed *yeshivot* of Mainz and Worms. His commentaries, which focus on the simple understanding of the text, are considered the most fundamental of all the commentaries that preceded and followed. Since their initial printings, the commentaries have appeared in virtually every edition of the Talmud and Bible. Many of the famed authors of the *Tosafot* are among Rashi's descendants.

Text 2b

הקדים להם אזהרת שבת לצווי מלאכת המשכן לומר שאינה דוחה את השבת.

רש"י, שם

He prefaced the instruction regarding the work of the Tabernacle with the commandment of Shabbat to teach that [the building of the Tabernacle] does not supersede the Shabbat.

Rashi, ad loc.

Text 2c

אבות מלאכות ארבעים חסר אחת כנגד מי. אמר להו רבי חנינא בר חמא: כנגד עבודות המשכן.

תלמוד בבלי, שבת מט,ב

To what do the thirty-nine *melachot* correspond? Rabbi Chanina bar Chama said, "They correspond to the labors of the Tabernacle."

Talmud, Shabbat 49b

Text 3

גבי שבת תנן: אבות מלאכות ארבעים חסר אחת; אבות מכלל דאיכא תולדות.
תלמוד בבלי, בבא קמא ב,א

The Mishnah says regarding Shabbat, "There are thirty-nine 'parent labors.'" "Parents" implies that there are children as well.

Talmud, Bava Kama 2a

Learning Activity 2

Try to match the secondary labors listed below to their root primary labor:

1. Milking a cow	**A. Plowing**
2. Gluing together papers	**B. Threshing**
3. Plucking eyebrows	**C. Kneading**
4. Mixing water and earth to make mud	**D. Shearing**
5. Fertilizing a field	**E. Sewing**

Learning Activity 3

Consider the following four technologies, which of the primary labors they most resemble, and whether the resemblance is sufficient to prohibit it on Shabbat:

Technology	Which Primary Labor Does It Most Resemble?	Status on Shabbat (circle one)
Driving a motorcycle		permitted / prohibited
Velcro		permitted / prohibited
Assembling a Pack 'N Play		permitted / prohibited
Photographing (with a film camera)		permitted / prohibited

Figure 5.2
Av, *Toladah*, and *Shevut*

Av
planting

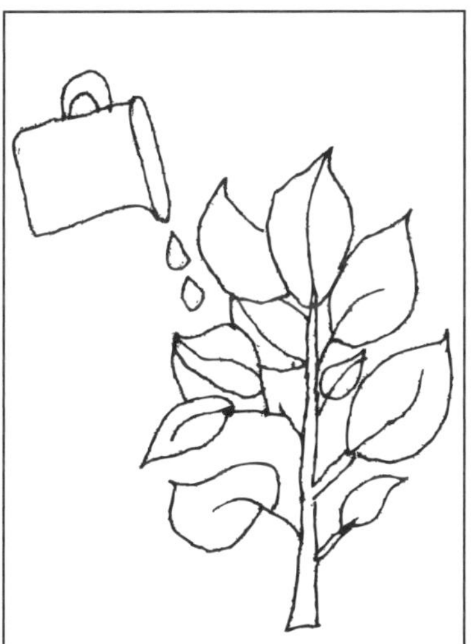

Toladah
watering plants

Shevut
putting water in a vase with flowers

The Message of Rest

Text 4

Dayan Dr. Isidor Grunfeld (1900–1975). Rabbi and author. Born in Tauberettersheim, Bavaria, Grunfeld studied law and philosophy at the universities of Frankfurt and Hamburg. He settled in England in 1933 where he studied for the rabbinate and was ordained. From 1939 until 1965 he served as *dayan* (chief rabbinical magistrate) of the London Rabbinical Court. Among his numerous communal activities were those on behalf of European Jewish war orphans, and the British Council for Jewish Relief and Rehabilitation. He was also active in Amnesty International and various peace movements. Grunfeld's literary work is chiefly concerned with Rabbi Samson Raphael Hirsch's, editing English translations of his work with extensive introductions and notes. His work, *The Sabbath*, has been a fundamental work for appreciating Shabbat in the modern world.

Sabbath testifies to God as the supreme Creator of heaven and earth and all they contain. Man, however, is engaged in a constant struggle to gain mastery over God's creation, to bring nature under his control. By the use of his God-given intelligence, skill and energy, he has in large measure succeeded in this. He is thus constantly in danger of forgetting his own creaturehood—his utter and complete dependence on the Lord of all things. He tends to forget that the very powers he uses in his conquest of nature are derived from his Creator, in whose service his life and work should be conducted. . . .

God willed therefore that the Jew, while subduing and controlling his environment like every other human being, must recognize, *and show that he recognizes*, that his powers are derived from One higher than himself. This recognition he is to express by dedicating one day in every week to God, and by refraining on this day from every activity which signifies human power over nature.

On this day we renounce every exercise of intelligent, purposeful control over natural objects and forces, we cease from every act of human power, in order to proclaim God as the Source of all power. By refraining from human creating, the Jew pays silent homage to the Creator. . . .

Melakhah thus includes within its scope any activity of a constructive nature which makes some significant change in our material environment—significant, that is, in relation to its usefulness for human purposes. Any act, however small, which demonstrates man's mastery of nature in this way is a *melakhah*, be it striking a light or washing clothes, tying a knot or building a house.

Dayan Dr. Isidor Grunfeld, *The Sabbath* [Jerusalem: Feldheim Publishers, 1981] pp. 27–29

Questions for Discussion

1. According to this text, how does man come to recognize God as the source of all power?

2. Practically speaking, what might you do differently in your life as a result of being mindful that God is the One Who provides and Who makes all your achievements possible?

Understanding *Hotsa'ah*

The Odd Man Out

Text 5

הם העלו את הקרשים מקרקע לעגלה, ואתם לא תכניסו מרשות הרבים לרשות היחיד.
הם הורידו את הקרשים מעגלה לקרקע, ואתם לא תוציאו מרשות היחיד לרשות הרבים.
תלמוד בבלי, שבת מט,ב

The [Levites] hoisted the [Tabernacle's] beams from the ground to the wagon;

hence, you must not carry from a public to a private domain.

The [Levites] lowered the [Tabernacle's] beams from the wagon to the ground;

hence, you must not carry from a private to a public domain.

Talmud, Shabbat 49b

Text 6a

הוצאה גופה היכא כתיבא?
תלמוד בבלי, שבת צו,ב

Where is [the prohibition against] carrying [from one domain to another] written in the Torah?

Talmud, Shabbat 96b

Text 6b

וַיֹּאמְרוּ אֶל מֹשֶׁה לֵּאמֹר מַרְבִּים הָעָם לְהָבִיא מִדֵּי הָעֲבֹדָה לַמְּלָאכָה אֲשֶׁר צִוָּה ה׳ לַעֲשֹׂת אֹתָהּ.
וַיְצַו מֹשֶׁה וַיַּעֲבִירוּ קוֹל בַּמַּחֲנֶה לֵאמֹר אִישׁ וְאִשָּׁה אַל יַעֲשׂוּ עוֹד מְלָאכָה לִתְרוּמַת הַקֹּדֶשׁ
וַיִּכָּלֵא הָעָם מֵהָבִיא.
שמות לו,ה–ו

They said to Moses, "The people are bringing much more than is needed for the work that God commanded to do."

Moses gave orders to make an announcement in the camp, "Let no man or woman do any more *melachah* for the sacred offering." So the people stopped bringing [offerings].

Exodus 36:5–6

Text 6c

משה היכן הוה יתיב? במחנה לויה, ומחנה לויה רשות הרבים הואי, וקאמר להו
לישראל, לא תפיקו ותיתו מרשות היחיד דידכו לרשות הרבים.
תלמוד בבלי, שבת צו,ב

Where was Moses stationed? In the camp of the Levites, which was a public domain. And he said to the Israelites, "Do not take out and bring [materials] from your private dwellings into the public domain."

Talmud, Shabbat 96b

Text 7

בעי הוצאה היכא כתיבה, ולא בעי למילפה ממשכן אף על גב דהויא במשכן, משום . . .
דמה מלאכה עשה שהוציאו מרשות. מעיקרא חפץ והשתא נמי חפץ.

אור זרוע ב,פב

Rabbi Yitschak ben Moshe of Vienna (ca. 1180–1250). Student of the German tosafists. His fame stems primarily from his influential halachic work and commentary to the Talmud, *Or Zaru'a*, which was subsequently quoted by many halachic authorities. His son Rabbi Chaim wrote a compendium of his father's work, which for many generations was the only widely used version of the *Or Zaru'a*. In the 19th century, the original work was found and published. Among his students was the Maharam of Rothenburg.

The Talmud asks, "Where is [the prohibition against] carrying [from one domain to another] written in the Torah?" and does not suffice with deriving it from the Tabernacle, though indeed it was performed in the Tabernacle. Because . . . what creative labor is accomplished by transferring [an object] from a domain? It originally was an object, and now too it is [the very same, unchanged] object!

Rabbi Yitschak ben Moshe of Vienna, *Or Zaru'a* 2:82

Text 8

If the other *melakhoth* show us man mastering and controlling his natural environment, this one shows him active in the social realm, carrying on the intercourse of the community, circulating its material good between house and house, through street and thoroughfare; not for trade only, but also for the personal and social ends of everyday life. "Carrying" is the characteristic *melakhah* by which man pursues and attains his purposes in society. By ceasing from each of the other *melakhoth*, we proclaim God as the source of our power over nature. By ceasing from "carrying" we acknowledge Him our Master in the sphere of human society. This vast, complex world of social organization—the world of house, street and city—needs above all else the realization of God's presence and God's purpose, the sanctification and dedication which ceasing from *melakhah* expresses. The community whose members refrain from "carrying" on Sabbath places the seal of God upon its social life.

Dayan Dr. Isidor Grunfeld, *The Sabbath* [Jerusalem: Feldheim Publishers, 1981] p. 36

The Prototypical *Melachah*

Text 9

טורנוסרופוס הרשע שאל את רבי עקיבא . . . אם כדבריך שהקדוש ברוך הוא מכבד את השבת, אל ישב בה רוחות, אל יוריד בה גשמים, אל יצמיח בה עשב. אמר ליה . . . אמשול לך משל . . . אם היה אחד דר בחצר הרי הוא מותר בכל החצר כולה, אף כאן הקדוש ברוך הוא לפי שאין רשות אחרת עמו וכל העולם כולו שלו מותר בכל עולם כולו.

בראשית רבה יא,ה

The wicked Tineius Rufus asked Rabbi Akiva, ". . . If it is true as you say that God honors the Shabbat, then on it He should desist from making the wind blow, making the rain fall, and making the grass grow!"

Rabbi Akiva responded, ". . . Let me illustrate with a parable. . . . One who lives in an enclosed courtyard is permitted to carry [on Shabbat] throughout the yard. So too, regarding God: there is no domain but His for the whole world is His. Therefore, He may [carry] throughout the entire world."

Midrash, *Bereishit Rabah* 11:5

Learning Activity 4

Tineius Rufus: (derisive) I don't know about this Shabbat thing. I think you Jews made it all up to sabotage the progress of the empire.

Rabbi Akiva: Why do you say that?

Tineius Rufus: Well, you say that God honors the Shabbat.

Rabbi Akiva: Correct.

Tineius Rufus: Can you Jews plant on Shabbat?

Rabbi Akiva: No.

Tineius Rufus: Can you carry things from a private domain to a public domain?

Rabbi Akiva: No, of course not.

Tineius Rufus: (triumphantly) So, how come God breaks His own rules? He does the same thing on Shabbat as the rest of the week. If He is honoring Shabbat, why does He make the wind blow? Wouldn't that be considered carrying? If He cares for Shabbat, why does He make the rain fall and the grass grow? I thought planting was not allowed!

Rabbi Akiva: You know, of course, that we Jews can carry within our own houses or property.

Tineius Rufus: (mocking) What's that got to do with anything?

Rabbi Akiva: The whole world is God's property, you know.

Tineius Rufus: (back-tracking) Okay, you got me there. But that only explains why He can make the wind blow. But what about planting? I got you there!

Rabbi Akiva: Let's talk some more about the carrying first. Tell me, why is carrying prohibited on Shabbat?

Tineius Rufus: (confused) Because . . . because . . . wait—I ask the questions around here. . . . (In accusing, mocking voice) So, tell me, where did you get the carrying thing from? What's that got to do with Shabbat?

Rabbi Akiva: Let me explain it to you. We refrain from work on Shabbat because we recognize that behind the very many things in this world there is really only one force in charge—God.

Tineius Rufus: And therefore?

Rabbi Akiva: When we carry from the private domain to the public domain, we betray the central message of Shabbat, which is seeing everything in the world as part of God's private domain, under His personal control. God, however, can carry on Shabbat, because He never fails to see the world as His private domain.

Tineius Rufus: But you didn't explain why He can do all that other stuff, like bringing the rain.

Rabbi Akiva: *All* of the prohibited labors are there to help us recognize that we are in God's private domain. When we stop creating, we realize that He is the owner of the universe. He is in charge of everything; but because God is the owner of the universe, in His private domain, there is no reason for Him to refrain from any other labor either.

Tineius Rufus: So, once I accept that the whole world is God's domain . . . then it is obvious that He can engage in the other acts as well?

Rabbi Akiva: Exactly. In fact, if on Shabbat God would not allow the wind to blow, the rain to fall, and so forth, you would have used that as proof that God abandons the world on Shabbat and that people can therefore do whatever they want!

Tineius Rufus: (sputtering) Well, you've won the argument this time; but I'm not done with you yet. . . . (evil laugh) There's always tomorrow.

Lesson Conclusion
Bringing Shabbat into Your Life

Text 10

The Sabbath is more than a mere set of rules. It is another way of life completely, totally divorced from weekday life. When put in handbook form, a different life style may seem very difficult and complex. When lived, however, it is really very easy.

A good example is going off to college. Every university prints a catalog, telling of all its rules and regulations and including a list of courses. If your sole impression of campus life were to be based on this catalog, it would seem impossibly complicated. After all, it takes a 200-page book just to describe it! But once you get there, you learn to live it.

The same is true of Shabbat. You learn to keep the Sabbath by reading books, but that makes it seem impossibly difficult. It is almost like learning about love from a marriage manual. You have to live it to see its true dimensions of beauty.

Rabbi Aryeh Kaplan, *Sabbath: Day of Eternity* [New York: NCSY, 1982], p. 44

Rabbi Aryeh Kaplan (1934–1983). Noted American rabbi and prolific author. During his short life, he authored over 50 volumes on Torah, Talmud, Jewish mysticism, and philosophy, many of which have become modern-day classics. He is best known for his popular translation and elucidation of the Bible, *The Living Torah*, and his translation of the Ladino biblical commentary, *Me'am Lo'ez*.

Key Points

1. We derive the various *melachot* of Shabbat by looking at the significant activities needed in order to build the Tabernacle.

2. The thirty-nine *melachot* are categories of prohibited labor. There are many other forms of labor, called *toladot*, that serve similar creative functions and are therefore prohibited as well.

3. On Shabbat, we refrain from *melachah* in order to renounce our control over the natural order and to show that God is the source of all our accomplishments.

4. The thirty-nine *melachot* are necessary for procuring food, clothing, and shelter. By refraining from activities necessary to produce these necessities, we demonstrate that even our most basic accomplishments depend on God's providence.

5. By ceasing from carrying from domain to domain, we acknowledge God as our Master in the social organization of life.

6. The purpose of all forbidden labor on Shabbat is to allow a person to experience God's point of view in which all of reality is a unified reflection of His will. On Shabbat, we are not to take ourselves out of this "private domain" to the "public domain."

7. Reading about Shabbat can be complex. In order to appreciate its true beauty, one must live it.

8. Shabbat is a storehouse of positive energy that has the ability to infuse the entire week with the Shabbat sensibility. Instead of being consumed by the public domain, we can chip away at it, gradually infusing the public domain with a greater consciousness of the true reality.

Appendix
The Thirty-Nine *Melachot*: A Brief Overview

Much of the following material is adapted from *The 39 Melochos* (Feldheim Publishers, 2003) by Dovid Ribiat

1. Producing Bread

The first subset of *melachot* that are forbidden on Shabbat derives from the process of producing dyes to color the Tabernacle's tapestries. The dyes were manufactured from herbs which were planted, harvested, gathered, husked, and purified from all other debris. The herbs were then ground, sifted, and mixed with water to create a paste, and then cooked in water in order to create the dye solution.

Considering that for ordinary people making bread is much more common than dye manufacture, the sages worded these *melachot* in terms of bread production (hence, they speak of "baking," rather than "cooking").

אב מלאכה *Av Melachah*	Definition and Underlying Principle	Examples
זורע **1. Sowing**	**Initiating or promoting plant growth**	Planting, pruning, or watering plants
חורש **2. Plowing**	**Preparing and optimizing soil for the purpose of planting**	Plowing, digging, hoeing, raking (soil), fertilizing, adding soil enhancers
קוצר **3. Reaping**	**Uprooting or severing plant life from its source of growth**	Picking fruits, vegetable, or flowers; removing moss from a rock
מעמר **4. Sheaving**	**Collecting or combining scattered fruits or produce**	Stringing figs, gathering a bushel of apples, raking leaves into a heap

אב מלאכה *Av Melachah*	Definition and Underlying Principle	Examples
דש **5. Threshing**	**Pounding kernels to loosen them from their husks; separating a fruit, vegetable, or earth-grown commodity from its natural shell or similar attachment**	Threshing grain, beating flax to extract fibers from their husks, extracting peas from inedible pods, removing the thick outer shel of a walnut
זורה **6. Winnowing**	**Separating loosened kernels from their husks; separating or removing undesired matter by means of wind (natural or artificial)**	Blowing at peanuts to remove their thin covering
בורר **7. Selecting**	**Removing pebbles and debris from grain kernels that have been husked; sorting or selecting from an assorted mixture or combination**	Removing spoiled cherries from a bowl of cherries, removing unwanted cashews from mixed nuts, straining impurities from liquids, trimming away a brown spot on a fruit, separating mixed cutlery and placing into separate drawer compartments, sorting soile laundry from fresh laundry
טוחן **8. Grinding**	**Breaking down and reducing a sizable entity into small parts, thereby making it suitable for a new use**	Grinding wheat, chopping lumber into wooc chips, crushing rocks into gravel, cutting reec into thin strips
מרקד **9. Sifting**	**Separating and removing unwanted matter from a mixture by sifting it through a sieve or similar device**	Sifting flour, sifting pebbles from sand to produce fine sand, allowing dressing to drair from salad in a slotted salad spoon, sifting granulated sugar from larger clumps
לש **10. Kneading**	**Causing granules to coalesce into a single mass by introducing a liquid**	Adding flour to dough, kneading dough, pouring water on sand to produce mud or cement, mixing water into a powder and creating a paste
אופה **11. Baking**	**Causing a change in the properties of a food or substance by way of heat**	Cooking, baking bricks, using heat to melt wax, stirring food to distribute heat

2. Weaving Fabric

The second category of *melachot* includes thirteen labors that are employed in the production of clothing. The Tabernacle's sanctuary contained several tapestry coverings, one of which was made of sheep's wool. The wool had to be shorn, washed, combed, and dyed. The fleece was then spun into thread and woven on a loom; the sheets of fabric were then sewn together. (If and when the tapestries sustained damage, it would be necessary to tear out the damaged area, creating an even hole, which could then be repaired.)

Tying and untying were necessary in order to create the fishing nets to catch the *chilazon* sea creatures, from whose blood the blue dye (*techelet*) for the tapestries was produced.

אב מלאכה *Av Melachah*	Definition and Underlying Principle	Examples
גוזז **12. Shearing**	**Severing or uprooting any part of the body of any creature (even if it is no longer alive)**	Shearing wool, cutting or tweezing hair, pulling a hair from a natural fur, feathering a chicken, paring finger- or toenails, removing a wart
מלבן **13. Washing**	**Cleansing absorbent materials from soil, grime, or other impurities**	Washing, soaking, or squeezing clothing or other absorbent materials; pouring water on a carpet to dilute a stain, scraping dried food or a stain out of a fabric, brushing dust off a hat or jacket
מנפץ **14. Combing**	**Separating entangled fibers to make it possible to spin them into thread**	Separating fibers by means of beating, picking apart by hand, or combing—for the purpose of making the fibers spinnable
צובע **15. Dyeing**	**Coloring any material or substance**	Dyeing wool, painting a wall, coloring in a coloring book, adding food coloring to water, causing a chemical to change colors for clinical testing
טווה **16. Spinning**	**Twisting hairs or fibers into a continuous thread, or twining thin strands into yarn**	Twisting a ball of cotton-wool to form a wick

אב מלאכה *Av Melachah*	**Definition and Underlying Principle**	**Examples**
מיסך **17. Warping**	**Mounting threads on to the warp beam of a loom**	Setting loops in a potholder frame, arranging and laying out reeds for basket making, aligning slats on the floor for lattice making
עושה שתי בתי נירין **18. Making Loops**	**Making loops on threads to allow the weft (horizontal) threads to pass across (i.e., under and over) the warp (vertical) threads**	Weaving baskets, sieves, or strainers out of reeds
אורג **19. Weaving**	**Completing the creation of a fabric by interlacing the perpendicular threads**	Knitting, making objects out of lanyard, making a lattice work
פוצע **20. Breaking Thread**	**Cutting the threads that attach the completed fabric from the loom**	Pulling out threads from the end of a weave, pulling loose threads from a fabric.
קושר **21. Tying**	**Binding of two separate pliant objects (usually string or rope) by twisting one around the other in a skilled or permanent manner**	Tying a permanent knot, tying a knot that requires particular skill, sealing a bag of food by tying its neck into a knot
מתיר **22. Untying**	**Untying a skilled or permanent knot**	Untying a permanent knot or a knot that requires particular skill, unraveling a hemp rope
תופר **23. Sewing**	**Attaching panels of fabric**	Sewing, gluing, pinning, stapling, taping, tightening a loose seam by tugging the end of the stitching, sealing an envelope
קורע **24. Tearing**	**Detaching sewn panels of fabric for the purpose of resewing them**	Opening a hem or seam to lengthen or widen it

3. Tanning Leather

The layers of tapestries that covered the Tabernacle included leather produced from ram's hides and the colorful fur of a now-extinct animal called *tachash.* The third category of *melachot* thus includes the labors required to produce leather and furs. The animals had to be trapped, slaughtered, and skinned. The hide was then tanned, smoothed, and cut to size.

אב מלאכה *Av Melachah*	Definition and Underlying Principle	Examples
צד **25. Trapping**	**Forcibly confining an animal or living creature**	Trapping an animal, trapping a bird in a closet, catching flies, placing a bowl over a bee
שוחט **26. Slaughtering**	**Terminating the life of a living being by any method, drawing blood**	Stepping on insects, spraying insecticide on an insect, drawing blood, causing a bruise
מפשיט **27. Skinning**	**Removing an animal's hide**	Removing the skin of raw chicken, peeling apart natural layers of leather
מעבד **28. Tanning**	**Preserving hides and transforming them into leather or fur**	Rubbing leather preserver into shoes, putting fresh gherkins into brine or pickle juice for pickling purposes
ממחק **29. Smoothing**	**Scraping or sanding any surface to achieve smoothness**	Removing hair from a hide, removing bark from a log, sanding wood or metal, scrubbing a pot with steel wool, lathering with a bar of soap, sharpening a knife
משרטט **30. Scoring**	**Marking or scoring lines on a surface in preparation for cutting it to size**	Drawing a line on paper to cut along it, folding a sheet of paper in order to tear it along the fold, scoring a line around a newspaper article to cut it out
מחתך **31. Cutting**	**Cutting an object to a specific size**	Tearing paper towel along the perforated lines, cutting or tearing out a newspaper article, cutting a sheet of foil or plastic wrap to a measured size

4. Constructing a Building

Once all the materials were produced, the Tabernacle had to be assembled. Each time the Jews traveled from one location in the desert to another, the Tabernacle was dismantled and then erected again in the new encampment. The Tabernacle's walls were comprised of forty-eight wooden planks; every time the Tabernacle was reconstructed, the planks had to be returned to the same position (relative to the others) that they had previously occupied. For this purpose, symbols were inscribed on each plank, indicating its proper position. The wooden planks were each overlaid with a gold sheath, which was secured to the plank with golden nails (hence, the labor of "striking the final hammer blow").

Fire was used for smelting and metal working; extinguishing was used to produce charcoal for use in the smelting process.

אב מלאכה *Av Melachah*	Definition and Underlying Principle	Examples
כותב **32. Writing**	**Forming any kind of letter, symbol, picture, or design that conveys a particular meaning or represents an idea**	Writing two letters with an ink pen or lead pencil, drawing a sketch, assembling a puzzle that depicts a picture
מוחק **33. Erasing**	**Erasing letters for the purpose of rewriting; cleansing a surface to render it fit for writing**	Erasing penciled writing to allow for corrections, whiting out penned characters in order to rewrite on that spot
בונה **34. Building**	**Creating or assembling a permanent structure (or part of one)**	Pressing a loose brick tightly into place in a brick patio wall, stamping down a loose tile or floorboard that came up, screwing hooks into a wall, erecting fencing
סותר **35. Demolishing**	**Tearing down or disassembling a permanent structure for the purpose of rebuilding**	Removing an old window to install a new one, breaking down a wall to use its bricks, detaching a loose pole to firmly reinsert it

אב מלאכה *Av Melachah*	Definition and Underlying Principle	Examples
מכה בפטיש **36. Striking the Final Hammer Blow**	**Any act of completion (in creating, perfecting or repairing an item)**	Sharpening a knife, replacing an eyeglasses lens by snapping it into place or adjusting the frames by bending them into the correct shape, straightening the prongs of a fork
מכבה **37. Extinguishing**	**Extinguishing or diminishing the intensity of a fire**	Blowing out a candle, lowering a gas flame, disconnecting an electric light
מבעיר **38. Kindling**	**Igniting a fire or refueling and spreading an existing fire**	Lighting candles, turning on or adjusting a gas flame, turning on central heating, striking a match

5. The Odd Man Out

אב מלאכה *Av Melachah*	Definition and Underlying Principle	Examples
הוצאה **39. Transferring**	**Transferring objects from one domain to another**	Transporting an object in one's hand or pocket through the street, pushing a carriage in the street, throwing a ball from the street into a fenced-in backyard or vice versa

Additional Readings

The Sabbath: A Day of Rest Ordained by God

by **Rabbi Samson Raphael Hirsch**

"When the Sabbath comes, comes rest."

And were it nothing more than this, nothing more than a day of rest ordained by God, recurring every seventh day, as it presents itself in its outward appearance to the most superficial observer, what a blessing it would even bring in its train!

If you had not this Sabbath, this day of rest, ordained by God, when would you rest, when would you come to your self, come to your wife and child, when would you attend to your mind and spirit, to your heaven upon earth? "When [would you have] had the time to spare?"—but *when* would you have the time, when would you *dare* to have time to spare?

Incessantly is the material world around you at work, it never rests, unceasingly it struggles on for its material existence, irresistibly it marches on. He who does not go forward, goes backward, he who stands still is trodden down: "by day and by night they never stand still"—and could you, would you, dare to cry "halt" to your labor; "halt" to your cares for your daily existence? Would or could you dare once in the way proclaim a rest for your hand, your head, your mind; once in the way wipe away the perspiration, smooth your forehead, shake off from you the dust of the arena of life? Dare you once stop looking forward with earnest intent to the goal which you have to gain, and instead gaze back for once, look around you and down into your inner self, look joyously and calmly at the hope which you cherished, the ideals which you strive after and partly realized, and for once in the way step out from the restless and afflicted world of "That is to be" into the blissful world of "Being," into the enjoyment of a paradise on Earth?

"Paradise"? Who dares still to speak of a paradise on Earth? The gates of paradise were closed behind us long ago. The tree of life blossoms of itself now for no one. Thorns and thistles cumber the way; our bread is gained in the sweat of the brow, and is eaten with sorrow and sighing. Without the Sabbath, without rest, man is fated but to toil; without the Sabbath, without rest, he is tormented by worry. And though a thousand minds were thinking day by day how to increase Knowledge; though a man's thousand inventions were day by day adding to his power, this knowledge would make him no richer or happier, this power would bring him no greater freedom or ease. "The more knowledge, the more care." The more inventions, the more wants; the more strength, the more work. The father had to contend only with his neighbor; but on the wings of the clouds the son has to battle with the whole world. The father had but his village to look round, but with flashes of lightning the son sets about to explore the whole world. Numberless possessions and pleasures unknown to the simple father, the wise son must win for himself and his family in the sweat of his brow, at the highest strain on output of his nervous system, at the greatest demand on his time. He has to provide so much for himself, so much for his wife and child, that he has no time to think of himself, of wife and child; and the cares for the house estrange him from the home. The word "existence" has assumed such gigantic proportions that life is entirely absorbed in the task of securing the existence, and no time is left to enquire into its purpose and aim, its value and meaning. The word "existence" has become so immense a problem that the sum total of all human wisdom, the exploration of the heavens and the earth, of countries and seas, and even virtue and morality, and even charity and benevolence, have to provide themselves with the industrial hallmark of economic utility in order to obtain recognition and notice from a bread-earning humanity. And man, created to be in God's image in wisdom and kindness, in love and justice;

created to rejoice, like God, in his work, pants under the yoke of the toil of the earth, dripping with sweat, seeking for food, and no longer hears the "Where art thou?" of God's voice wandering up and down in search of him.

But then appears the messenger from Eden, the angel of God, the Sabbath approaches him and says, "In the name of God: no further!" You must not only care for earthly bread for yourself and your family. You sin against yourself, your wife and child, if your hand is always busy only to procure food, if your foot is always moving only to find, if your head is always meditating only how to gain the means of a livelihood. Have you no mind, no heart, no soul which in this temporal life are to blossom forth into eternal salvation, and dare you let your soul starve and wither while you keep on only feeding and clothing your bodies? Enough of labor! Your God commands that you *shall* no longer labor, and that is a guarantee that you *need* not labor, that you have done enough when you have honestly worked for six days. "If you do not wish to deny your better, eternal self, and your God, then desist from working, and enter your home with me." You now stand still, and the panting breast ebbs and flows more calmly, the pulse of life beats more placidly, and you return to yourself. You lay down the yoke of labour, you wipe the sweat from your dripping brow, and shake off the dust from your garments, your forehead regains its smoothness, you raise your eyes, you look above and around—you smile. And now you hear the searching voice from Eden calling you home to the delightful attractions of your family circle; to the cheering side of wife and children. It introduces the Sabbath to your souls, to your home; and your dwelling becomes transfigured. No house is so small, or poor, in which God's splendor does not enter with the Sabbath! The light that shines in you, doubles the brightness of the Sabbath-light; the peace that dwells in you, flavours the Sabbath meal; care, tears, grief and sorrow, all these the Sabbath banishes from the poorest home. "Sabbath has come, you must not weep!" "Sabbath has come, you must not mourn!" The Sabbath has balm and comfort for all, makes all rich and equal. The Sabbath says to each one:

"Place upon God the burden of your way, and He will accomplish it!" If you have done your duty, God will do the rest. This the Sabbath guarantees you, because it bids you, in *His* name to cry a halt to your cares and troubles and labours. It shows Him to you as your Father in heaven, the omnipotent Ruler and Guide of the times, shows Him to you as your God, who fights your battles with and for you, who knows your troubles and feels your cares, and would gladly take from you the greater and heavier part of your life's burden, would you but wish and entrust it to Him.

The Sabbath makes all rich—and *equal.* The gains for which the battle of the week is fought, separate men according to the amount which each one acquires. Not all are successful in the struggle, and there is infinite variety in the results achieved. But the treasures of paradise which the Sabbath dispenses, the peace, the divine bliss, the repose, these are granted to all in equally rich abundance, and "if all of us would but once keep the Sabbath truly, it would mean redemption for all" (Yalkut on Psalm 95, 7).

But it is *only to God's Sabbath* that such a wonderful result is vouchsafed, only when *God* bids you pause in your labour, can you gain rest. In vain do you choose for yourself another day of rest during the week, your hand may be idle, your foot may rest, your body may feast, but it is only God that calms the mind, soothes the heart, revives the soul. *Only when God ordains* the repose you have the assurance that you may repose, and find in God the consummation of your life.

Only God's Sabbath brings you rest.

The Jewish Sabbath. Trans. Josephussoro, B. (Newport: Mullock and Sons, 1911), pp. 9–12
Reprinted by permission of the publisher

The Jewish Sabbath Movement in the Early Twentieth Century

by **Benjamin Kline Hunnicutt**

During the first three decades of the twentieth century and especially the 1920's, Jewish groups and individuals paid an increasing amount of attention to questions of the Sabbath, how it should be observed and what its larger place was in American culture. The Sabbath also became an important cause for a number of Jews, combining religious purpose with social reform goals. The Sabbath had a practical social dimension since it directly involved the reduction of the work week and as such coincided with labor's demands for the five-day week. Spokesmen for the Sabbath movement supported labor's shorter-hour cause, reasoning that modern industrial developments made jobs harder, more stressful, specialized and unrewarding, and as such increased the practical need for more time off. But concerns about workers' health, safety, and social well-being were joined in the Sabbath movement by larger, more idealistic, and religious motives. Individuals and groups saw in the idea of the Sabbath some profound truths that transcended the workaday world and opened up a new kind of human reform and a new field for "genuine" progress. They came to believe that the Sabbath, as a special time set aside for real human needs and apart from material concerns, provided the model and rationale for the "progressive shortening of the hours of labor"—a labor clause that began to outrun practical reform goals with the beginning of the five-day week. They also saw values contained by the Sabbath that countered modern materialism, "spurious progress," mass, cheap culture, and the philistinism of the "gospel of consumption." Hence these people represented twentieth century's Sabbatarianism as combining a very real improvement of the worker's life (a shorter workweek), a general criticism of a culture and economy sunk in materialism, without a transcendent vision, and a new direction for a qualitatively different type of progress.

One of the main difficulties that Jews faced in America during the nineteenth and early twentieth centuries was the loss of Saturday as the historical Sabbath. By law and custom, Americans worked six days a week and, if possible, took Sunday off. Paradoxically, the reason why most Americans worked the six-day week was due in part to a social reform which was sparked by religious concerns, the nineteenth-century Christian Sabbatarian movement. This movement, in the 1820's and 1830's, had a strong social reform motive and a stronger result, although it was heavily sentimental and designed for the most part for religious purposes. But even though Jews and Christians alike shared its social benefits, Jews were denied its religious possibilities. Any deviation from the six-day–Sunday-off pattern was difficult, almost impossible unless one worked the full seven days (even though this was exceptional since blue laws augmented the Sabbatarian's reform). Although the Jewish concern for keeping the Sabbath was as keen as the Christian, Jews were practically prohibited this religious freedom and forced by society and their jobs to observe Sunday as what amounted to a national religious holiday.[1]

Throughout the nineteenth and early twentieth centuries, Jews faced this problem but never resolved it. The problem also caused a rift among Jews between the Orthodox and Reform leadership. Orthodox spokesmen were afraid that the Sabbath as a unique part of their religion was dying out—being observed more in the breach than in the keeping. Often they would predict that the Sabbath was doomed because of the constraints of the American culture. They saw in the death of the Sabbath one more force that would speed up the assimilation and even the conversion of the Jewish people. For example, Rabbi Israel Herbert Levinthal argued that "if we see Jewish life crumbling before our very eyes in America it is mainly due to the fact that we have lost our Sabbath."[2] That this view was widely held was demonstrated by a joint statement issued

---

[1] David Philipson, *The Reform Movement in Judaism* (New York: 1931), pp. 195-214, 373; *Historical Statistics of the United States from Colonial Times to the Present* (Washington D.C.: 1975), pp. 155, 172; Robert Moats Miller, *American Protestantism and Social Issues* (Chapel Hill: 1958), p. 172.

[2] *New York Times,* January 10, 1925, p. 15:2.

by the Union of Orthodox Rabbis of the United States and Canada, the Rabbinical Assembly of America, the Union of Orthodox Jewish Congregations of America, and the United Synagogue of America: ". . . this violation of the Sabbath, if continued indefinitely, must inevitably lead to the gradual disintegration of our people."[3] For the Orthodox and a number of Conservatives, the preservation of the Sabbath was a precondition to the preservation of American Judaism. The Sabbath also contained ideals and values central to their religion. It was the special, holy time for ritual matters, for community, for family, for tradition, and for the individual and his God, set aside from the busy, materialistic and profane world. A strict observance of that day preserved the forms and institutions of Judaism to be sure, but it also contained central truths that were timeless.

The importance of the Sabbath cannot be overstated. Since prominent Jews were later to graft the traditional ideas associated with the Sabbath onto the larger social reform cause of the "progressive shortening of the hours of labor," some insight into how the Sabbath was viewed during this period is useful. A fine, poetic example may be found in Ben Eliezer's book, *Letters of a Jewish Father to his Son.* In the chapter, "Princess Sabbath," Ben Eliezer stated that "the Sabbath is probably the greatest cultural contribution that the Jews have made to the world," even surpassing "the gift of the idea of the unity of God." The Sabbath has acted both as "a national unifying and cementing influence" for Jews as well as a "universal humanizing factor." Its place in the tradition was assured in talmudic literature with such passages as: "The Sabbath outweighs the whole of the Torah and he who observes it properly has all his sins forgiven." Ben Eliezer, as did many Jews, believed that the observance of the Sabbath put man into contact with his real needs and his true nature, and put the material world into perspective.

> What does . . . give the Sabbath its sacred significance is the fact that during its 24 hours, there is an abandoning of all material interests, followed by complete retirement into a self-contained spiritual world, free from earthly cares and worries . . . For it is only in such an environment, free from the thoughts of daily affairs, that the highest religious and ethical sentiments can come uppermost to mind . . . By cultivating such an atmosphere . . . [modern Jews] would also grow in knowledge possessed by their forefathers . . . that our souls are capable of deriving more lasting pleasure from other joys which raise man beyond the level of mere animal enjoyment, drawing him nearer to the source of the great unknown from which he emanates.[4]

The Sabbath was, in fact, the goal of work and material concerns: the time "longed for . . . with the same fervor as a prince awaiting his bride." Labor and "the thought of labor" were important chiefly because they led to the Sabbath and to "its self-contained spiritual world." In this Jews and Christians agreed. The Sabbath was a kind of "escathon" in this world, a taste of that eternal Sabbath described by St. Augustine at the end of his *Confessions.*

On the other hand, during the last half of the nineteenth and first quarter of the twentieth century, many progressive rabbis, in an attempt to "modernize" Judaism, held Sunday services and argued that all American congregations should permit Sunday observances. The rabbinical conference at Pittsburgh in 1885 unanimously agreed that:

> Whereas we recognize the importance of maintaining the historical Sabbath as a bond with our great past and a symbol of the unity of Israel the world over; and,
>
> Whereas, on the other hand, it cannot be denied that there is a very large number of Jews who, owing to economic and industrial conditions, are not able to attend services on our sacred day of rest; be it:
>
> Resolved, that in the judgment of this conference there is nothing in the spirit of Judaism to prevent the holding of divine services on Sunday, or any other day of the week, where the necessity of such services is felt.[5]

This resolution was reaffirmed in 1902, 1905, 1906 and afterwards, periodically until the 1920's in the Committee on "Weekday Services," by the Central

[3] *New York Times,* September 17, 1926, p. 9:2.

[4] Ben Eliezer, *Letters of a Jewish Father to His Son* (London: 1928), pp. 214, 216-217.

[5] Philipson, *op. cit.,* p. 375.

Conference of American Rabbis. The Central Conference also watered down the Orthodox notion of how the Sabbath should be kept, agreeing that activities like tramrides, work at necessary jobs, shaving, and secular amusements were permissible given the realities of the American environment.[6]

In addition, the more radical leadership pressed for the total transfer of the Sabbath to Sunday immediately following the Pittsburgh Conference. The center for this movement seems to have been the *Jewish Tidings*, a publication out of Rochester, New York, which espoused the cause.[7] This notion remained viable in Reform Judaism until 1902 when in New Orleans, after a long and heated debate, the Central Conference committed itself to a struggle for the Saturday Sabbath. The Conference resolved that it was "in favor of maintaining the historical Sabbath as a fundamental institution of Judaism and exerting every effort to enforce its observance."[8]

Despite their disagreement, Orthodox and Reform groups joined together in the struggle for the Saturday Sabbath as it developed from 1903 to 1920. The two most important groups engaged in this movement were the Central Conference of American Rabbis and the Orthodox Jewish Sabbath Alliance. On the one hand, the Central Conference did not vigorously pursue its 1902 commitment. It continued to promote Sunday services (rearranging rituals accordingly) and to interpret Sabbath laws in a more "liberal" manner and seems to have held little hope that Saturday observance and traditional rules could be revived in America. But the Sabbath Alliance took the initiative in the movement and was much more active, fully committing itself to the ideal of the traditional Sabbath.[9]

Nevertheless, during this early period, both groups used the same two techniques. Both endorsed the broader social reform of one day's rest out of seven (a cause supported originally by the Federal Council of Churches of Christ in 1908 and afterwards), but argued that industry and business should make special accommodations for their Jewish workers by allowing them to take Saturday instead of Sunday off. In contrast to the Central Conference's passive endorsement of the scheme (it never got far beyond Conference resolutions), the Sabbath Alliance actively promoted the staggered work week in New York, Boston, Philadelphia, and other major cities where Jews were employed by specific industries in large numbers. Both groups also joined together in opposition to Sunday blue laws. Again the Sabbath Alliance was more active, launching what the *New York Times* called a national "campaign" against these laws. Hence Jewish Sabbatarianism faced two fronts at first: the rearranging of the work week to allow for free Saturdays and the defeating of blue laws to open up Sunday work. Both were necessary if the Sabbath was to be observed on Saturday in a country where the six-day week was standard.[10]

This original and narrowly focused struggle seemed doomed from the start. The Alliance had little success in promoting the staggered work week since industrial managers were unwilling or unable to administer the production and personnel problems that would have resulted from a reduced and changed work force for two days a week. Progressive businessmen, who supported the six-day work week, were not willing to extend its potential religious benefit to Jews by altering the work force and thereby the very means of production. Even Jewish employers, the target for most of the Sabbatarians' efforts, were not ready to disrupt their businesses for this cause. In addition, some members of the Sabbath Alliance conceded that even in the best of circumstances, the staggered work week could be instituted only by special industries in large cities and

6 *Yearbook of the Central Conference of American Rabbis,* XY (1905), 60, 61, 72-74; XVI (1906), 87-113; XXIV (1914), 84-91.

7 Stuart E. Rosenberg, "The *Jewish Tidings* and the Sunday Services Question," *Publications of the American Jewish Historical Society,* XLII (June, 1952), 371-385.

8 *Yearbook of CCAR*, XIII (1902), 77, 102-122.

9 *Ibid.,* XVI (1906), 87-113; Frank T. DeVyver, "The Five-Day Week," *Current History,* XXXIII (November, 1930), 223-227.

10 John A. Hutchinson, *We Are Not Divided: A Critical and Historical Study of the Churches of Christ in America* (New York: 1941), p. 104; *New York Times,* May 31, 1909, p. 16:1; December 1, 1920, p. 36:1.

would not solve the Sabbath problem for the majority of Jews.[11]

Consequently, during these early years, the Central Conference of the Sabbath Alliance devoted most of their efforts against enforcement of the nineteenth-century blue laws and the passing of new ones. But again, in this effort they faced great difficulty. Beginning around 1918 the Lord's Day Alliance, the Central Sabbath Crusade Committee, the International Reform Bureau, and several other Christian organizations were promoting a new and militant campaign for the strict observance of Sunday. The original social gospel concern with the six-day week as a constructive labor reform had by this time deteriorated into a new and repressive drive to eliminate by local and state ordinances and even federal laws all sorts of Sunday activities including movies, newspaper publications, sports, voluntary recreation pursuits, as well as most commerce and all manufacturing. As with Prohibition and immigrant restriction the dark side of modern reform was exhibited by the wave of blue laws passed in the 1920's. In many cases the campaign for strict Sunday observance had anti-Semitic overtones. For example, blue laws in Boston and New York were often enforced selectively against Jews. In addition, leaders of the Lord's Day Alliance such as H. L. Bowlby attacked the Jewish Sabbath Alliance, charging that its efforts were motivated by the desire to give Jews an unfair business advantage on Sunday or else were a front for the movie trade, which, according to Bowlby, was dominated by Jewish interests. The result of the new campaign for strict Sunday observance was a vigorous enforcement of existing blue laws and the passing of numerous new laws by city councils and state legislatures.[12]

In this situation supporters of the Jewish Sabbath could do little except fight a rearguard action. Nevertheless, beginning in 1920, the Jewish Sabbath Alliance began its national "campaign" against blue laws. Its major argument was that such legislation "forced Jews to observe a Christian holiday" and as such violated the Constitutional provision for the separation of church and state. Acting on this assumption, the Sabbath Alliance promoted the introduction of the Dickstein Bill in the New York legislature in 1920, a bill that would have allowed Jews to operate commercial concerns on Sunday (a law similar to statutes in New Jersey and Oklahoma). But because of the rising tide of public sentiment about Sunday reform, this bill was defeated in March, 1921. Several other such bills were introduced in state legislatures in the 1920's, including one proposed by Bernard Downing, senator from New York City, that would have prohibited on Saturday all activities prohibited on Sunday. Downing supported his bill by declaring, "if this bill becomes law, it will give 1,600,000 Jews . . . no further justification for saying that legislation designed to compel them to observe our Sunday laws involves discrimination, placing them at an economic disadvantage, . . . and a little more rest and leisure will do us no harm." But these bills had little chance in state legislatures that were passing new blue laws in record numbers.[13]

Moreover, in their fight against blue laws, the Jewish organizations had little help from the courts, although the Sabbath Alliance at first considered them to be a major hope for redress. By the 1920's, the Supreme Court of the United States had twice accepted the constitutionality of Sunday laws, with *Hennington vs. Georgia* (163, U.S. 299, 1896) and *Pettit vs. Minnesota* (177, U.S. 164, 1900), even though never ruling on the First Amendment issue of separation of church and state involved. However, lower courts were laying the foundations for the secular interpretation of these laws, ruling in over fifteen instances that the police power of localities permitted enforcement of Sunday laws, and that they were civil, not religious in purpose, since they permitted everyone to have one day of rest in the week, essential for public order, rest, recreation, health, and welfare. The New Jersey court, for example, held in *Kislingbury vs. Treasurer of Plainfield* (160A. 654, 10 NJ

[11] *New York Times,* February 7, 1924, p. 20:4.

[12] *New York Times*, December 11, 1920, p. 3:8; July 12, 1921, p. 27:2; June 13, 1922, p. 20:3; May 27, 1927, p. 16:2; January 7, 1921, p. 18:3; March 14, 1923, p. 3:5; January 21, 1925, p. 1:4; January 31, 1925, p, 17:1; January 21, p. 5:3; March 7, 1921, p. 28:2; April 3, 1921, p. 14:4; June 27, 1921, p. 15:3; January 17, 1921, p. 28:2; March 5, 1924, p. 17:3.

[13] *New York Times*, February 9, 1921, p. 3:2; March 24, 1921, p. 3:2; March 24, p. 36:3; March 11, 1924, p. 21:8; *American Jewish Year Book*, XXVI (1924), 24-26.

misc. 798) that the New Jersey law exempting Jews and others who observed Saturday from prosecution under the state's Sunday closing ordinance was unconstitutional in its exemption and that the First Amendment did not speak on the issue of Sunday laws.[14]

Hence in their first attempts to free American Jews to observe the traditional Sabbath, the Sabbath Alliance and Central Conference seemed blocked by the nature and requirements of industry, the wave of Christian Sunday reform, legislatures more interested in passing Sunday blue laws than exempting people from them, and courts not willing to apply the First Amendment to this issue. It was only when the Sabbath Alliance began to concentrate on larger labor reform matters that it was able to make headway in its first, primarily religious cause. In the five-day week its members found what seemed to be a natural vehicle for both their concern for the Sabbath and their hopes for more general social justice achievements. Again in support of the five-day week, the Orthodox Sabbath Alliance led the way. It is interesting to note that other more liberal groups were slow to recognize the coincidence of this labor reform and the religious cause. Historians have always supposed that the liberal, reform groups such as the Central Conference were those who advocated this program of social reform, but in the struggle for the Sabbath/five-day week, it was Orthodox Jewry which demonstrated its own brand of social consciousness.

As early as 1910, Rabbi Bernard Drachman, president of the Sabbath Alliance, told that group that the problem of the Sabbath was so interwoven with American conditions that the issue could be resolved only if both Saturday and Sunday were observed as days of rest by "Christians and Jews alike." As the efforts to exempt Jews from Saturday work failed and the attempts to open up Sunday work proved fruitless and generated hard feelings among Christian Sabbatarians, more people came to appreciate the wisdom of Drachman's original vision. Beginning in 1919, the Sabbath Alliance supported local unions in New York, Boston, Philadelphia, and other cities which were launching their campaigns for the five-and-a-half day week, a campaign that worked directly toward the institution of Saturday holidays.[15]

It is hard to judge religion's influence on this new labor cause. But since the unions that first pressed for the five-day week were composed mostly of Jews, the desire to revive Saturday observance was very prevalent in Jewish groups, and national Jewish organizations as well as local congregations endorsed the five-day week, a prima facie case has been made that religion was a motive of union members in this cause. But union leaders did not stress the five-day week's religious benefit. In fact, they seldom mentioned it. Instead, they represented their unions with economic and social arguments that were applicable to all workers. There is no way of telling whether economic and social consideration of the desire for the traditional Sabbath was more important for the Jewish union members who were beginning to demand and strike for the five-day week. But since the religious and the economic/social purposes coincided in a practical fashion, and the union's economic/social arguments were endorsed by religious groups and even given a theological dimension, the question of union members' motives may be left unanswered for the purpose of this essay.[16]

The first national union to propose the five-day week was the Amalgamated Clothing Workers Union of America, which passed resolutions for this goal in their biennial conventions, beginning in 1920. Led by Sidney Hillman, this national union worked with local unions, especially in New York, during the decade to incorporate 40-hour clauses in trade agreements, or a clause

14 *New York Times,* June 16, 1924, p. 16:3; John J. McGrath, *Church and State in American Law* (Milwaukee: 1962); Code Virginia 1930 and 4570, Broad-Grace Arcade Corporation v. Bright, 48 F. 2d 348, affirmed 52 S. Ct. 137, 284 U.S. 588, 76 L. Ed. 507; Ky. St and 1321—Stand Amusement Co. v. Commonwealth, 43 S.W. 2d 321, 241 Ky. 48; Code Pub. Loc. Laws 1930, art. 4 and 6 (18); Const. art. 11A.—Ness V. Ennis, 160 A. 8, 162 Md. 529; Komen v. City of St. Louis, 289 S.W. 838, 316 Mo. 9; *New York Times*, October 12, 1924, Section VIII, p. 11:3, State v. Dean, 184 N.W. 275, 149 Minn. 410; Pirkey Bros. v. Commonwealth 114 S.E. 764, 134 Va. 713, 29, A.L.R. 1290.

15 DeVyver, *loc. cit.,* p. 223.

16 Marion C. Cahill, *Shorter Hours: A Study of the Movement Since the Civil War* (New York: 1932), p. 253; National Industrial Conference Board, *The Five-Day Week in Manufacturing Industries* (New York, 1929), p. 28; *American Jewish Year Book,* XXVI (1924), 24.

that committed manufacturers to institute this reform "as soon as possible." But for several local Jewish unions, progress through trade agreements and resolutions was too slow. Strikes were called by the needle trade, the New York City clothing workers, and the Patterson, New Jersey silk workers and several other local unions between 1920 and 1924, which included demands for either the five-and-a-half-day or five-day week. These early strikes were settled for the most part by compromise, the workers agreeing to give up the hours' benefit for higher wages. But beginning in 1924, a series of major successful strikes were called by 50,000 New York City Ladies' Garment Workers' Union members (the largest strike in the nation that year), 40,000 clothing workers in New York City in 1926, 5,000 fur workers in New York and 3,000 in Boston (both in 1926) and all members of the New York and Philadelphia Cloth Hat and Cap Workers' Union in 1927, as well as other smaller unions in children's dresses, bathrobes, and kimonos. In these strikes, the 40-hour/five-day week was a major issue. When coupled with demands for higher wages, the issue dominated. For example, observers of the 17-week strike of the New York furriers concluded that "the main difficulty [prolonging the strike] seems to have been what points the union should barter away in order to gain the forty-hour week." These strikes were successful, so much so that by 1927 the Bureau of Labor Statistics concluded that the five-day work week was "practically the rule in trade agreements in the clothing industry."[17]

Together with the painters' and plasterers' unions, other building trades such as plumbers and carpenters, and printing and publishing unions, these unions in the clothing industry with large, Jewish memberships initiated the five-day week movement. That their efforts were productive was demonstrated by the fact that before the war, less than twenty manufacturing establishments nationally had adopted the five-day week. Nearly all of these were managed and staffed by Jews. But during the 1920's, over 240 manufacturers adopted this plan. By 1929, approximately 400,000 to 500,000 employees were working on a five-day pay basis. The 1920's was truly the decade of the beginning of the five-day work week.[18]

Between 1920 and 1925, the American Federation of Labor had its hands full mopping up "pockets of long hour resistance." Even though the eight-hour day/six-day week had become the norm by the 1920's, enough unions were still struggling to catch up with this standard to occupy the AFL's attention. Although it had endorsed the Amalgamated Clothing Worker's five-day week drive in 1920, it was not until 1926 that the AFL was ready to turn its full attention to this cause as the next logical step in the century-long process of shorter hours. The AFL supported the five-day week as one of its primary goals. But enough options were before it—the six- or seven-hour day and the five-and-a-half-day week—that it chose to commit itself to the larger cause of "the progressive shortening of the hours of labor" during the 1926 Convention.[19]

Jewish organizations actively supported these labor developments. In February, 1924, the convention of Orthodox Rabbis of New York, New Jersey and Connecticut met in New York City and endorsed the five-day week. This convention's efforts to "further the establishment of the five-day-week system" was an outgrowth of the Sabbath Alliance and the local congregations' original support of clothing, fur, and needle trade unions and the joint efforts of several Jewish groups to combat blue laws. A new note of optimism and conciliation was present at the convention.

17 Matthew Josephson, *Sidney Hillman: Statesman of American Labor* (New York: 1952), pp. 177-180; *Monthly Labor Review,* XVI (August, 1923), 503; XVIII (June, 1924), 1366-1368; XXIII (December, 1926), 1153; XX (June, 1925), 1390-1391; Bureau of Labor Statistics *Bulletin #439* (June, 1924), 373, 374, 573-575; *Bulletin #435*, 20-21.

18 National Industrial Conference Board, *op. cit.* pp. 15-24. *Monthly Labor Review,* XXIII (December, 1926), 1153-1169; John P. Frey, "Labor's Movement for a Five-Day Week," *Current History Magazine,* XXV (December, 1926), 369-373.

19 Chester M. Wright, "Epoch-Weakening Decisions in the Great American Federation of Labor Convention at Detroit," *American Labor World,* (1926), 22-24; American Federation of Labor, *Report of the Proceedings of the 46th Annual Convention* (Washington D.C.: 1926), see especially the Report of the Committee on the Shorter Workday, pp. 195-207; Sidney Hillman, "Attitude of Organized Labor Toward the Shorter Work Week," *Monthly Labor Review,* XXIII (December, 1926), 1167-1168.

Several speakers (among them Drachman) noted that since opposition of blue laws was failing and bringing "protests from Christians," the five-day week offered a compromise. The convention concluded "so, to please both Jews and Christians, the plan for two days of rest each week was adopted."[20]

The idea gained ground rapidly among Jews and others. In 1925, the Sabbath Alliance formed an interdenominational committee to promote the cause, composed of such men as Drachman, Carlyle B. Haynes, Cyrus Adler, and N. Taylor Phillips. Spokesmen for this group agreed that "this great public reform ... will ... tend to remove the greatest causes of friction and religious intolerances existing in America today." Also, in 1925, representatives of several rabbinic bodies (Orthodox, Reform, and Conservative) met in New York to "further the five-day week in American industry." They launched what they called "a vigorous campaign in publications, lobbying, and promotion." Included in these efforts as leaders were M. Z. Margolies, Chaim Block and A. B. Burak of the Union of Orthodox Rabbis, Samuel Schulman and Nathan Stern of the Central Conference of American Rabbis, and "lay organizations" such as the Union of Orthodox Jewish Congregations of America, the Sabbath Alliance, and Young Israel. In addition, beginning in 1924, the United Synagogue of America planned a series of conferences between employers and labor unions "with a view to the establishing of a five-day week in as many industries as possible." By 1927, the Union of Orthodox Jewish Congregations, the Central Conference of American Rabbis, the Rabbinic Assembly, the United Synagogue, and the Union of Orthodox Rabbis of the United States and Canada had endorsed this cause as a general labor reform and in several instances actually encouraged the efforts of local unions, such as the needles trade and the Ladies' Garment Workers'. However, it was the Orthodox groups that took the active leadership role while the Reform group, such as the Central Conference, acted mostly as a cheering section.[21]

The primary concern of all the groups and individuals was, of course, the revitalization of the Sabbath observance on Saturday. The five-day week cause and its successes turned the original pessimism of Reform Jews into a new enthusiasm and proved to be a justification for the Orthodox leadership's holding onto the cause. But Jewish Sabbatarianism was altered and expanded by the five-day week issue. The issue led naturally to larger concerns: broad scale labor reforms and general questions about economic development and cultural progress. The five-day week served the practical cause of Jewish Sabbatarianism to be sure; but Jewish Sabbatarianism, as expanded by the issue, served in turn to justify the broader labor reform of the "progressive shortening of the hours of labor" and to inform the cultural, social, and economic debate about the decreasing importance of work and the increasing importance of free time.

Rabbi Israel Herbert Levinthal expressed the logical broadening of the argument for the Sabbath in this way:

> I can see but one way to save the Sabbath for the Jew, and that is through the establishment of the five-day week. . . . I would favor the five-day week even if I were not interested in the preservation of the Jewish Sabbath. I would favor it because it would add health and strength to the American people. It would promote the home and home life, giving the father an added opportunity to become more intimately acquainted with . . . his children.[22]

In a like manner, other prominent Jews who supported the five-day week agreed with the social and economic arguments of union leaders. During the struggle for the ten-hour day, the eight-hour day, and the six-day week, unions relied on fairly simple, common sense arguments. They had stressed safety factors, health benefits, moral considerations, and increased production in their defense of the earlier advances. But with the beginning of the 40-hour/five-day week drive and the commitment to "the progressive shortening of the hours of labor" these earlier, generally acceptable goals were less applicable. It was not clear at all that Saturdays off improved production, was necessary for rest, or made

---

20 *New York Times,* February 7, 1924, p. 20:4.

21 *New York Times,* May 10, 1926, 21:4; January 14, 1925, 5:3; September 17, 1926, p. 9:2; *Yearbook of CCAR,* XXIV (1924), 51; *American Jewish Yearbook,"* (1925), 26-28.

22 *New York Times,* January 10, 1925, p. 15:2.

the work place safer. Union leaders found that they had to discover new arguments to justify this new reform.

To do this men such as William Green, president of the American Federation of Labor, Matthew Woll, vice-president of the AFL, A. O. Whorton, president of the International Association of Machinists, and Sidney Hillman, founder and president of the Amalgamated Clothing Workers of America turned their attention to the larger economy. They suggested that shorter hours were essential in order to deal with chronic unemployment and with general overproduction—new problems of the new era. These union leaders, and others, especially in the New York garment industry, firmly believed that with increasing mechanization, the economy was beginning to be overbuilt and the demand for goods such as textiles was being saturated. As production "outran the rate of natural consumption," general overproduction and chronic, acute unemployment would soon follow. In order to deal with these two new developments, they stressed two solutions—higher wages and shorter hours. Higher wages would allow workers to buy the necessities of life and as such increase the consumption of certain types of traditional products. Shorter hours, on the other hand, would create more jobs and would act to increase wages.[23] But they would also limit production that was beginning to outstrip demand. As A. O. Wharton put it:

> Increased production accentuates the problem of overproduction or underconsumption. Increased wages and reduced hours go hand in hand with increased production. . . . Economic balance can be maintained only if . . . wages advance and leisure hours increase. If some sort of balance is not maintained, we are headed straight for disaster.[24]

Unions were perhaps the first major group in American history to suggest that economic growth had a limit, a limit being reached in the 1920's and as such made the limiting of production necessary to stabilize the new, mature economy.

Bernard Drachman echoed the arguments of the union officials. He pointed out "the only cure for overproduction is limitation of production" since "it is perfectly possible under modern methods of production, that commodities can be produced in quantities greater than can be consumed. . . ." He also suggested that as a result, technological unemployment, especially in the garment industry was increasing and would continue to increase as technology outran the "rate of natural consumption. . . . The machines invented in recent years . . . with uncanny, almost demoniacal super ability . . . accomplish . . . tasks formerly requiring the labor of thousands and for the . . . displaced multitudes no opportunities of employment present themselves." Drachman saw shorter hours as a way to improve the workers' bargaining position for higher wages (by making labor scarce and hence more valuable) and also to deal with unemployment caused by overproduction. Shorter hours would distribute fairly the available work which was diminishing and would limit production to "reasonable levels." He concluded that he supported "the idea of the shorter work week, not only on economic grounds, but also on social, cultural, and spiritual grounds." This reform would stabilize the economy and help deal with unemployment. But it would also provide a new kind of freedom from material concerns and a new opportunity for human achievements by the masses.[25]

Union leaders also stressed the fact that work had lost its ethical and human dimensions and was becoming increasingly hard and "dehumanizing." As such, it had increased the importance of leisure. Formerly, they believed, work had been a place for creativity, community, craftsmanship, the way for social mobility, and the vehicle for self expression, personal fulfillment, and individualism. But modern means of production had changed all that, creating jobs that were specialized, repetitive,

23 William Green, "The Five Day Week," *American Federationist,* XXXIII (November, 1926), 1299, 1300; for Green and Woll's attitudes see also American Federation of Labor, *op. cit.,* pp. 195-207; for Hillman's view see "Attitude of Organized Labor Toward the Shorter Work Week," *Monthly Labor Review,* XXIII (December, 1926), 1167-1168; William Green, "Leisure for Labor," *Magazine of Business,* LVI (August, 1929), 136-137; James M. Lynch, "Shorter Working Day Urged as Alleviation for Depression Cycles," *American Labor World* (November, 1926), 28, 29.

24 James L. Wright, "Is the Machine Replacing Men?" *Nation's Business* (September, 1927), 79.

25 Bernard Drachman, *Looking at America* (New York: 1934), pp. 97-102.

boring and routine as well as establishing a permanent industrial labor force. As William Green put it,

> there must be a progressive reduction of the hours of labor, so that men and women may have time to rebuild their exhausted physical energies. This is more than ever important in the highly specialized process of modern industry, where speed and monotony tax physical existence to the utmost.

He saw the AFL policy as a "complement of labor's long struggle to prevent work from becoming deading toil." Sidney Hillman agreed that the "speed and strain of American industry was always greater."[26]

Green, Woll, and Hillman also defended the "leisured proletariat" by criticizing the "devitalized nature of modern work" and by renewing their support of traditional values that had been lost in modern occupations. Green, for example, insisted in order that " . . . our social and human values may not be merged with the machines until, they too, become mechanical, shorter hours [were] essential because they safeguard our human nature" and "lay the foundation for the higher development of spiritual and intellectual powers." He predicted "a dawn of a new era, leisure for all" and "a revolution in living" because of reduced hours. He saw leisure as a new opportunity for craftsmanship, creativity, community development, for fellowship, the "finer things in life" such as "music, art, literature, and travel," as a way "to worker's education" and "increased knowledge of technological principles," and for "recreation and recuperation . . . necessary to sustain vigor." For Green, gradually increasing leisure could redeem traditional values that had been lost at work, as well as open up new democratic vistas for the masses.[27]

Matthew Woll, like other union leaders, criticized work in new forms and looked to leisure to compensate workers for human values that they had lost. But he also criticized that fact that "unfortunately, our industrial life is dominated by the materialistic spirit of production, of work and more work, giving little attention to the development of the human body, the human mind, or the spirit of life. . . . All the finer qualities of life are entirely ignored." The dehumanized nature of modern jobs was complicated by the "materialistic spirit" of the business community. For Woll, increasing leisure was both a "restraining influence" limiting production to basic needs as well as a hedge against the material values of the "New Era."[28]

Jews active in the Sabbath movement agreed with the idea that work was becoming less rewarding and meaningful and that leisure offered the opportunity to recover some of the old values that work once had. Felix Cohen, for example, offered a parable of the modern economy that was able to provide the necessities of life and still supported work as a prime virtue.

> Adam's children inherited the [curse of work] and soon learned to make a virtue of necessity. Idleness came to be regarded as a sin rather than a source of love, art, inspiration, and wisdom.

Offered a chance by "God's messenger" or by the machine to slip the bonds of toil, men chose instead to "sing new hymns in praise of the sweetness of chains" and hold onto work because "they had so long praised each other . . . for industriousness. . . . The message of the machine is that we shall work without end."

According to Cohen, much of that work was useless. It no longer had the firm, external sanction of necessity. Work was being channeled in absurd directions: the production of useless or shoddy articles, advertising and a new industry, war. If useless work were abolished, then the work week could be reduced to "thirty hours immediately" and a "general working week of ten hours is then a fairly immediate possibility," given the rate of increased productivity. For Cohen, work's new forms—specialization, mechanization, and impersonal organization—destroyed the old nineteenth-century ideals about work's value, such

26 William Green, "Leisure for Labor," *loc. cit.,* pp. 136-137; William Green, *The Five-Day Week: Inevitable* (New York: 1932), pp. 1-6; Wright, "Is the Machine Replacing Man?" *loc. cit.,* p. 79.

27 Green, "Leisure for Labor," *loc. cit.,* pp. 136-137; Green, "The Five-Day Week," *loc. cit.,* pp. 567-574.

28 Matthew Woll, "Labor and the New Leisure," *Recreation,* XXVII (1933), 418; Matthew Woll, "Leisure and Labor," *Playground,* XIX (1925), 322.

as creativity, craftsmanship, self-fulfillment. In this he agreed with the union leaders. But he also suggested that work's purpose—its product—had been undercut by the machine. Much of modern work was useless, was without a firm purpose because there was "no natural" use for its product. Consequently work had been made a demigod—a thing worshipped for its own sake. It mattered little if its products were useless. One consumed them out of respect for this supreme virtue, like it or not.[29]

Sabbatarians, such as Cohen, extended the union leaders' arguments and engaged in the larger economic debates about overproduction with a new breed of economic businessmen. In contrast to the union and some pessimistic businessmen who were stressing limited production, most businessmen and economists were entering, practically and ideologically, a new age of mass consumption. They did not accept the argument that human needs for industrial products were finite or set by some nineteenth-century idea of human nature. Instead they took a new view of economic growth. They promoted what Edward Cowdrick called the "new economic gospel of consumption." In their view, the best way to deal with unemployment and overproduction was not to limit production by reducing working hours, but by stimulating demand. For many businessmen, if supply exceeded demand, then the reasonable response was to increase and insure consumption of those goods in oversupply through new domestic and foreign markets, advertising and even higher wages. They were sure that Americans would naturally (or be convinced to) buy those things produced by industry which they had never needed before and consume goods and services, not in response to some set of economic motives, but according to a standard of living that constantly improved. They concluded that human needs were social and plastic, capable of being molded to fit the needs of a growing economy by the hard work of marketing experts, advertisers and business leaders.[30]

Businessmen's new interest in consumption had been well documented as well as their optimism that demand could be stimulated. Herbert Hoover's Committee on Recent Economic Changes, however, presented one of the first and finest examples of this documentation. The Committee pointed out that "economists have long declared that consumption, the satisfaction of wants, would expand with little evidence of satiation, if we could so adjust our economic processes as to make dormant demands effective." But businessmen had proven this assumption in the 1920's. This "almost insatiable appetite for goods and services, this abounding production of all things which almost any man could want, which is so striking a characteristic of the period covered by the survey" eliminated suspicion that the demand could be saturated and markets limited. The Committee found that

> people . . . have become steadily less concerned about the primary needs—food, clothing, shelter. . . . The slogan of the "full dinner pail" is obsolete. . . . Our wants have ranged more widely and we now demand a broad list of goods and services which come under the category of optional purchases.

It is in the area of "optional purchases" that the Committee saw the best hope for economic advance. Criticizing the pessimists' ideas about "remote saturation points" the Committee observed that

29 Felix Cohen, "The Blessing of Unemployment," *The American Scholar,* II (1933), 203-214.

30 Report of the 15th Annual Meeting of the Chamber of Commerce, "Prosperity and Production," *Nation's Business,* XV (May 20, 1927), 40, 41; William Foster and Waddill Catchings, "What is Business Without a Buyer?" *Nation's Business,* XIV (June, 1926), 27; William Craig, "Digest of the Business Press," *Nation's Business,* XIV (June, 1926), 14; Glen Buck, "This American Ascendancy," *Nation's Business,* XV (March, 1927), 15; "Business Views in Review," *Nation's Business,* XV (July, 1927), 117; (August, 1927), 95; Edward Cowdrick, "The New Economic Gospel of Consumption," *Industrial Management,* LXXIV (October, 1927), 208; Irvin S. Paull, "When is Industry's Job Complete?" *Nation's Business,* XV (December, 1927), 28, 29; James L. Wright, "Is the Machine Replacing Man?" *Nation's Business,* XV (September, 1927), 78-80, for views about increased consumption by James Maloney and Secretary of Labor David, who argued that "the luxuries of yesterday become the necessities of today"; Merle Thorpe, "The Amazing Decade," *Nation's Business,* XVI (September, 1928), 9; J. H. Collins, "Producer Goes Exploring for the Consumer," *Saturday Evening Post,* CXCV (April 7, 1923), 8; T. C. Sheehan, "Must We Limit Production?" *Magazine for Business,* LIII (February, 1928), 150-152.

> the survey has proved conclusively what was long held to be theoretically true, that our wants are almost insatiable, that one want satisfied makes way for another. The conclusion is that economically we have a boundless field before us; that there are new wants that will make way endlessly for newer wants as fast as they are satisfied. . . . As long as the appetite for goods and services is practically insatiable, as it appears to be, and as long as productivity can be consistently increased, it seems that we can go on with increasing activity.[31]

Union leaders did not meet this argument head on. But some Jewish supporters of the five-day week did. For example, Abba Hillel Silver, later president of the Central Conference of American Rabbis, saw in the Sabbath movement a direct counter argument—one that justified the "progressive shortening of the hours of labor" and opposed what he called the "philistine" gospel of consumption. He began by describing the Sabbath as representing "the day of rest, the consecrated covenant between God and man." As such it was "much more than mere relaxation from labor. It is a sign and symbol of man's higher destiny."[32] The five-day week could help solve the economic problem of overproduction and unemployment to be sure. But the progressive shortening of the hours of labor could open up a new field of human progress. Increased leisure could provide a time for culture, for learning, for individual creativity and freedom, for the appreciation of life and creation, for spiritual exercise, and for essential rituals, those things which Ben Eliezer ascribed to the Sabbath as the "universal humanizing factor." Silver suggested "we must say to ourselves . . . so far shall I go in my pursuit of the things of life and no further. Beyond that I am a free man, a child of God. Beyond that I have a soul and I must give to it time, energy, and interest." He saw in the gospel of consumption a new way in which "our population has been victimized." Just when the opportunity for real human development had been opened through technology and increased free time, it had been closed again by businessmen intent on selling the "golden fleece" of useless luxuries and "excessive wealth." For Silver, human needs for industrial products could still be defined—they were not infinite. Increased productivity and job specialization had created two potential avenues of progress, one spurious and one genuine. If Americans chose to pursue "success" defined in terms of the piling up of useless luxuries, they would turn their backs on the more human form of progress offered by reduced working hours. For Silver, the Sabbath was the pattern for a new form of progress, being cut in the American economy by shorter hours and increased leisure for human, nonmaterial needs.[33]

The job preparing individuals for "worthy use of leisure" was great. But Silver saw the new wealth of free time as a force revitalizing the church, the family, and the school. As people who were able to spend more of their time and energy in these more human institutions, they would naturally learn how to use their time to develop their higher potentials and humane interests.

Moreover, according to Silver, it was no longer possible to assume that all work was valuable because of its extrinsic results. The relationship between work and the necessities of life was becoming increasingly tenuous. Businessmen and economists ignored this problem. Instead, they had begun to understand work and increased wealth as indeterminant values, relative to no set of given, basic or higher standards. Yet, they continued to support and value these things. As such, work, increased production and consumption were redefined as ends in themselves, values to be used to judge other economic and social needs. Losing extrinsic justification, these things took on intrinsic values during the decade. For Silver, these ideas were a corruption of that which was truly valuable in itself—that which Ben Eliezer describes as "the highest religious and ethical sentiments." For him, the Sabbath was the only true "telos" in its "self-contained spiritual world," the model for a qualitatively new kind of progress through increased leisure. Businessmen and economists had entered the realm of philosophy and theology in their "gospel of consumption," promoting the old virtue of

31 Report of the President's Committee on Recent Economic Changes, *Recent Economic Changes* (New York: 1929), pp. xv, xviii, 52, 59, 80, 81, 574-578.

32 Abba Hillel Silver, "Leisure and the Church," *Playground,* XX (January, 1927), 539.

33 Abba Hillel Silver, *Religion in a Changing World* (New York: 1930), pp. 63, 77, 143-146, 184-187, 190-194.

work and economic growth by new, virtually existential arguments. Silver believed that work and increased productivity were still instrumental in that they could meet rational needs and then lead to real virtues through shorter hours of work—to human activities that were really worth doing for their own sake.[34]

The Jewish Sabbath movement, beginning as a narrowly focused attempt to allow Jewish workers to have free Saturdays and to work on Sunday, broadened in two stages. Failing in the first limited attempt, the movement flourished in the second stage as a supportive part of the general labor movement for the five-day week. Finding practical success in this reform, individuals in the Sabbath movement then went on to engage in even larger economic and social debates about modern progress and work, using the Sabbath model as a philosophical base. Certainly many Jews were content with the five-day week's practical accomplishments. It did, after all, satisfy their original purpose and constitute a significant social reform. But others such as Drachman, Cohen, and Silver went on to support the "progressive shortening of the hours of labor," reasoning that as human needs for industry's products were met, increased technology and productivity should free the worker from his job for other, "higher" pursuits. They understood the economy as beginning to offer two avenues for progress—increased wealth and luxuries or increased leisure. Rejecting the first option as a philistine "chasing after the phantom of insatiable desires," they supported the second as the way to authentic progress, humanistic rather than materialistic, individualistic rather than collective. They saw in the Sabbath the "symbol of man's higher destiny" and in increased leisure the practical opportunity to broaden and spread the Sabbath's values and truths.

American Jewish History 79:2 (Dec. 1979), pp. 196–225
Reprinted by permission of the publisher

[34] Samuel Strauss, "Things are in the Saddle," *Atlantic Monthly* (November, 1924), 577-588; *idem, American Opportunity* (Boston: 1935), pp. 182-193.

Orthodox Answers to Unusual Questions: Rabbi Rules on Sabbath Skating and Other Issues

by **Brian Murphy**

Caesarea, Israel

The full scope of Jewish texts and traditions couldn't help the rabbi sort this one out: Could he skate to synagogue on the holy day of rest and prayer?

Dov Kaplan decided he should go straight to the top for an answer—a religious sage in Jerusalem who rules on what's acceptable, and what's not, under Orthodox Jewish law. His verdict on the in-line skates? Roll on, including Saturdays.

The recent case was more than just a quirky display of Torah scholarship.

The modern world of gadgets and hobbies makes being true to faith increasingly difficult for Jews who strictly observe Shabbat, or the Sabbath, and its detailed list of forbidden activities. The ban includes any type of commercial labor, nearly all modes of transportation and anything construed as igniting or extinguishing "fire," such as cooking or even flicking a light switch.

Any Shabbat problem—like the roller-skating question—probably will find its way to a crammed wedge of offices on a Jerusalem hilltop. The space serves as a kind of one-stop answer factory: the staff responding to letters and e-mails, the head rabbi issuing religious decrees, and amateur inventors tinkering at work tables to find Shabbat-acceptable devices. Among the latest projects is a doorbell that uses air pressure instead of electricity.

"We believe the Torah is a living document and needs to address modern issues, especially with the incredible pace of change," said Rabbi Levi Yitzchak Halperin, who directs the Institute for Science and Halacha, Halacha being the body of Jewish law. "But we are not an institute that is looking for loopholes."

On roller-skating? "That wasn't a real hard one," he said with a smile.

Kaplan's problem arose after plans were made for a second synagogue in Caesarea, a town of 5,000 people on the Mediterranean coast that has the feeling of a Florida resort, right down to bike paths and an 18-hole golf course.

Cars are out on Shabbat. Bicycles are banned because of the risk of fixing a chain or flat, which would be considered work. So Kaplan thought of zipping between the two synagogues using in-line skates—even though he needs beginner-level lessons.

"We must have respect for Jewish law and traditions," said Kaplan, 45, who was raised in Long Beach, N.Y., and immigrated to Israel when he was 11. "But we also have to show that Orthodox rabbis are not distant, unapproachable and closed to new ideas. Who knows if I'll actually skate. It's more about making a point."

Halperin saw no problem. He decided that skates can't break down the way bikes do.

The institute is a mix of library, workshop and warehouse. In one room, Orthodox rabbinical students pore over books. Next door is a workshop loaded with switches and wires, a place to experiment with ways around using electricity on Shabbat. Other Jewish groups in Israel and abroad also offer guidance on Shabbat and other matters, but Halperin is widely considered the definitive voice.

When the institute opened in the 1960s, electricity was the main source of inquiries and innovations—which some ultra-Orthodox dismissed as diluting Jewish law. About a third of Israel's Jewish population either strictly adheres to Shabbat codes or follows them to some degree, such as not watching television on the holy day but traveling by car to synagogue. In the United States, about 7 percent of Jews identify themselves as Orthodox.

Under Orthodox views, it's forbidden to "close" an electrical circuit on Shabbat—for example turning on a light, dialing a phone or hitting an elevator button.

The solution was developing appliances, phones and other electrical devices with preset open-and-close cycles. The institute's Shabbat phone is a prime example: It has a constant "on-off" cycle so the caller is not directly dialing a number, but allowing the phone to make the connection.

It's no longer so straightforward. Halperin is peppered with requests of all kinds.

Can the institute develop a TV remote for Shabbat? Not interested in even trying.

Is stem cell research acceptable? Yes, Halperin says, as long as the process will not alter the genetic makeup of the patient. Cloning, however, is considered wrong.

The use of sperm banks? There are many obstacles, Halperin says. But in some cases—such as a husband who froze his sperm before he died or was rendered sterile—it's allowable because reproduction remains within the family.

The queries have even reached beyond this world.

Shabbat questions about space travel were raised when Israeli astronaut Ilan Ramon was aboard the space shuttle *Columbia*, which broke apart during reentry in 2003. When, it was asked, is Shabbat in outer space, given that the observance begins and ends with sunset? Halperin's conclusion: Calculate when Shabbat would occur at the launch pad.

Other solutions require a bit more elbow grease. One of them was tucked into a corner: an attempt to create a Shabbat wheelchair that uses pneumatic power as an alternative to electric power. There are still some bugs, said the institute's key researcher, Rabbi Shmuel Strauss.

"It still doesn't have the efficiency of a battery," Strauss said. "We're working on it."

The Washington Post, October 29, 2005

The Shabbos Queen to the Rescue

The story we are going to tell you here came to pass over a hundred and fifty years ago in the year 1831. It was the year of the Polish uprising, when Polish patriots organized a rebellion against their Russian overlords. They drove the Russians out of Warsaw and proclaimed independence (Jan. 1831). But later that year, the Russians recaptured Warsaw and crushed the revolt.

In a small Polish town near Kovno, there lived at that time a Jewish innkeeper. His name is not known to us, but we will call him Yosef. He was well known in the surrounding countryside as an honest and God-fearing Jew, whose wife could prepare delicious Jewish dishes. Members of the Polish nobility frequented Yosef's inn, where there was never a shortage of good food and wine.

One day, on a late Friday afternoon, a Russian General and his troops arrived in town. They were returning from the fighting around Warsaw, and settled in the town for a rest after the long march. The sun had already set when the General sent his assistant to fetch some wine. The General had been told about the good reputation of the local Jewish innkeeper, and to him he directed his aide.

From every Jewish house, the Shabbos candles were shining forth, which cast an air of festivity and holiness in the otherwise dark and deserted streets, through which the general's aide made his way. He finally found the inn, but it was closed. He went around to the private entrance and knocked at the door.

The innkeeper, dressed in his Shabbos clothes, welcomed the adjutant into his house.

"The General sent me to buy some of your best wine," the aide said, taking out a roll of money.

"I am sorry indeed," Yosef replied. "We are now celebrating the Sabbath. I do not do business on our holy day of Sabbath."

Nothing the adjutant said could make the Jew change his mind. The adjutant returned to his general and told him that the Jew had refused to sell him wine because of the Sabbath.

The general flew into a rage. He immediately dispatched two soldiers to the innkeeper to warn him that if he still refused to sell them wine for the General, he would face the most serious consequences.

After a time, the soldiers returned to the thirsty General—without wine.

"Why didn't you bring me wine?!" the General roared.

"The Jew said he could not sell any wine to anybody on his Sabbath. However, he sent the key to his wine cellar, and suggested that perhaps the General might wish to help himself to any of the wine as his guest," the soldiers reported.

The fury of the General began to evaporate as he contemplated the strange situation. "How strange that Jew is!" the General thought. "He would not sell me a bottle of wine because of the Sabbath, yet he is prepared to give away his entire wine-cellar. That little Jew has a great deal of brazenness, or perhaps courage is more to the point."

Such were the thoughts that crossed the General's mind at that moment, and he decided to meet the Jew in person! When the General entered Yosef's house, he remained standing at the door as he absorbed the wonderful scene that met his eyes. The table was covered with a white cloth and laden with tasty dishes. The Shabbos candles shone brightly. Yosef and his wife and children were dressed in their Shabbos clothes, all faces aglow with delight. The General almost felt sorry to have disturbed this beautiful atmosphere and to have frightened the children.

Yosef rose to meet the General and respectfully invited him to join in the feast.

The General, who had burst into the house with the intention of teaching the Jew a lesson, felt his anger melt away. He sounded quite human, even polite, when he asked Yosef why he had refused to sell him some wine. "Don't you know that refusing to sell provisions to the army in times of war is tantamount to rebellion?"

"Your gracious Highness surely knows that we Jews are forbidden to do business on our holy Shabbos day," Yosef replied. "To keep the Shabbos day holy is one of the Ten Commandments given to us by God, the Supreme King of kings. His command we must obey before any command by human kings and princes. However, now that your Highness has been so gracious as to honor our humble house with your presence, allow us the opportunity of fulfilling another great commandment—that of hospitality. We shall indeed consider it a privilege if you and your adjutant would join us at the table. Please be our guests."

The General was greatly impressed. He sat down at the table and motioned his aide to do the same. Never in their lives had they enjoyed such delicious dishes before—gefilte fish with horseradish, roast chicken with tzimmess, kugel, and kishka, with plenty of excellent wine to wash down each course. It was a feast fit for royalty.

Before leaving, the General took from his pocket a handful of golden pieces and offered them to Yosef. Politely but firmly Yosef refused to accept any money. "Have I not told your Highness that we consider it a special mitzvah to offer hospitality. You were our guests, not clients. We are grateful to you for the privilege."

The General warmly shook hands with Yosef and departed in a happy mood.

Several years later, some militiamen suddenly appeared in Yosef's inn and arrested him. Together with other dangerous rebels and criminals, Yosef was brought to Vilna in chains.

During the long investigation that followed, Yosef learned that he was accused of taking part in a new Polish conspiracy to overthrow the Russians and drive them out of Poland. It so happened that the leader of the local rebels, Pan Kanarski, was captured, and in his documents, Yosef's inn was mentioned as the place where members of the Polish nobility frequently met to plan their revolt. This was proof enough that Yosef, too, was part of the conspiracy.

Yosef sat in prison awaiting trial, fully aware of the serious sentence that would be meted out to him—lifelong deportation to Siberia with hard labor, from which very few ever returned alive; or perhaps more mercifully a quick death by a firing squad. In addition to his own plight, Yosef knew that if he were found guilty, it would cast a shadow on all the Jews of his town, with endless repression and persecutions.

While he knew that all efforts would be made by his fellow-Jews to establish his innocence, he could not feel very confident about the outcome. His only hope was to trust in the Heavenly Father. There was nothing for Yosef to do but to pray fervently and recite Tehillim, which he did constantly, tearfully, and with a broken heart.

One day, as he was in the midst of such supplication, the heavy door of his solitary cell opened, and a high official appeared. He was the Chief Inspector of prisons, on a routine check of the prison cells. The tears that filled Yosef's eyes blurred his vision, and he could not see the Inspector very well. But the Inspector gazed at him intently, and then exclaimed, "Why, this is my good friend Yosef the innkeeper. Good heavens, what are you doing here?"

Yosef wiped his tears and looked in astonishment at the Inspector. It suddenly dawned on him that this was none other than the General whom he had entertained in his house that Friday night many years before!

"Believe me, your Highness, I have done no wrong. I have always minded my own business, and taken no part in any politics. I am as innocent as a baby," Yosef cried.

"I have no doubt about it, Yosef," the Chief Inspector assured him. "Rest assured that I shall leave no stone unturned to get you out of here. At last I shall be able to repay you for the friendship and hospitality you showed me that Friday night. I have never forgotten the experience of that evening."

The General, now Chief Inspector, personally appeared before the investigating committee and vouched for the innocence of the Jewish innkeeper. He told them in detail of his experience with the innkeeper, and assured them that from his personal knowledge, he had not the slightest doubt that Yosef had no part in any conspiracy.

"He is nothing more than an innkeeper, whose inn is open to all. In between serving his customers, he was always busy with his sacred books. How can he be held responsible for the actions of customers who found his inn a very attractive place to have a good meal?"

The Chief Inspector's words, and his great influence in the highest spheres of the Russian government, dispelled all the suspicion directed against Yosef, and he was promptly released and sent home.

Great was the joy of Yosef's family when he suddenly returned home, a free man.

"How did this wonderful thing happen?" his wife asked.

"The Queen has intervened in my behalf," said Yosef.

"What Queen?"

"The Shabbos Queen, of course," replied Yosef with a smile.

www.jewishchildren.com/badge/mb/stories/shabbos_stories.pdf
Reprinted with permission

Lesson 6

Afterglow

Introduction

The skies have darkened and the sun has set . . . yet the evening sky is ablaze with a magnificent afterglow.

In this lesson we will explore the effects of Shabbat on the week once the hectic pace of life has resumed. Memory of the Shabbat experience lingers in our senses, and its inspiration continues to illuminate our days and our lives.

Bonds of Love

Text 1a

אֶת שַׁבְּתֹתַי תִּשְׁמֹרוּ.
ויקרא יט,ל

You shall observe My Sabbaths.

Leviticus 19:30

Text 1b

מהו את שבתותי תשמורו תרין, אלא שבת דמעלי שבתא ושבתא דיומא.
זהר א, ה,ב

What is [implied when the verse says] "You shall observe My Sabbaths"?

The plural form indicates the Sabbath of Friday night and the Sabbath of Shabbat day.

Zohar 1:5b

Separation Anxiety

Text 2a

אמר רבי שמעון בן לקיש: נשמה יתירה נותן הקדוש ברוך הוא באדם ערב שבת,
ולמוצאי שבת נוטלין אותה הימנו.
תלמוד בבלי, ביצה טז,א

Rabbi Shimon ben Lakish said, "On the eve of Shabbat, God gives a person extra soul; at the close of Shabbat it is withdrawn from the person."

Talmud, Beitsah 16a

Text 2b

כיון ששבת ווי אבדה נפש.
תלמוד בבלי, שם

Once one has finished celebrating Shabbat, woe that the [extra] soul has been lost!

Talmud, ibid.

Drawing from the Wellsprings of Salvation

Text 3

Rabbi Moshe ben Maimon (1135–1204). Better known as Maimonides or by the acronym Rambam; born in Cordoba, Spain. After the conquest of Cordoba by the Almohads, he fled Spain and eventually settled in Cairo, Egypt. There, he became the leader of the Jewish community and served as court physician to the vizier of Egypt. His rulings on Jewish law are considered integral to the formation of halachic consensus. He is most noted for authoring the *Mishneh Torah*, an encyclopedic arrangement of Jewish law, and for his philosophical work, *Guide for the Perplexed.*

מצות עשה מן התורה לקדש את יום השבת בדברים שנאמר (שמות כ,ח) זכור את יום השבת לקדשו, כלומר זכרהו זכירת שבח וקידוש, וצריך לזכרהו בכניסתו וביציאתו, בכניסתו בקידוש היום וביציאתו בהבדלה.

רמב"ם, הלכות שבת כט,א

The Torah commands us to sanctify the day of Shabbat with a verbal statement, as it says (Exodus 20:8), "Remember the day of Shabbat to sanctify it." This means to verbally declare its sanctity and praise. This declaration must be made at Shabbat's start and finish: at the day's start with Kiddush and at its finish with *Havdalah*.

Maimonides, *Mishneh Torah*, Laws of Shabbat 29:1

Text 4

יין תחלה לפי שחוש הטעם הוא יותר עב שבשאר החושים שאינו משיג אלא בפגישה אל המוחש. וחוש הריח יותר דק ממנו כי מרחוק יריח וחוש הראות יותר דק שהוא משיג עד לשמים יגיע בהשגת הכוכבים. והבדלה היא חכמה להבדיל בין הקדש ובין החול . . . והוא יותר דק משאר החושים שהוא משיג המלאכים . . . וכן הם מסודרים החושים הלשון הטועם תחתון והחוטם המריח למעלה ממנו והעינים לראות למעלה ממנו והמוח להשכיל למעלה מכלם.

מאמר חמץ לרשב״ץ, נדפס ביבין שמועה לד,ג

Wine comes first because the sense of taste is the least refined of all the senses. It can only perceive when it comes in direct contact with that which is being sensed.

The sense of smell is more refined because one can smell something from afar.

The sense of sight is yet more refined in that it can even see the stars and the sky.

One requires wisdom in order to distinguish between the sacred and the mundane. . . . This sense is the most refined of all the senses because it can perceive spiritual realities.

And so the senses are ordered in this way:

The tongue, which tastes, is the lowest [on the face]. Above it is the nose, which smells. Above it are the eyes, which see. And above them all is the mind, which comprehends.

Rabbi Shimon ben Tsemach Duran, *Ma'amar Chamets* (printed in *Yavin Shemu'ah* 34c)

Rabbi Shimon ben Tsemach Duran (1361–1444). Known by the acronym Rashbats; born in the Spanish island of Majorca; famed rabbi, physician, and authority on Jewish law. Due to forced conversions and the massacre of Jews in Spain, the Rashbats fled to Algiers in 1391 where he was able to resume his role as a rabbi. He is best known for his responsa, which address all aspects of Jewish life.

Text 5a

הִנֵּה אֵל יְשׁוּעָתִי אֶבְטַח וְלֹא אֶפְחָד.
כִּי עָזִּי וְזִמְרָת יָ-הּ ה׳, וַיְהִי לִי לִישׁוּעָה.
וּשְׁאַבְתֶּם מַיִם בְּשָׂשׂוֹן מִמַּעַיְנֵי הַיְשׁוּעָה.
לַה׳ הַיְשׁוּעָה, עַל עַמְּךָ בִרְכָתֶךָ סֶּלָה.
ה׳ צְבָאוֹת עִמָּנוּ, מִשְׂגָּב לָנוּ אֱלֹהֵי יַעֲקֹב סֶלָה.
ה׳ צְבָאוֹת, אַשְׁרֵי אָדָם בֹּטֵחַ בָּךְ.
ה׳ הוֹשִׁיעָה, הַמֶּלֶךְ יַעֲנֵנוּ בְיוֹם קָרְאֵנוּ.
לַיְּהוּדִים הָיְתָה אוֹרָה וְשִׂמְחָה וְשָׂשׂוֹן וִיקָר, כֵּן תִּהְיֶה לָּנוּ.
כּוֹס יְשׁוּעוֹת אֶשָּׂא וּבְשֵׁם ה׳ אֶקְרָא.
הבדלה, סדור תהלת ה׳

ndeed, God is my deliverance; I am confident and shall not fear.

For God the Lord is my strength and my praise, and He has been my salvation.

You shall draw water with joy from the wellsprings of salvation.

Deliverance is the Lord's; may Your blessing be upon Your people forever.

The Lord of Hosts is with us; the God of Jacob is our everlasting stronghold.

Lord of Hosts, happy is the man who trusts in You.

Lord deliver us; may the King answer us on the day we call.

For the Jews there was light and joy, gladness and honor—so let it be with us.

I will raise the cup of salvation and invoke the name of the Lord.

Havdalah, Sidur Tehilat Hashem

Text 5b

בָּרוּךְ אַתָּה ה׳ אֱלֹקֵינוּ מֶלֶךְ הָעוֹלָם בּוֹרֵא פְּרִי הַגָּפֶן.

נוסח הבדלה, שם

lessed are You, Lord our God, King of the Universe, Who creates the fruit of the vine.

Havdalah, ibid.

Text 5c

בָּרוּךְ אַתָּה ה׳ אֱלֹקֵינוּ מֶלֶךְ הָעוֹלָם בּוֹרֵא מִינֵי בְשָׂמִים.

הבדלה, שם

lessed are You, Lord our God, King of the Universe, Who creates various kinds of spices.

Havdalah, ibid.

Text 5d

בָּרוּךְ אַתָּה ה׳ אֱלֹקֵינוּ מֶלֶךְ הָעוֹלָם בּוֹרֵא מְאוֹרֵי הָאֵשׁ.
הבדלה, שם

Blessed are You, Lord our God, King of the Universe, Who creates the lights of fire.

Havdalah, ibid.

Text 6a

ל״ו שעות שימשה אותה האורה, שנים עשר של ערב שבת, וי״ב של לילי שבת וי״ב של שבת,
כיון ששקעה החמה במוצאי שבת התחיל החושך ממשמש ובא ונתירא אדם הראשון.
בראשית רבה יא,ב

The [sublime] light shone [for Adam and Eve] for thirty-six hours: twelve hours on Friday, twelve on Friday night, and twelve on Shabbat day. When the sun set on Saturday night and the darkness became increasingly palpable, Adam was frightened.

Midrash, *Bereishit Rabah* 11:2

Text 6b

אמר: אוי לי, שבשביל שסרחתי עולם חשוך בעדי.
תלמוד בבלי, עבודה זרה ח,א

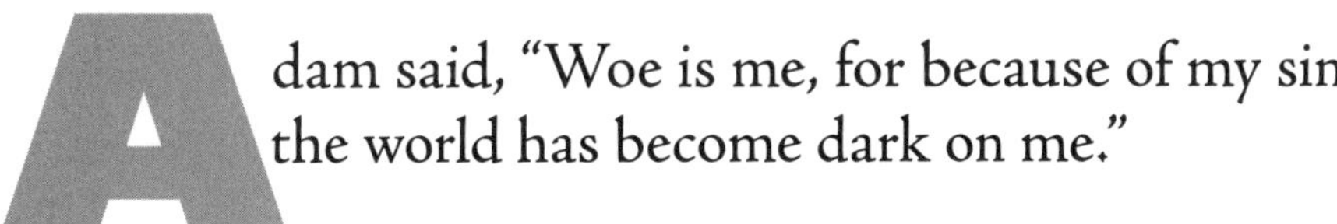

Adam said, "Woe is me, for because of my sin the world has become dark on me."

Talmud, Avodah Zarah 8a

Text 6c

ובמוצאי שבת נתן הקדוש ברוך הוא דיעה באדם הראשון מעין דוגמא של מעלה,
והביא שני אבנים וטחנן זו בזו ויצא מהן אור.
תלמוד בבלי, פסחים נד,א

On Saturday night, God imparted to Adam a glimpse of His wisdom. Adam took two [flint] stones and rubbed them together, and fire sprang forth.

Talmud, Pesachim 54a

Text 7

בָּרוּךְ אַתָּה ה׳ אֱלֹקֵינוּ מֶלֶךְ הָעוֹלָם. הַמַּבְדִּיל בֵּין קֹדֶשׁ לְחוֹל. בֵּין אוֹר לְחשֶׁךְ. בֵּין יִשְׂרָאֵל לָעַמִּים. בֵּין יוֹם הַשְּׁבִיעִי לְשֵׁשֶׁת יְמֵי הַמַּעֲשֶׂה. בָּרוּךְ אַתָּה ה׳ הַמַּבְדִּיל בֵּין קֹדֶשׁ לְחוֹל.

הבדלה, סדור תהלת ה׳

Blessed are You, Lord our God, King of the Universe, Who makes a distinction between sacred and mundane, between light and darkness, between Israel and the nations, between the seventh day and the six days of labor. Blessed are You Lord, Who makes a distinction between sacred and mundane.

Havdalah, Sidur Tehilat Hashem

The Power of Fire

Text 8a

Rabbi Dr. Jonathan Sacks (1948–). Born in London, chief rabbi of the United Hebrew Congregations of the Commonwealth. Attended Cambridge University and received his doctorate from King's College, London. A prolific and influential author, his books include *Will We Have Jewish Grandchildren?* and *The Dignity of Difference.* Recipient of the Jerusalem Prize in 1995 for his contributions to enhancing Jewish life in the Diaspora. Knighted in 2005.

There is, in other words, a fundamental difference between the light of the first day ("And G-d said: Let there be light . . .") and that of the eighth day. The light of the first day is the illumination G-d makes. The light of the eighth day is the illumination G-d teaches us to make. It symbolizes our "partnership with G-d in the work of creation." There is no more beautiful image than this of how G-d empowers us to join Him in bringing light to the world. On Shabbat we remember G-d's creation. On the eighth day (motsei Shabbat) we celebrate our creativity as the image and partner of G-d.

To understand the full depth of what the sages were saying, it is necessary to go back to one of the great myths of the ancient world: the story of Prometheus. To the Greeks, the gods were essentially hostile to mankind. Zeus wanted to keep the art of making fire secret, but Prometheus stole a spark and taught men how to make it. Once the theft was discovered, Zeus punished him by having him chained to a rock, with an eagle pecking at his liver.

Against this background we can see the revolutionary character of Jewish faith. We believe that G-d wants human beings to exercise power: responsibly, creatively, and within limits set by the integrity of nature. The rabbinic account of how G-d taught Adam and Eve the secret of making fire is the precise opposite of the story of Prometheus. G-d seeks to confer dignity on the beings He made in His image as an act of love. He does not hide the secrets of the universe from us. He does not seek to keep mankind in a state of ignorance or dependence. The creative G-d empowers us to be creative and begins by teaching us how. He wants us to be guardians of the world He has entrusted to our care. That is the significance of the eighth day. It is the human counterpart of the first day of creation.

Rabbi Jonathan Sacks, *Covenant and Conversation, Shemini* 2008

Text 8b

Rabbi Samson Raphael Hirsch (1808–1888). Born in Hamburg, Germany; rabbi and educator; intellectual founder of the *Torah Im Derech Eretz* school of Orthodox Judaism, which advocates combining Torah with secular education. Beginning in 1830, Hirsch served as chief rabbi in several prominent German cities. During this period he wrote his *Nineteen Letters on Judaism*, under the pseudonym of Ben Uziel. His work helped preserve traditional Judaism during the era of the German Enlightenment. He is buried in Frankfurt am Main.

The element by which man can extract objects from Nature and by which he gains control over things (and by which night subtly transforms itself into day), thus averring and confirming man's mastery over Nature, is fire.

And so, as soon as you again enter your working week, and you commence your struggle to control the forces of the world and to make things follow your behest, you should assert, as the Sabbath has taught you, that you are active only by the power of God and by the strength given you by God and by His will. You should therefore declare that the element let loose so ingeniously, which is the product helping you to master the world, is a gift presented to the world by God. It is incumbent upon you, therefore, to will and to implement this mastery of the forces of the world only in accord with God's will. That you have this intention very much at heart you manifest by uttering the expressive benediction over a meaningful symbol of the content and intent of your mission in life, as the Sabbath has taught you.

Rabbi Samson Raphael Hirsch, *Horeb* (London: Soncino Press, 1962), p. 105

Text 9a

מצוה להרבות קצת בנרות במוצאי שבת, ולומר הזמירות ללוות את השבת ביציאתו דרך כבוד, כדרך שמלוין את המלך ביציאתו מן העיר, ומזכירין אליהו הנביא ומתפללין שיבא ויבשר לנו הגאולה . . .

מי שאפשר לו יקיים סעודת מלוה מלכה בפת ותבשיל חם, ויסדר שלחנו יפה לכבוד הלוית השבת, ומי שאי אפשר לו לאכול פת יאכל לכל הפחות מיני מזונות או פירות.

קיצור שולחן ערוך צו,יב–יג

It is a mitzvah to brighten the room and recite songs upon Shabbat's departure to escort it with respect, as one escorts the king when he departs from the city. We mention Elijah the Prophet and pray that he will come to herald the redemption. . . . One who is able, should escort the departing [Shabbat] queen with a feast of bread and hot food, and should set the table beautifully to honor the departing Shabbat. One who cannot eat bread should at least eat cake or fruits.

Rabbi Shlomoh Ganzfried, *Kitsur Shulchan Aruch* 96:12–13

Rabbi Shlomoh Ganzfried (1804–1886). Hungarian rabbi and authority on Jewish law. Best known for his *Kitsur Shulchan Aruch*, a user-friendly summary of Rabbi Yosef Caro's *Shulchan Aruch* and the observations of subsequent halachic commentators. This highly acclaimed work quickly became a classic, a mainstay in every Jewish home. Rabbi Ganzfried was born in Uzhhorod (today part of Ukraine), and after being orphaned at a very young age was adopted by Uzhhorod's chief rabbi, Rabbi Tzvi Hirsh Heller. Eventually Rabbi Ganzfried was appointed *dayan*—chief rabbinical magistrate—of Uzhhorod, a position he retained until his passing.

Text 9b

שזהו התוכן הפנימי דסעודת מלוה מלכה, תיקון חטא עץ הדעת, כי בסעודה זו ישנו החיבור דשבת וחול, דמחד גיסא הרי הוא לאחרי גמר קדושת שבת, אבל לאידך יש בה הברכה (וההמשכה) דיום השבת, שעל ידי זה נמשך הכח דשבת גם בסעודה של חול.

לקוטי שיחות לו, עמ׳ 76

Rabbi Menachem Mendel Schneerson (1902–1994). Known as "the Lubavitcher Rebbe," or simply as "the Rebbe." Born in southern Ukraine. Rabbi Schneerson escaped from the Nazis, arriving in the U.S. in June 1941. The towering Jewish leader of the 20th century, the Rebbe inspired and guided the revival of traditional Judaism after the European devastation, and often emphasized that the performance of just one additional good deed could usher in the era of Mashiach.

This is the deeper meaning of the *melaveh malkah* meal: [We are able] to repair the sin of the tree of knowledge because at this meal, there is a connection between Shabbat and the weekday. On the one hand, this meal begins only after the holiness of Shabbat has departed. On the other hand, it is an extension of Shabbat and through it, the spirit of Shabbat is drawn into a weekday meal.

Rabbi Menachem Mendel Schneerson, *Likutei Sichot* 36:76

Course Conclusion

Text 10

כל שיתא יומין מתברכאן מיומא שביעאה.

זהר ב, סג,ב

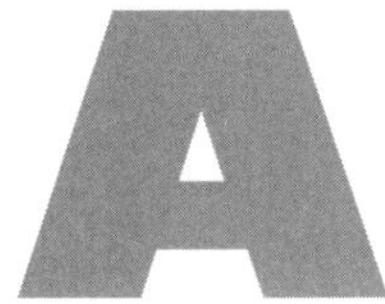

All six days are blessed [with manna] from the seventh.

Zohar 2:63b

Learning Activity 1

Over the past weeks we explored six different aspects of Shabbat. The following exercise will enable you to review and internalize what you have learned in this course so as to enrich your experience of Shabbat and of life itself.

1. Consider each lesson in the course. (You may want to refer to the key points at the end of each lesson to help jog your memory.) Think of something you learned that was new to you, or something that made an impression on you that you could incorporate to enhance your Shabbat experience. Compose a short sentence or phrase that summarizes this idea and record it in the chart on the next page.

2. Now consider a way in which you could incorporate one idea from each lesson into your everyday life. Record this insight in the chart on the next page.

(For example: From Lesson Two I learned that how I prepare for Shabbat will affect my experience of Shabbat.

The everyday application: I can value preparation, not just as a burden, but as an integral part of every end goal.)

	Enhancing Shabbat	Enhancing Everyday Life
1. The Gift		
2. Beginning with the End in Mind		
3. Walking with Angels		

	Enhancing Shabbat	Enhancing Everyday Life
4. Pure Pleasure		
5. Working Definitions		
6. Afterglow		

Key Points

1. As Shabbat continues, our transcendent state intensifies and reaches its peak on Shabbat afternoon.

2. The departure of Shabbat is traumatic. For *Havdalah*, we drink wine, smell fragrant spices, and cite biblical verses that comfort and gladden us.

3. The light of the *Havdalah* candle reminds us that God provides for us in the same way that He provided for Adam and Eve when they were enveloped in darkness.

4. The fire of the *Havdalah* candle reminds us that God shares His wisdom with us so that we can partner with Him in developing the physical universe.

5. On the one hand, Shabbat is separated from the six days of the week. At the same time, this division is not absolute. We must bring Shabbat into our week, thereby elevating the mundane.

6. The week and Shabbat complement each other. The week enables us to enjoy a proper Shabbat and Shabbat helps us live properly during the week.

Course Summary

Lesson	Summary
1. The Gift	There are numerous benefits to Shabbat rest, starting with the most simple and proceeding to the most holy and transcendent.
2. Beginning with the End in Mind	How we prepare for Shabbat is essential in defining how we will experience it.
3. Walking with Angels	Shabbat theory and practice alludes to secrets for achieving peace.
4. Pure Pleasure	The body is part of the Shabbat celebrations. The goal is to share the soul's experience with that of the body.
5. Working Definitions	Through careful analysis of the prohibited work on Shabbat, we recognize that all of our success comes from God's blessing.
6. Afterglow	Faith, joy, and discernment are key to conveying the blessings of Shabbat to the other days of the week.

Simply Shabbat: *Havdalah*

We sanctify Shabbat by distinguishing it from the weekdays that precede and follow it. We mark the onset of Shabbat with a cup of wine. When Shabbat departs, we do the same: over a cup of wine, we bless God for distinguishing Shabbat from the weekdays. We call this ceremony *Havdalah* (literally, "separation").

For the *Havdalah* ceremony, you'll need: a **prayer book** (or print out the *Havdalah* text at **tinyurl.com/3mf69bw**), a **cup** (that holds at least 3 fluid ounces), **wine** or grape juice, **aromatic spices** (whole cloves are popular), and a multi-wick **candle**.

The Ceremony:

Fill your cup with wine until it overflows slightly. Lift the cup in your right hand (unless you are left-handed) and begin to recite *Havdalah.*

The *Havdalah* opens with joyous verses from Psalms and Isaiah so that we begin the new week on a positive note. Also included is the verse from the Book of Esther, which everyone recites in unison: "For the Jews there was light, happiness, joy, and honor"—to which we add: "So may it be for us!" Following these verses, recite the *hagafen* blessing over the wine.

Now place the cup down, take the spices in your hand, say the blessing on the spices, and smell them. Allow the fragrant aroma to comfort and soothe your soul, which feels forlorn when Shabbat departs.

Now say the blessing on the candle to commemorate the creation of fire and to thank God for giving us its light. (According to the Midrash, fire was created on the first Saturday night.) After the blessing, hold your fingernails up to the candle's light and gaze at them.

Lift up the cup of wine again, and recite the concluding *Havdalah* blessing, praising God for separating between the holy and the mundane.

Sit down and drink at least 1.5 ounces of the wine.

Related Notes and Customs:

After *Havdalah*, the candle is traditionally extinguished by dipping it in the wine that overflowed onto the tray when the cup was overfilled. Once the *Havdalah* candle has been extinguished, many have the custom of dipping a finger into the wine in the tray, and running the finger just above the eyelids, as per the verse, "The *mitzvot* of God are clear, enlightening the eyes" (Psalms 19:9).

In the absence of wine or grape juice, certain other beverages can be used. Consult with your rabbi about which beverage should be used.

If one did not make *Havdalah* on Saturday night, it can still be done until sunset of the following Tuesday evening. A candle and spices are not used if reciting *Havdalah* after Saturday night.

The Shabbat Afterglow:

The Shabbat afterglow does not completely end with the *Havdalah*. It is customary to continue wearing Shabbat finery on Saturday night, and many have the custom of lighting candles on the table after reciting *Havdalah*.

Sometime on Saturday night it is customary to partake of a meal, called *melaveh malkah*, the "escorting the [Shabbat] queen" meal. Ideally, one should wash and eat bread or challah at this meal. It is customary among *chasidim* to tell stories of *tsadikim* (righteous people) at the *melaveh malkah* meal.

Shavua Tov!

Additional Readings

Shabbat in the Shtetl

by **Elie Wiesel**

On Shabbat, if poverty did not vanish altogether, it was attenuated. One can never speak enough of what Shabbat was like in the shtetl—and what it did for its inhabitants. Shabbat helped people endure the other six days of the week, often gray and dark, heavy with sorrow and anxiety. Hence the waiting for Shabbat, which actually began much earlier. Thursday evening or early Friday morning, the housewife would already be busy preparing the hallah, gefilte fish, and cholent, the traditional elements of a Shabbat meal in the shtetl. The white tablecloth, the white shirt: everything had to be ready, and everything was the housewife's responsibility. One easily forgets that we owe the gift of Shabbat to the queen of the home, *Shabbat malka*, the Shabbat queen. We couldn't wait for her arrival.

In the stores, business was conducted with haste. Sellers and customers were equally in a hurry to go home. Men would go to the *mikvah*, then dress and prepare to be worthy of welcoming the Shabbat, already on the horizon. The first to spot her would be the beadle, the shammash: he would go around stores and homes shouting *"Yiden, greit zicht tzu Shabbes!"*—Jews, ready yourselves for the Sabbath! Or a variation on the same theme: *"Yiden, s'is bald Shabbes oif der velt!"*—Jews, it's almost Shabbat in the world! At home, one did not need these reminders: the mother, mine too, lit the candles honoring Shabbat, one for each member of the family, and blessed them silently, with gestures of grace and tenderness. Suddenly, her face would be illuminated by a light coming from another world, from another time, a light at once frail and eternal. And her beauty was multiplied sevenfold. So that even now as I am writing these words, the tears well up in my throat.

In the shul also, everything was different. More luminous, the candelabras. More serene, the faces. More melodious, the prayers. The Talmud is right: on Shabbat, one gains an added soul, the *neshama yeteira*.

Then, at the end of the service, many worshipers began running toward the visitors in shul. If there were none the shammash would yell aloud, "Are there strangers here?" It was forbidden, absolutely forbidden, to allow anyone to be without an invitation to partake with some family in a Shabbat meal. Frequently people would fight over a visitor. It was an honor to invite him or her to their table. I myself can hardly remember a Shabbat without an honored guest in our home.

Whenever my maternal grandfather, Reb Dodye, was with us, we would feel double honored. And I was three times as happy. I have sworn never to forget him, nor his return from the Shabbat-eve office. He would stop on the threshold, kiss the mezuzah, and, his face burning with delight, start the Wizsnitzer *"Sholem aleikhem malakhei ha'shareit"*—Be blessed, angels in the service of peace. And it was as if peace now reigned over the heaven and earth, a peace that brought together men and women of all nations, of all ages, a dream of which Shabbat remains the uplifting and inspiring symbol.

The end of Shabbat was signaled by mother and grandmother. Shortly before the Havdalah ceremony, which separates light from darkness and the sacred from the profane, the Shabbat from the weekdays, both women, like all mothers, would recite the special prayer attributed to the great Rebbe Levi-Yitzhak of Berditchev: *"Gott fun Avrohom, Yitzhok un Yankev . . ."* God of Abraham, Isaac, and Jacob, extend your protection over Thy children and ours . . . When the prayer ends, the Havdalah begins.

Whereupon another song takes hold of my memory: *"Bobeshi, zog nokh nit Gott fun Avrohom . . ."* It's a little child pleading with his grandmother not to recite her prayers, not yet, let her wait a bit longer, the sun hasn't set yet in the west, let Shabbat last a while longer . . . The little child loves the Shabbat and refuses to leave it behind—to be left behind.

Which, of course, recalls an old Hasid or rebbe who, during the mystical Third Meal, is doing in his way what the grandmother could have done in hers. He sings a song: *"Ven ich volt ge'hat koi'ekh,"* if I had the strength, *"volt ich in di gassen gelofen,"* I would run through the streets, *"un ich volt geshere'in hoikh,"* and I would yell with all my might, *"Shabbess, heiliger shabbess,"* Holy, holy Sabbath . . . And legend has it that as long as he sang, the Shabbat would remain with him and his followers. So he sang and sang . . .

Wise Men and Their Tales (New York: Schocken Books, 2003), pp. 328–330
Reprinted by permission of the publisher

Hasidic Warsaw

by **Rabbi Joseph B. Soloveitchik**

The Jewish yearnings for sanctity and spirituality found their expression in the Halakhah. This is the concept of *"Tosefet Shabbat,"* or the requirement that "we add from the profane on to the holy" (Rosh Hashana 9a). Why must we rush into the Sabbath? For example, the sunset is 6:45 P.M. Why do we recite the prayers welcoming the Sabbath at 6 P.M.? Let us wait until the Sabbath actually begins! Why do some Jews retain the Sabbath until two or three hours after nightfall on Saturday night? They postpone the recitation of the Havdalah until well into the night!

Once again, I return to my childhood memories. In Warsaw we lived three houses away from the Modzhitzer shtiebel. Generally, I would go to the Modzhitzer shtiebel for the seudah shlishit [third meal] of the Sabbath. They would sing all the zemirot for the seudah shlishit. Poor Jews would be seated around the table in the shtiebel. The Modzhitzer shtiebel was located in a poor district in Warsaw called the Grzybowska district. My father could not afford to live in a more affluent district. This was a neighborhood where many of the Jews worked as porters. There was a large iron gate in Warsaw where all the porters looking for employment gathered. I always say that in Warsaw I saw sights that I never saw since. You would see a large closet or a buffet that seemed to be walking on its own. The Jewish porter who was carrying the furniture was totally bent over in a ninety degree angle. It seemed as if the furniture was walking along with feet coming out of the closet.

I knew these Jews well and I constantly spoke with them. They were sincerely pious Jews who willingly sacrificed for their spiritual commitments. I once spoke with one of them who was frail and short. He constantly carried heavy metal pieces and I wondered where he got the physical strength to support this weight. His load was always tied around him with a thick cord and he totally resembled a "coolie." On the Sabbath, I saw this very Jew and I did not recognize him. He came over to me in his tattered kapote. It was covered with endless patches, and even the patches had patches. Yet his face shone with the joy of the Sabbath. I recognized in a tangible fashion that a person's Sabbath countenance is totally different than his weekday appearance.

So, I asked him: When will we daven Ma'ariv [pray the evening prayer for the conclusion of the Sabbath]? He answered: What is with you? Are you already longing for the weekdays to begin? What do you mean when will we daven Ma'ariv, are we lacking anything now?

When these Jews would sing the *"Bnei Heikhalah"* ["The dwellers of the Sanctuary who wish to experience the Divine Presence"] at the end of the seudah shlishit, they were singing about themselves. When they sang "He maketh me lie down in green pastures" [from the twenty-third Psalm (23:2)], they knew that there were no "green pastures" outside of the shtiebel. There were many vicious Poles out there who were anxious to participate in pogroms against the Jews. They were desirous of taking away any chance for the Jews to earn a livelihood. The Jews knew all this and therefore they could not depart from the Sabbath. They sang a refrain and repeated it. They only wanted to remain with the Sabbath. They lived the concept of *"Tosefet Shabbat."* This was truly the fulfillment of the Halakhah that we "add from the profane on to the holy." This Halakhah represented a deep exposition and a great experience. It represented the overwhelming longings and yearnings of the Jews for the sanctity of the Sabbath.

Transcript of Rabbi Joseph B. Soloveitchik, September 23, 1974, printed in Rakeffet-Rothkoff, Aaron. *The Rav: The World of Rabbi Joseph B. Soloveitchik*, vol. 1 (Jersey City, NJ: Ktav Publishing House, Inc., 1999) pp. 159–161

The Kabbalah of Havdalah

by **Yanki Tauber**

> *If there is no* daat *(discriminating intelligence), how can there be differentiation?* (Jerusalem Talmud, Berachot 5:2)

In the Jewish home, the close of the Shabbat is marked with a special ceremony, called *Havdalah* ("differentiation"). Over a brimming cup of wine, to the multi-flamed light of a braided candle and the smell of aromatic spices, we recite: "Blessed are You, L-rd our G-d . . . Who differentiates between the holy and the mundane, between light and darkness, between Israel and the nations, between the seventh day and the six days of work."

Differentiation is at the heart of what we call morality. If theft or adultery are wrong, it is only because there is a real difference between mine and yours and between the wedded and the unwedded state. If ceasing work on Shabbat or eating matzah on Passover are meaningful deeds, this is only because Shabbat is truly different from Friday and matzah is truly different from leavened bread. If there is meaning and purpose to our actions, there must be true significance to the differences between things.

Differentiation, however, also implies a sameness to the things being differentiated. If Shabbat and Sunday looked, smelled and tasted differently to our physical senses, there would be no need to actively differentiate between them. Indeed, when the Torah employs the verb "to differentiate" (*lehavdil*), it is to distinguish between things that are essentially similar. A case in point is the concluding verse of Leviticus 11, the chapter which lays down the kashrut dietary laws. The verse reads: "To differentiate between the pure and the impure; between the animal that may be eaten and the animal that may not be eaten," regarding which our sages remark:

> Need this be said regarding the difference between a donkey and a cow? . . . Rather, this is to tell us to differentiate between the animal which had half its windpipe cut [during the slaughtering] and the animal which had most of its windpipe cut. . . . Need this be said regarding the difference between a wild ass and a deer? Rather, this is to tell us to differentiate between an animal in which there developed a defect yet remains fit to be eaten and an animal in which there developed a defect which renders it unfit to be eaten (Rashi on verse, from Torat Kohanim).

In other words, *havdalah* requires the ability to look at two similar things and appreciate that, despite their elementary similarity, they are to be differentiated and held apart. In the words of our sages, "If there is no *daat* (discriminating intelligence), how can there be *havdalah*?"

A World of Words

The capacity to differentiate, as we have noted, is the basis for any moral vision of life. Chassidic teaching takes this a step further, demonstrating how *havdalah* is the essence of the created existence, of what we call reality.

An axiom of the Jewish faith is that G-d is infinite—without beginning and without end. This raises the problem, addressed by all major Jewish philosophers, of how our world can possibly exist, since a truly infinite being precludes the existence of anything other than itself. Indeed, the Torah asserts that "There is nothing else besides Him." But what about ourselves, our world, our reality? Are these not existences besides Him?

In his Tanya, Rabbi Schneur Zalman of Liadi lays the groundwork for a resolution of this problem by defining the created reality as divine speech. In the first chapter of Genesis, G-d's creation of the world is described as a series of (ten) utterances: G-d said, "Let there be light!" and there was light; G-d said, "Let the earth send forth vegetation," "Let there be luminaries in the heavens," "Let the waters spawn living creatures," and plants, stars and fish emerged into existence. Citing teachings from the Midrash, the Kabbalist Rabbi Isaac Luria and Chassidism's founder Rabbi Israel Baal Shem Tov, Rabbi Schneur Zalman deduces that these divine utterances are not merely the cause of these existences—they *are* these existences. What we experience as "light" is but the embodiment of G-d's articulated desire that there be light; what we experience as a "tree" is but the embodiment of G-d's articulated desire that there be a tree.

So the created reality is not, in truth, something else besides Him, any more than our spoken words are things distinct from ourselves. Speaking is a creative act; but when we speak we are not creating anything that is other than ourselves—we are giving vocal form to our own ideas, feelings and desires. In describing G-d's creation of the world as a series of divine utterances, the Torah wishes to convey the idea that the world is not something distinct from its Creator, but His spoken words—His articulation of concepts and potentials which are an integral part of His being.

The implications of such a conception of ourselves and our world—of reality as divine speech—are numerous and manifold. One is the realization that the differences between things are secondary to a primary sameness that embraces them all. A language might include millions of words, but these are all variations on a handful of consonants and vowels. On a more basic level, these consonants and vowels are just variations on how a minute expulsion of breath is bounced off the speaker's vocal cords, tongue, palate, teeth and lips.

A tree might seem very different from a ray of light, as might a fish from a star. But each of these objects is, in essence, the same thing: a divine word, an articulation of divine will. In origin, they share a singular essence; their differentiation occurs at a later stage, as they pass through the divine mouth that imparts to them their respective forms and characteristics.

Thus the Torah relates how, on the first day of creation, "G-d differentiated between light and darkness." What can be more different than light and darkness? What differentiation is necessary between such obviously different phenomena? But light and darkness are both creations of G-d; both are divine words, formulations of the same surge of divine will. Their distinction is the product of a divine act of *havdalah*, of a deliberate differentiation between two essentially synonymous realities.

Daat

In light of this, we can better understand the above-quoted Talmudic dictum regarding the connection between *daat* and *havdalah*. The Talmud is discussing the fact that in the evening prayers recited after the close of Shabbat, the text of the *Havdalah* is inserted in the prayer which begins: "You grant *daat* to man, and teach the human being understanding; grant us, from You, wisdom, understanding and knowledge . . ." The reason for this placement, says the Talmud, is that "If there is no *daat*, how can there be *havdalah*?"

On the most basic level, the Talmud is saying that an act of *havdalah* requires the discriminating intelligence of *daat*. On a deeper level, it is saying that *havdalah* is possible only because "*You* grant *daat* to man"—only because G-d Himself grants us the capacity to differentiate between various elements of His creation.

For if the world is divine speech, if all created things are essentially the same, how can we differentiate between them? And if we do differentiate, what significance can there be to our differentiation? We might discern light and darkness; we might identify certain things as holy and others as mundane; we might designate the first six days of the week for material achievement and its seventh day for spiritual rest; but if all of these are, in essence, divine words, what power have we to differentiate between them?

But G-d wanted a moral world—a world in which the deeds of man are purposeful and meaningful. So He imparted variety, diversity and distinction to His creation, decreeing that the differences between things should possess import and significance. His act of creation was an act of *havdalah*—of differentiating between essentially similar entities. And He granted the human being a mind capable of appreciating the paradox of *havdalah*—the paradox of meaningful difference imposed upon intrinsic synonymy—thereby empowering us to implement, through our awareness and our actions, the differentiations He decreed in His world.

The Second Paradox

Havdalah carries another paradox—that its ultimate function is to join and unite the very things it comes to differentiate.

The Torah commands us to remember and to preserve the day of Shabbat—to distinguish it, in mind, word and deed, from the six days of work. Yet Shabbat is integrally bound to the other days of the week. It is the culmination of our weekday endeavors—the day on which all that we labored for and achieved in the preceding six days ascends on high, attaining its most complete and perfect realization. And Shabbat is the day from which all days are blessed—the source of the fortitude and energy that drives our efforts of the work-week that follows it.

We are told to preserve our uniqueness as Jews—to safeguard the delineation between Israel and the nations. Yet the people of Israel are designated to serve as "a light unto the nations," as the conveyers of the ethos and ideals of Torah to all inhabitants of the earth.

We are instructed to differentiate between the holy and the mundane—to embrace what is sacred and G-dly in our lives while exercising wariness and restraint in the material aspects of life. At the same time, we are told that "the purpose of man's creation, and of the creation of all worlds, spiritual and material is to make for G-d a dwelling place in the lowly realms"—to involve our everyday material pursuits in the quest to know and serve G-d, thereby making Him at home in the lowliest, most mundane stratum of creation.

For it is only through our awareness and enforcement of the boundaries within creation that these objectives can be achieved. Only if Shabbat is preserved in its distinctiveness and transcendence can it elevate and empower the other six days of the week. Only in their uniqueness as G-d's chosen people does the nation of Israel have anything of true value to offer the peoples of the world. Only when our spiritual life is kept inviolably apart from the coarsening influence of the material can it in turn sanctify the material by enlisting it to serve its spiritual aims.

From Unity to Symphony

Havdalah is the substance of our daily lives, as every hour and moment confronts us with the challenge to define and differentiate—to distinguish between right and wrong, between holy and mundane. But these delineations are merely a means to an end, a process springing from a primordial unity and leading toward a future synthesis.

In origin and essence, all is one. But an even deeper unity is achieved when differentiations and demarcations are imposed upon the primordial oneness, and its component parts are each given a distinct role in creation's symphonious expression of the goodness and perfection of its Creator.

Based on the teachings of the Lubavitcher Rebbe, Rabbi Menachem Mendel Schneerson

Week in Review, Published by The Meaningful Life Center
Reprinted by permission of the publisher

Night of the Righteous

by **Meir Michel Abehsera**

It is a prevalent custom among observant Jews to gather on Saturday night, singing and dancing and telling stories until dawn. We extend the Shabbat that has technically passed, carrying some of its holiness with us into days of the week, the realm of the profane. It is the ideal time to speak about the righteous (in Hebrew, *"tzadikim"*). Any story or anecdote about them is a Shabbat in itself, a rest-stop for the Jew who is preparing to confront the weekdays. It is a place of transition where the mind is given ample time to ready itself for the mundane.

The spiritual forces of darkness have been starving during the entire length of the Shabbat. Therefore, you can only expect that as soon as Shabbat draws to its end, these forces will reach out to devour the defenseless. They lie in wait by the doors of every house of prayer and grab congregants by the dozen. One bite from the beast, and they are infused with an acute sense of the Saturday night blues.

Saturday night is a most sacred time, when exile is boxed in by redemption. It is a time when the nourishment of the spirit is most varied, when all duality is resolved. Intelligence is heightened, and everyone who celebrates the occasion is instantly wise. Doubts wane. Impossible questions are easily answered. The night exhausts itself, depositing a block of resolutions.

It is the night when the true face of the Jew emerges. The subtle mixture of light and darkness gives a brightly hued, vibrant luminosity to the ambient air in which the face reveals ancient wisdom. The image is somewhat grainy, because neither light nor darkness is yet settled in their respective vessels. But in their eager jockeying for position, in that play of volatile contrasts, the true face is exposed.

Shabbat bathes the Jew in a bright and homogenous light which is not necessarily conducive to revelations of individual character. Shabbat is much too full, and therefore permits no contrast. Shabbat is the reservoir, not the conduit. It is contained within specific limits which allow no explosions to occur. Saturday night's light however, flickers relentlessly. It is a black fire whose pulsating luminescence disturbs and disperses the obtrusive layers that camouflage the soul. The Jew is never more conscious of his mission than during these hours. It is on this night that the world was created and on the very same night that light was made. Now, light is again renewed through our actions. As Shabbat draws to its end, and the obscurity of night begins to cover us with its black mantle, we burn a braided candle, whose variegated and animated flame rekindles the light of Creation.

Our holy masters say that the feeling of sadness we experience at Shabbat's end is caused by our subconscious sense of the primordial Shattering of the Vessels—that timeless, spaceless juncture in the history of Creation when the divine light fell into the lower worlds. We are given a taste of that decline. The light of Shabbat has flown back to its nest, and we search for it within. Some mystical writings compare that departure of the light to a deer fleeting from its pursuer, running with its head tilted under and to the side, staring back into your eyes. In that look of the deer, as the light recedes swiftly in the distance, we are given to retroactively appreciate the hidden reality of Shabbat.

It is said that at the beginning of Creation—meaning on Saturday night—the vessels prepared to hold the infinite light of Creation broke. On that same night, the repair of the vessels also began. Thus, we can only assume that there is no more opportune time to repair our own. Darkness was formed when work was left undone. The mundane week lies before us like an open abyss, auguring a reprise of that tragedy. The abyss beckons, and its pull is far out of proportion to our fragilities. The disparity is the main cause of Saturday night melancholia. The threat is real.

The threat is so real in fact, that one cannot possibly remain insensitive to it, since all of us descend from Adam, who was the first to experience the fall. It is said that upon seeing the sun set for the first time, he experienced a great anguish, certain that darkness had settled on the world because of his sin. That very same night, he took two stones and struck them one against the other until sparks flew. Though such a simple act seemed to hold little promise of transcendence, it was, in fact, the initial stroke that impelled him to return to the Garden of Eden. Poor though it may have been, the light of the fire gave him comfort, and so he blessed it. The memory of that past makes of Saturday night a most opportune time for new beginnings. Anticipation of something new happening is never so great, which is the reason why this night is known as the "Night of the Redeemer."

According to tradition, the Redeemer (*Mashiach*) will reveal himself in the wink of an eye, even when all the signs and estimations will concur to proclaim his coming. He will surprise everyone, wicked or wise, and also the cautious, those who prefer not to speak about him, from fear of exacerbating other's skepticism, or from taking the risk of spoiling the suspense of his coming. Above all, he will most likely surprise those who think and speak of him constantly, even those who serve him. In accordance with that, we are left with no other alternative than to opt for the obvious. The Redeemer will surprise primarily those who expect him the most—as a mother is surprised by the presence of her child, the same with couples, or true friends—for the simple reason that true surprise hits more strongly those who have much life in them. Others, who have less, will most likely find it hard to react enthusiastically to the news.

It is precisely in such an atmosphere of anticipation—namely, that we could at any moment be taken unaware by something already known—that past faults can be corrected. If folly so treacherously intrudes inside us, to have us commit an error, it is perfectly sensible, therefore, to utilize such means which would take the intruder by surprise. What better scheme is there than to confront the faults during moments that seem so uncertain as to confound them? Being that a fault is, on the whole, of an accidental nature, it is logical that it be exposed to an atmosphere that suits its character. Saturday night's incomplete light makes it an ideal host. No judgment is passed.

But take heed. Don't be so readily fooled by such a display of leniency. The diminished light does not indicate some sort of deficiency or weakness. In truth, the reason why the light has dimmed is because it has traveled a distance to gather momentum, before coming back with a force that renews Creation. Kabbala calls such a light *"Or Chozer,"* "Returning Light." It comes to wake us up from sleep. It says, "Where were you while I was there in your midst? I was a willing guest and you were such a distracted host." It is Shabbat speaking. Distance makes it talk; it has divested itself of its clothing of effervescent gold, and donned a humbler robe to travel lightly.

As the night advances, our faults change aspect. The deeds that are performed for selfish gain are released from bondage. There is no visible trace of corruption in any of them. This occurs because the night makes us more compassionate on ourselves. Or else it is making us so wise that we can discern some of the workings of redemption. In any event, the fact is that at such times, faults greatly contribute to enriching the atmosphere, while the night kindly obliges by returning the favor with a gift all its own. It broadens the scope of each fault as far as the twilight of Creation. There the fault becomes deed, the instant it re-enters its original mold. You can imagine how much such a moment of good-will can benefit anyone, stranger or friend. What appears to him most improbable will resolve itself in the warmth of companionship. His faults experience a loss of identity. They have become new entities altogether. They are enriching reality. The interaction between each fault and the specific hour of the night, formulates the mode of the celebration at hand.

On Saturday night, it is quite visible that the guests experience change the moment they enter the house. However, no transmutation will really begin to take place before the food is served. The animation of the voices generates enough warmth to fecundate the most sterile of thought. The multitude of bodies produces more than enough pressure to wring out bothersome ruminations. The heart is jolted by Chasidic chanting. Music, which usually follows, tears all worries apart. But nothing appears more catalyzing than dance, when every remnant of pain—that of dancer and onlookers alike—is shaken off with each change of cadence. The highlight of the celebration, however, will take place in the calm before dawn, when most people have left. By then everyone is weary. Words are few and the movements slow. Silence prevails in spite of the resonance of voices or the fracas of pots being washed. Not even the dissonant chords played by dilettante musicians are able to disrupt the quiescence of the moment. At this stage, incidental noises are put at the service of silence to give it a new depth. Thus nested, thought is given to witness how the passing of time has fulfilled the night's promises—the cycle of transmutations is virtually completed—and that subsequently, the slowest of metabolism has benefited as well. At any moment, all this abundance of human exchange ignites time, which shoots back far into the past, to redeem it. The past, in turn, redeems the present. Creation has just begun.

www.kabbalaonline.org
Reprinted with permission

Yedid Nefesh—Beloved of the Soul

Rabbi Eliezer Azikri (1533-1600 CE) lived in Safed, Israel, during its zenith in Torah and Kabbalah. A student of Rabbi Moses Cordovero, and colleague of Rabbi Chaim Vital and Rabbi Avraham Galanti, Rabbi Azikiri wrote Sefer Chassidim, *and composed this poem. The poem uses the imagery of lovesickness to describe our intense longing for closeness with G-d. Traditions vary from community to community, but many sing this before* Kabbalat Shabbat, *and during the Shabbat afternoon meal.*

Beloved of [my] soul, merciful Father,
draw Your servant to Your will.
[Then] Your servant will run as swiftly as a deer;
he will bow before Your splendor;
Your acts of affection will be sweeter
than honeycomb and every pleasant taste.

Glorious, resplendent One, Light of the world,
my soul is lovesick for You;
I beseech You, O God, pray heal it
by showing it the sweetness of Your splendor.
Then it will be strengthened and healed
and will experience everlasting joy.

O pious One, may Your mercy be aroused
and have compassion upon Your beloved child.
For it is long that I have been yearning
to behold the glory of Your majesty.
These my heart desires,
so have pity and do not conceal Yourself.

Reveal Yourself, my Beloved, and spread over me
the shelter of Your peace.
Let the earth be illuminated by Your glory;
we will rejoice and exult in You.
Hasten, Beloved, for the time has come; and
be gracious unto us as in days of yore.

Siddur Tehillat Hashem with English Translation, Annotated Edition.
(Brooklyn, NY: Merkos L'Inyonei Chinuch, 2002), p. 151

Author's Acknowledgments

First and foremost, I owe thanks to G-d Almighty for the gift of Shabbat, and to the Lubavitcher Rebbe, whose wisdom and guidance have opened my eyes to appreciate that gift.

To **Rabbi Levi Kaplan**, for introducing me to **JLI** and for suggesting that I write this course.

To **Dr. Chana Silberstein**, for her academic and editorial genius, and to her entire team, for their expert preparation and rendering of the material.

To our executive director, **Rabbi Efraim Mintz**, for the privilege of partaking in his vision; and to our chairman, **Rabbi Moshe Kotlarsky**, and principal patron, **Mr. George Rohr** and family, for seeing the value in this enterprise.

To **Rabbi Altein, Rabbi Loschak**, and **Rabbi Nemes** of the editorial board, whose valuable feedback and teaching experience helped anchor the ideas in the course and kept them from flying too high.

To my wife, **Leah**, for her constant patience, support, and companionship throughout this project, and for her help in filtering through the hundreds of ideas that never made it into the course.

To my colleagues at JLI Central, to dedicated JLI instructors everywhere, and to the students of JLI for this incredible opportunity.

Thank you,

Rabbi Zalman Abraham

Brooklyn, NY
Rosh Chodesh Nisan, 5771

Acknowledgments

Shabbat, says the Talmud, is G-d's gift to the Jewish people—and what a gift it is! It anchors time, creating cycles of meaning and being. It offers respite from hard labor and a break from the intrusion of our ubiquitous technologies. It allows family and community the time to connect and reflect without distraction. The warm smell of challah, the glowing candles, the comfort of ritual, all leave their imprint, shaping forever the meaning of family, peoplehood, and one's place in the universe.

Yet to many, Shabbat seems complex, daunting, restrictive, or sterile. The objective of this course is to remove the barriers that keep people from enjoying what Shabbat has to offer. We invite students of every level of observance to experience the mystery of this most precious of Jewish treasures. The course provides multiple entry points so that students at every level of affiliation can explore meaningful ways to enrich their lives with the lessons of Shabbat.

Every JLI course is a vast collaborative effort. We are grateful first and foremost to our course author, **Rabbi Zalman Moshe Abraham.** Rabbi Abraham's erudition and creative perspective have provided extraordinary depth and texture to the course matter. In keeping with the course's objectives, he has masterfully integrated philosophical, inspirational, and practical elements in order to appeal to the diverse demographic served by JLI. Rabbi Abraham wears many hats, and as marketing director of JLI, he brings to his writing a sensitivity to audience and message that has been invaluable.

The JLI Editorial Board has guided the development and revision of our course and ensured that the course material is sensitive to the needs of our students. Many thanks to **Rabbi Yisrael Altein**, **Rabbi Yosef Loschak, Rabbi Yossi Nemes, Rabbi Shalom Raichik**, and **Rabbi Avraham Steinmetz** who provided extensive comments and review at various stages of course production.

"Two are better than one" (Ecclesiastes 4:9). Over the past year, the flagship department has been fortunate to add a number of exceptional staff members. The masterful collaboration of the team has allowed for an exponential advance in terms of our course development and has allowed us to lend support to curricular initiatives in other departments, most notably the newly forged Department of Continuing Education and the JLI Academy.

We are greatly indebted to **Rabbi Mordechai Dinerman**, our associate editor, who served as leading editor on this course, for his extensive contributions and guiding vision. His careful precision and clear, logical analysis have left their imprint on every page, resulting in lessons that are thoughtful, compelling, and powerfully structured. **Rabbi Naftali Silberberg**, our developmental editor, brings clarity, accessibility, and warm humor to his work. Rabbi Silberberg introduced a number of new features to ease the reader into sophisticated ideas in a manner that is open and inviting.

The multimedia and instructional support team create extraordinary enhancements to ensure the effective delivery of our course material. We are grateful to **Ms. Neria Cohen**, who carefully reviewed the document, made many suggestions for improvement, and provided many of the learning activities that enhance the teachability of the course. Ms. Cohen also scripted and reviewed the weekly videos accompanying the course, which were creatively developed and produced by **Rabbi Levi Teldon**. We thank **Mrs. Chana Lightstone** for her contributions to the initial planning and drafting of the video series. We also thank her for extensive contributions to the production and final review of the text. **Mrs. Lea-Perl Shollar** contributed to the selection of our additional readings, as well as to the creation of the promotional course teaser. In addition, Mrs. Shollar is our JLI blogmaster, bringing rich supplementary perspectives to our students via Facebook, Twitter, and our JLI blog (www.myjli.com/blog). **Rabbi Avraham Bergstein** is a master of using the visual to enhance conceptual understanding. Rabbi Bergstein creates the slides that accompany each lesson and also crafts the lesson maps that serve as a powerful guide to lesson preparation.

We warmly welcome **Ms. Chava Zviklin**, the flagship department's project manager, who masterfully coordinates numerous initiatives that intersect with the work of the flagship department. Ms. Zviklin's thoughtful research and analysis allow us to ensure continued refinement of best practice.

JLI's efficient and talented production team is responsible for the outstanding quality of our printed materials. **Rabbi Mendel Sirota**, production manager, sets perfection as JLI's baseline standard. He orchestrates the myriad tasks that are necessary to our overall operation, including posting and personalizing marketing materials, overseeing the delivery of our books, and ensuring that our affiliates receive all support materials in a timely manner. **Mrs. Rachel Witty**, our proofreader, meticulously prepares our manuscript for print. **Nachman Levine**, our layout designer and research editor, brings to his work not only an artistic eye but also a scholarly one.

Thank you, **Spotlight Design**, for proving that you *can* judge a book by its cover. Finally, we would like to acknowledge the efforts of Shimon Leib Jacobs, who oversees our printing and shipping.

We extend our thanks to **Rabbi Zalman Abraham**, director of marketing, and to **Rabbi Moshe Teldon**, administrator of marketing, as well as to the members of our JLI marketing board, **Rabbi Simcha Backman, Rabbi Ronnie Fine, Rabbi Ovadia Goldman, Rabbi Mendel Halberstam**, and **Rabbi Yehudah Shemtov**. Our thanks go as well to **Rabbi Shraga Sherman**, who reviews our marketing materials.

The hardworking support staff at JLI Central is critical to our success and growth.

JLI's administrative staff, **Mrs. Musie Kesselman, Mrs. Mindy Wallach, Mrs. Fraydee Kessler**, and **Mrs. Chana Shaffer-Minkowitz**, attend to the many details that hone our professional edge to perfection. **Mrs. Shaina Basha Mintz, Mrs. Nechama Shmotkin**, and **Ms. Musie Karp** oversee our accounts. **Rabbi Mendel Bell**, webmaster *par excellence*, ensures the integrity of our online environment. **Rabbi Levi Kaplan** directs our international division and adapts our material for our Hebrew-speaking and Spanish-speaking markets. **Rabbi Mendel Popack**, director of JLI Academy, is the organizing force behind our annual JLI conference and is devoted to providing our affiliates with the development tools they need. **Dubi Rabinowitz**, chief operating officer, invites us to constantly rethink our roles and to reconfigure ourselves for efficiency and results.

We are immensely grateful for the encouragement of our chairman and vice chairman of Merkos L'Inyonei Chinuch—Lubavitch World Headquarters, **Rabbi Moshe Kotlarksy**. We are blessed to have the unwavering support of JLI's principal benefactor, **Mr. George Rohr**, who has fully invested in our work and has been instrumental in guiding the monumental expansion of the organization.

JLI's dedicated executive board—**Rabbi Chaim Block, Rabbi Hesh Epstein, Rabbi Yosef Gansburg, Rabbi Shmuel Kaplan, Rabbi Yisrael Rice,** and **Rabbi Avrohom Sternberg**—devoted countless hours to the development of JLI. Their dedicated commitment and sage direction have helped JLI continue to grow and flourish. We owe a particular debt of thanks to **Rabbi Yisrael Rice**, chairman of our flagship division, whose patient and thoughtful guidance has been an exceptional source of support throughout a period of rapid development.

The constant progress in JLI is a testament to the visionary leadership of our director, **Rabbi Efraim Mintz,** who is never content to rest on his laurels and who boldly encourages continued innovation and change.

Finally, JLI represents an incredible partnership of more than 300 *shluchim,* who give of their time and talent to further Jewish adult education. We thank them for generously sharing their thoughts, feedback, questions, and teaching experiences. They are our most valuable critics and our most cherished contributors.

Inspired by the call of the **Lubavitcher Rebbe** of righteous memory, it is the mandate of the Rohr JLI to allow all Jews throughout the world to experience and take part in the Torah learning that is their heritage. May this course succeed in fulfilling that sacred charge.

On behalf of the Rohr Jewish Learning Institute,

Chana Silberstein, PhD

Ithaca, New York
2 Nisan, 5771

The Rohr Jewish Learning Institute

An affiliate of
Merkos L'Inyonei Chinuch
The Educational Arm of
The Chabad Lubavitch Movement
822 Eastern Parkway, Brooklyn, NY 11213

Rabbi Berel Bell
Montreal, QC

Rabbi Hesh Epstein
Columbia, SC

Rabbi Zalman Aaron Kantor
Mission Viejo, CA

Rabbi Levi Kaplan
Brooklyn, NY

Rabbi Dr. Shmuel Klatzkin
Dayton, OH

Rabbi Yakov Latowicz
Ventura, CA

Rabbi Yosef Loschak
Goleta, CA

Rabbi Levi Mendelow
Stamford, CT

Rabbi Benzion Milecki
Dover Heights, AU

Rabbi Yossi Nemes
Metairie, LA

Rabbi Reuven New
Boca Raton, FL

Rabbi Dr. Shlomo Pereira
Richmond, VA

Rabbi Shalom Raichik
Gaithersburg, MD

Rabbi Benny Rapoport
Clarks Summit, PA

Rabbi Nochum Schapiro
Sydney, AU

Rabbi Shraga Sherman
Merion Station, PA

Rabbi Avraham Steinmetz
S. Paulo, BR

Rabbi Avrohom Sternberg
New London, CT

Rabbi Aryeh Weinstein
Newton, PA

Rabbi Motti Wilhelm
Portland, OR

Multimedia Development

Rabbi Avrohom Bergstein
Ms. Neria Cohen
Rabbi Chesky Edelman
Mrs. Chana Lightstone
Moshe Raskin
Mrs. Leah-Perl Shollar
Rabbi Levi Teldon

Administration

Rabbi Mendel Sirota
Mrs. Chana Shaffer-Minkowitz
Mrs. Mindy Wallach

Affiliate Support

Rabbi Mendel Sirota
Mrs. Musie Kesselman
Mrs. Fraydee Kessler
Mrs. Mindy Wallach

Online Division

Rabbi Mendel Bell
Dovid Ciment
Rabbi Mendel Sirota

Marketing

Rabbi Zalman Abraham
Director

Rabbi Moshe Teldon
Administrator

Marketing Committee

Rabbi Simcha Backman
Glendale, CA

Rabbi Ronnie Fine
Montreal, QC

Rabbi Ovadia Goldman
Oklahoma City, OK

Rabbi Mendy Halberstam
Miami Beach, FL

Rabbi Reuven New
Boca Raton, FL

Rabbi Yehuda Shemtov
Yardley, PA

Marketing Consultants

J.J. Gross
New York, NY

Warren Modlin
MednetPro, Inc.
Alpharetta, GA

Alan Rosenspan
Alan Rosenspan & Associates
Sharon, MA

Alan M. Shafer
Alliant Marketing Solutions
Stamford, CT

Gary Wexler
Passion Marketing
Los Angeles, CA

Graphic Design

Spotlight Design
Brooklyn, NY

Friedman Advertising
Los Angeles, CA

Yossi Graphic Design
Brooklyn, NY

Publication Design

Nachman Levine
Detroit, MI

Printing

Shimon Leib Jacobs
Point One Communications
Montreal, QC

Shipping

Mary Stevens
Market Tech
Nixa, MO

Accounting

Ms. Musie Karp
Mrs. Shaina B. Mintz
Mrs. Nechama Shmotkin

JLI Departments

Dubi Rabinowitz
Chief Operating Officer

JLI Flagship

Rabbi Yisrael Rice
Chairman
S. Rafael, CA

Dr. Chana Silberstein
Dean of Curriculum
Ithaca, NY

Rabbi Mordechai Dinerman
Associate Editor

Rabbi Naftali Silberberg
Developmental Editor

Mrs. Leah-Perl Shollar
Instructional Designer

Rabbi Avraham Bergstein
Instructional Support

Mrs. Chana Lightstone
Research Associate

Rabbi Mendel Sirota
Production Manager

Ms. Chava Zviklin
Project Coordinator

Mrs. Rachel Witty
Proofreader

Nachman Levine
Research Editor
Detroit, MI

Department of Continuing Education

Mrs. Mindy Wallach
Director

Ms. Musie Karp
Registrar

Mrs. Rivka Sternberg
Administrative Support

Dr. Michael Akerman, MD
Consultant
Continuing Medical Education
Associate Professor of Medicine,
SUNY–Downstate Medical Center

Bernard Kanstoroom, Esq.
Consultant
Continuing Legal Education
Bethesda, MD

JLI For Teens
in partnership with CTeeN: Chabad Teen Network

Rabbi Chaim Block
Chairman
San Antonio, TX

Rabbi Benny Rapoport
Director
Clarks Summit, PA

Mrs. Gani Goodman
Coordinator

Rabbi Beryl Frankel
Director, CTeeN
Yardley, PA

JLI International Desk

Rabbi Avrohom Sternberg
Chairman
New London, CT

Rabbi Levi Kaplan
Coordinator

JLI Teacher Training

Rabbi Berel Bell
Director
Montreal, QC

myShiur:
Advanced Learning Initiative

Rabbi Shmuel Kaplan
Chairman
Potomac, MD

Rabbi Levi Kaplan
Director

Rosh Chodesh Society

Rabbi Shmuel Kaplan
Chairman
Potomac, MD

Mrs. Shaindy Jacobson
Director

Mrs. Musie Kesselman
Administrator

Steering Committee
Mrs. Chanie Bukiet
Mrs. Simcha Fine
Mrs. Sara Lieberman
Mrs. Michla Schanowitz
Mrs. Bronya Shaffer

National Jewish Retreat

Rabbi Hesh Epstein
Chairman
Columbia, SC

Rabbi Mendy Weg
Founding Director

Rabbi Boruch Cohen
Director

Bruce Backman
Liaison

Mrs. Shaina B. Mintz
Administrator

Sinai Scholars Society
in partnership with Chabad on Campus

Rabbi Menachem Schmidt
Chairman
Philadelphia, PA

Rabbi Yitzchok Dubov
Director

Executive Committee
Rabbi Moshe Chaim Dubrowski
Rabbi Efraim Mintz
Rabbi Menachem Schmidt
Dr. Chana Silberstein
Rabbi Nechemia Vogel
Rabbi Eitan Webb

TorahCafe.com
Online Learning

Rabbi Levi Kaplan
Director

Mrs. Miri Birk
Adminisrator

Rabbi Simcha Backman
Consultant

Golan Ben-Oni
Rabbi Laibel Karp
Advisory Board

Mrs. Chana Lightstone
Mrs. Ani Lipitz
Editors

Rabbi Mendy Elishevitz
Rabbi Mendel Bell
Website Development

Rabbi Getzel Raskin
Director of Filming and Editing

Menachem Amos
Ms. Fraidy Bell
Avrohom Shimon Ezagui
Yosef Kramer
Yehuda Shaffer
Akiva Silberstein
Filming Crew

Moshe Raskin
Moshe Dunn
Yosef Schmalberg
Yehoshua Hayward
Video Editing

Torah Studies

Rabbi Yossi Gansburg
Chairman
Toronto, ON

Rabbi Meir Hecht
Director

Steering Committee
Rabbi Yaacov Halperin
Rabbi Nechemia Schusterman
Rabbi Ari Sollish

JLI Academy

Rabbi Hesh Epstein
Chairman

Rabbi Mendel Popack
Director

Dr. Gill Heart
Consultant

Steering Committee
Rabbi Yoel Caroline
Rabbi Mordechai Grossbaum
Rabbi Levi Mendelow

Beis Medrosh L'Shluchim
in partnership with Shluchim Exchange

Rabbi Sholom Zirkind
Administrator

Rabbi Mendy Rabin
Coordinator

Rabbi Mendel Margolin
Producer

Steering Committee
Rabbi Simcha Backman
Rabbi Mendy Kotlarsky
Rabbi Efraim Mintz

JLI Central
Founding Department Heads

Rabbi Zalman Charytan
Acworth, GA

Rabbi Mendel Druk
Cancun, Mexico

Rabbi Menachem Gansburg
Toronto, ON

Rabbi Yoni Katz
Brooklyn, NY

Rabbi Chaim Zalman Levy
New Rochelle, NY

Rabbi Elchonon Tenenbaum
Napa Valley, CA

Rohr JLI Affiliates

Share the **Rohr JLI** experience with friends and relatives worldwide

ALABAMA

BIRMINGHAM
Rabbi Yossi Friedman
205.970.0100

ARIZONA

CHANDLER
Rabbi Mendel Deitsch
480.855.4333

FLAGSTAFF
Rabbi Dovie Shapiro
928.255.5756

GLENDALE
Rabbi Sholom Lew
602.375.2422

PHOENIX
Rabbi Zalman Levertov
Rabbi Yossi Friedman
602.944.2753

SCOTTSDALE
Rabbi Yossi Levertov
Rabbi Yossi Bryski
480.998.1410

ARKANSAS

LITTLE ROCK
Rabbi Pinchus Ciment
501.217.0053

CALIFORNIA

AGOURA HILLS
Rabbi Moshe Bryski

BAKERSFIELD
Rabbi Shmuel Schlanger
661.835.8381

BEL AIR
Rabbi Chaim Mentz
310.475.5311

BRENTWOOD
Rabbi Boruch Hecht
Rabbi Mordechai Zaetz
310.826.4453

BURBANK
Rabbi Shmuly Kornfeld
818.954.0070

CALABASAS
Rabbi Eliyahu Friedman
818.585.1888

CARLSBAD
Rabbi Yeruchem Eilfort
Rabbi Michoel Shapiro
760.943.8891

CHATSWORTH
Rabbi Yossi Spritzer
818.718.0777

CONTRA COSTA
Rabbi Yaakov Kagan
Rabbi Dovber Berkowitz
925.937.4101

ENCINO
Rabbi Joshua Gordon
Rabbi Eli Rivkin
818.758.1818

FOLSOM
Rabbi Yossi Grossbaum
916.608.9811

GLENDALE
Rabbi Simcha Backman
818.240.2750

HUNTINGTON BEACH
Rabbi Aron Berkowitz
714.846.2285

IRVINE
Rabbi Alter Tenenbaum
Rabbi Elly Andrusier
949.786.5000

LAGUNA BEACH
Rabbi Elimelech Gurevitch
949.499.0770

LOMITA
Rabbi Eli Hecht
Rabbi Sholom Pinson
310.326.8234

LONG BEACH
Rabbi Abba Perelmuter
562.621.9828

MARINA DEL REY
Rabbi Danny Yiftach
Rabbi Mendy Avtzon
310.859.0770

MISSION VIEJO
Rabbi Zalman Aron Kantor
949.770.1270

MONTEREY
Rabbi Dovid Holtzberg
831.643.2770

MT. OLYMPUS
Rabbi Sholom Ber Rodal
323.650.1444

NEWHALL
Rabbi Elchonon Marosov
661.254.3434

NEWPORT BEACH
Rabbi Reuven Mintz
949.721.9800

NORTH HOLLYWOOD
Rabbi Nachman Abend
818.989.9539

NORTHRIDGE
Rabbi Eli Rivkin
818.368.3937

PACIFIC PALISADES
Rabbi Zushe Cunin
310.454.7783

PASADENA
Rabbi Chaim Hanoka
626.564.8820

RANCHO CUCAMONGA
Rabbi Sholom B. Harlig
909.949.4553

RANCHO PALOS VERDES
Rabbi Yitzchok Magalnic
310.544.5544

REDONDO BEACH
Rabbi Dovid Lisbon
310.214.4999

SACRAMENTO
Rabbi Mendy Cohen
916.455.1400

S. BARBARA
Rabbi Yosef Loschak
805.683.1544

S. CLEMENTE
Rabbi Menachem M. Slavin
949.489.0723

S. CRUZ
Rabbi Yochanan Friedman
831.454.0101

S. DIEGO
Rabbi Motte Fradkin
858.547.0076

S. FRANCISCO
Rabbi Peretz Mochkin
415.571.8770

S. MONICA
Rabbi Boruch Rabinowitz
310.394.5699

S. RAFAEL
Rabbi Yisrael Rice
415.492.1666

S. ROSA
Rabbi Mendel Wolvovsky
707.577.0277

SIMI VALLEY
Rabbi Nosson Gurary
805.577.0573

STOCKTON
Rabbi Avremel Brod
209.952.2081

STUDIO CITY
Rabbi Yossi Baitelman
818.508.6633

TEMECULA
Rabbi Yitzchok Hurwitz
951.303.9576

THOUSAND OAKS
Rabbi Chaim Bryski
805.493.7776

TUSTIN
Rabbi Yehoshua Eliezrie
714.508.2150

Ventura
Rabbi Yakov Latowicz
Mrs. Sarah Latowicz
805.658.7441

West Hills
Rabbi Avrahom Yitzchak Rabin
818.337.4544

Yorba Linda
Rabbi Dovid Eliezrie
714.693.0770

COLORADO

Aspen
Rabbi Mendel Mintz
970.544.3770

Boulder
Rabbi Pesach Scheiner
303.494.1638

Denver
Rabbi Yossi Serebryanski
303.744.9699

Highlands Ranch
Rabbi Avraham Mintz
303.694.9119

Longmont
Rabbi Yaakov Dovid Borenstein
303.678.7595

Vail
Rabbi Dovid Mintz
970.476.7887

Westminster
Rabbi Benjy Brackman
303.429.5177

CONNECTICUT

Branford
Rabbi Yossi Yaffe
203.488.2263

Glastonbury
Rabbi Yosef Wolvovsky
860.659.2422

Greenwich
Rabbi Yossi Deren
Rabbi Menachem Feldman
203.629.9059

Litchfield
Rabbi Yoseph Eisenbach
860.567.3609

New London
Rabbi Avrohom Sternberg
860.437.8000

Orange
Rabbi Sheya Hecht
Rabbi Adam Haston
203.795.5261

Simsbury
Rabbi Mendel Samuels
860.658.4903

Stamford
Rabbi Yisrael Deren
Rabbi Levi Mendelow
203.3.CHABAD

West Hartford
Rabbi Yosef Gopin
Rabbi Shaya Gopin
860.659.2422

Westport
Rabbi Yehuda L. Kantor
Mrs. Dina Kantor
203.226.8584

DELAWARE

Wilmington
Rabbi Chuni Vogel
302.529.9900

FLORIDA

Aventura
Rabbi Laivi Forta
305.933.0770

Bal Harbour
Rabbi Dov Schochet
305.868.1411

Boca Raton
Rabbi Moishe Denberg
Rabbi Zalman Bukiet
561.417.7797

Bonita Springs
Rabbi Mendy Greenberg
239.949.6900

Boynton Beach
Rabbi Yosef Yitzchok Raichik
561.732.4633

Bradenton
Rabbi Menachem Bukiet
941.388.9656

Brandon
Rabbi Mendel Rubashkin
813.657.9393

Coconut Creek
Rabbi Yossi Gansburg
954.422.1987

Coral Gables
Rabbi Avrohom Stolik
305.490.7572

Deerfield Beach
Rabbi Yossi Goldblatt
954.422.1735

Delray Beach
Rabbi Sholom Ber Korf
561.496.6228

East Boca Raton
Rabbi Ruvi New
561.417.7797

Fort Lauderdale
Rabbi Yitzchok Naparstek
954.568.1190

Fort Myers
Rabbi Yitzchok Minkowicz
Mrs. Nechama Minkowicz
239.433.7708

Hollywood
Rabbi Leizer Barash
954.965.9933

Rabbi Zalman Korf
Rabbi Yakov Garfinkel
954.374.8370

Kendall
Rabbi Yossi Harlig
305.234.5654

Key Biscayne
Rabbi Yoel Caroline
305.365.6744

Key West
Rabbi Yaakov Zucker
305.295.0013

Miami Beach
Rabbi Aron Rabin
Rabbi Mendy Halberstam
305.535.0094

Naples
Rabbi Fishel Zaklos
239.262.4474

North Miami Beach
Rabbi Moishe Kievman
305.770.1919

Orlando
Rabbi Yosef Konikov
407.354.3660

Parkland
Rabbi Mendy Gutnik
954.796.7330

Pinellas County
Rabbi Shalom Adler
727.789.0408

S. Petersburg
Rabbi Alter Korf
727.344.4900

Sarasota
Rabbi Chaim Shaul Steinmetz
941.925.0770

Satellite Beach
Rabbi Zvi Konikov
321.777.2770

South Palm Beach
Rabbi Leibel Stolik
561.889.3499

South Tampa
Rabbi Mendy Dubrowski
813.287.1795

Sunny Isles Beach
Rabbi Alexander Kaller
305.803.5315

Tallahassee
Rabbi Schneur Zalmen Oirechman
850.523.9294

Venice
Rabbi Sholom Ber Schmerling
941.493.2770

Walnut Creek
Rabbi Zalman Korf
954.374.8370

Weston
Rabbi Yisroel Spalter
954.349.6565

West Palm Beach
Rabbi Yoel Gancz
561.659.7770

GEORGIA

Alpharetta
Rabbi Hirshy Minkowicz
770.410.9000

Atlanta
Rabbi Yossi New
Rabbi Isser New
404.843.2464

Atlanta: Intown
Rabbi Eliyahu Schusterman
Rabbi Ari Sollish
404.898.0434

Gwinnett
Rabbi Yossi Lerman
678.595.0196

Marietta
Rabbi Ephraim Silverman
Rabbi Zalman Charytan
770.565.4412

IDAHO

Boise
Rabbi Mendel Lifshitz
208.853.9200

ILLINOIS

Chicago
Rabbi Meir Hecht
312.714.4655

Gurnee
Rabbi Sholom Ber Tenenbaum
847.782.1800

Glenview
Rabbi Yishaya Benjaminson
847.998.9896

Highland Park
Mrs. Michla Schanowitz
847.266.0770

Naperville
Rabbi Mendy Goldstein
630.778.9770

Northbrook
Rabbi Meir Moscowitz
847.564.8770

Peoria
Rabbi Eli Langsam
309.692.2250

Skokie
Rabbi Yochanan Posner
847.677.1770

Wilmette
Rabbi Dovid Flinkenstein
847.251.7707

INDIANA

Indianapolis
Rabbi Mendel Schusterman
317.251.5573

KANSAS

Overland Park
Rabbi Mendy Wineberg
913.649.4852

LOUISIANA

Metairie
Rabbi Yossi Nemes
504.454.2910

MARYLAND

Baltimore
Rabbi Elchonon Lisbon
410.358.4787

Rabbi Velvel Belinsky
Classes in Russian
410.764.5000

Bethesda
Rabbi Bentzion Geisinsky
Rabbi Sender Geisinsky
301.913.9777

Columbia
Rabbi Hillel Baron
Rabbi Yosef Chaim Sufrin
410.740.2424

Gaithersburg
Rabbi Sholom Raichik
301.926.3632

Potomac
Rabbi Mendel Bluming
301.983.4200

Silver Spring
Rabbi Berel Wolvovsky
301.593.1117

MASSACHUSETTS

Hyannis
Rabbi Yekusiel Alperowitz
508.775.2324

Longmeadow
Rabbi Yakov Wolff
413.567.8665

Newton
Rabbi Moshe Lieberman
617.965.1968

Sudbury
Rabbi Yisroel Freeman
978.443.3691

Swampscott
Mrs. Layah Lipsker
781.581.3833

MICHIGAN

Ann Arbor
Rabbi Aharon Goldstein
734.995.3276

Novi
Rabbi Avrohom Susskind
248.790.6075

West Bloomfield
Rabbi Kasriel Shemtov
248.788.4000

Rabbi Elimelech Silberberg
Rabbi Avrohom Wineberg
248.855 .6170

MINNESOTA

Minnetonka
Rabbi Mordechai Grossbaum
952.929.9922

Rochester
Rabbi Dovid Greene
507.288.7500

MISSOURI

S. Louis
Rabbi Yosef Landa
314.725.0400

MONTANA

Bozeman
Rabbi Chaim Shaul Bruk
406.585.8770

NEBRASKA

Omaha
Rabbi Mendel Katzman
402.330.1800

NEVADA

Henderson
Rabbi Mendy Harlig
Rabbi Tzvi Bronstein
702.617.0770

Summerlin
Rabbi Yisroel Schanowitz
Rabbi Tzvi Bronstein
702.855.0770

NEW JERSEY

Basking Ridge
Rabbi Mendy Herson
908.604.8844

Cherry Hill
Rabbi Mendy Mangel
856.874.1500

Clinton
Rabbi Eli Kornfeld
908.623.7000

Flanders
Rabbi Yaacov Shusterman
973.723.6868

Fort Lee
Rabbi Meir Konikov
201.886.1238

Franklin Lakes
Rabbi Chanoch Kaplan
201.848.0449

Hillsborough
Rabbi Shmaya Krinsky
908.874.0444

Madison
Rabbi Shalom Lubin
973.377.0707

Manalapan
Rabbi Boruch Chazanow
732.972.3687

Medford
Rabbi Yitzchok Kahan
609.953.3150

Mountain Lakes
Rabbi Levi Dubinsky
973.551.1898

North Brunswick
Rabbi Levi Azimov
732.398.9492

Randolph
Rabbi Avraham Bechor
973.895.3070

Rockaway
Rabbi Asher Herson
Rabbi Mordechai Baumgarten
973.625.1525

Sparta
Rabbi Shmuel Lewis
973.726.3333

Teaneck
Rabbi Ephraim Simon
201.907.0686

Tenafly
Rabbi Mordechai Shain
Rabbi Yitzchak Gershovitz
201.871.1152

Toms River
Rabbi Moshe Gourarie
732.349.4199

Wayne
Rabbi Michel Gurkov
973.694.6274

West Orange
Rabbi Mendy Kasowitz
973.731.0770

Woodcliff Lake
Rabbi Dov Drizin
201.476.0157

NEW MEXICO

S. Fe
Rabbi Berel Levertov
505.983.2000

NEW YORK

Albany
Rabbi Yossi Rubin
518.482.5781

Bedford
Rabbi Arik Wolf
914.666.6065

Binghamton
Mrs. Rivkah Slonim
607.797.0015

Brighton Beach
Rabbi Zushe Winner
Rabbi Avrohom Winner
718.946.9833

Brooklyn
Mrs. Shimona Tzukernik
718.493.2859

Cedarhurst
Rabbi Shneur Zalman Wolowik
516.295.2478

Dix Hills
Rabbi Yaakov Saacks
631.351.8672

Dobbs Ferry
Rabbi Benjy Silverman
914.693.6100

East Hampton
Rabbi Leibel Baumgarten
631.329.5800

Great Neck
Rabbi Yoseph Geisinsky
516.487.4554

Ithaca
Rabbi Eli Silberstein
607.257.7379

Kingston
Rabbi Yitzchok Hecht
845.334.9044

Larchmont
Rabbi Mendel Silberstein
914.834.4321

Long Island City
Rabbi Zev Wineberg
347.262.5540

New York
Rabbi Yisrael Kugel
212.799.0809

NYC Gramercy Park
Rabbi Naftali Rotenstreich
212.924.3200

NYC Kehilath Jeshurun
Rabbi Elie Weinstock
212.774.5636

Oceanside
Rabbi Levi Gurkov
616.764.7385

Ossining
Rabbi Dovid Labkowski
914.923.2522

Port Washington
Rabbi Shalom Paltiel
516.767.8672

Riverdale
Rabbi Levi Shemtov
718.549.1100

Rochester
Rabbi Nechemia Vogel
585.271.0330

Roslyn
Rabbi Yaakov Reiter
516.484.8185

Sea Gate
Rabbi Chaim Brikman
Mrs. Rivka Brikman
718.266.1736

Staten Island
Rabbi Moshe Katzman
Rabbi Shmuel Bendet
718.370.8953

Stony Brook
Rabbi Shalom Ber Cohen
631.585.0521

West Hempstead
Rabbi Yossi Lieberman
Rabbi Mordechai Dinerman
516.596.8691

NORTH CAROLINA

Asheville
Rabbi Shaya Susskind
828.505.0746

Charlotte
Rabbi Yossi Groner
Rabbi Shlomo Cohen
704.366.3984

Greensboro
Rabbi Yosef Plotkin
336 617 8120

Raleigh
Rabbi Aaron Herman
919.637.6950

Rabbi Pinchas Herman
Rabbi Sholom Ber Estrin
919.847.8986

OHIO

Beachwood
Rabbi Yossi Marosov
216.381.4736

Blue Ash
Rabbi Yisroel Mangel
513.793.5200

Columbus
Rabbi Areyah Kaltmann
Rabbi Levi Andrusier
614.294.3296

Dayton
Rabbi Nochum Mangel
Rabbi Dr. Shmuel Klatzkin
937.643.0770

Toledo
Rabbi Yossi Shemtov
419.843.9393

OKLAHOMA

Oklahoma City
Rabbi Ovadia Goldman
405.524.4800

Tulsa
Rabbi Yehuda Weg
918.492.4499

OREGON

Ashland
Rabbi Avi Zwiebel
541.482.2778

Portland
Rabbi Moshe Wilhelm
Rabbi Mordechai Wilhelm
503.977.9947

PENNSYLVANIA

Ambler
Rabbi Shaya Deitsch
215.591.9310

Bala Cynwyd
Rabbi Shraga Sherman
610.660.9192

Clarks Summit
Rabbi Benny Rapoport
570.587.3300

Devon
Rabbi Yossi Kaplan
610.971.9977

Newtown
Rabbi Aryeh Weinstein
215.497.9925

Philadelphia: Center City
Rabbi Yochonon Goldman
215.238.2100

Pittsburgh
Rabbi Yisroel Altein
412.422.7300 ext. 269

Pittsburgh: South Hills
Rabbi Mendy Rosenblum
412.278.3693

Reading
Rabbi Yosef Lipsker
610.921.2805

Rydal
Rabbi Zushe Gurevitz
215.572.1511

RHODE ISLAND

Warwick
Rabbi Yossi Laufer
401.884.7888

SOUTH CAROLINA

Columbia
Rabbi Hesh Epstein
803.782.1831

TENNESSEE

Bellevue
Rabbi Yitzchok Tiechtel
615.646.5750

Chattanooga
Rabbi Shaul Perlstein
423.490.1106

Knoxville
Rabbi Yossi Wilhelm
865.588.8584

Memphis
Rabbi Levi Klein
901.766.1800

TEXAS

Fort Worth
Rabbi Dov Mandel
817.263.7701

Houston
Rabbi Moishe Traxler
713.774.0300

Houston: Rice University Area
Rabbi Eliezer Lazaroff
Rabbi Yitzchok Schmukler
713.522.2004

Plano
Rabbi Mendel Block
Rabbi Yehudah Horowitz
972.596.8270

S. Antonio
Rabbi Chaim Block
Rabbi Yossi Marrus
210.492.1085

UTAH

Salt Lake City
Rabbi Benny Zippel
801.467.7777

VERMONT

Burlington
Rabbi Yitzchok Raskin
802.658.5770

VIRGINIA

Alexandria/Arlington
Rabbi Mordechai Newman
703.370.2774

Fairfax
Rabbi Leibel Fajnland
703.426.1980

Norfolk
Rabbi Aaron Margolin
Rabbi Levi Brashevitzky
757.616.0770

Richmond
Rabbi Dr. Shlomo Pereira
804.740.2000

Tysons Corner
Chapter founded by
Rabbi Levi Deitsch OBM

Rabbi Chezzy Deitsch
703.829.5770

WASHINGTON

Olympia
Rabbi Cheski Edelman
360.584-4306

Seattle
Rabbi Elazar Bogomilsky
206.527.1411

Spokane County
Rabbi Yisroel Hahn
509.443.0770

WISCONSIN

Mequon
Rabbi Menachem Rapoport
262.242.2235

Milwaukee
Rabbi Mendel Shmotkin
414.961.6100

PUERTO RICO

Carolina
Rabbi Mendel Zarchi
787.253.0894

ARGENTINA

Buenos Aires
Rabbi Hirshel Hendel
5411.4807.7073

Rabbi Mendy Grunblatt
5411.4772.1024

AUSTRALIA

Bondi
Rabbi Pinchas Feldman
Rabbi Eli Feldman
612.9387.3822

Brisbane
Rabbi Chanoch Sufrin
617.3843.6770

Double Bay
Rabbi Yanky Berger
612.9327.1644

Dover Heights
Rabbi Benzion Milecki
612.9337.6775

Melbourne
Rabbi Schneier Lange
613.9522.8222

Rabbi Shimshon Yurkowicz
613.9822.3600

North Shore
Rabbi Nochum Schapiro
Mrs. Fruma Schapiro
612.9488.9548

Sydney
Rabbi Levi Wolff
612.9389.5622

Victoria
South Yarra
Rabbi Yehuda Hoch
03.9613.0738

BRAZIL

Rio de Janeiro
Rabbi Yehoshua Goldman
Rabbi Avraham Steinmetz
55.21.3543.3770

S. Paulo
Rabbi Avraham Steinmetz
55.11.3081.3081

CANADA

ALBERTA

Calgary
Rabbi Mordechai Groner
403.238.4880

Edmonton
Rabbi Ari Drelich
Rabbi Mendy Blachman
780.851.1515

BRITISH COLUMBIA

Richmond
Rabbi Yechiel Baitelman
604.277.6427

Victoria
Rabbi Meir Kaplan
250.595.7656

MANITOBA

Winnipeg
Rabbi Avrohom Altein
Rabbi Shmuel Altein
204.339.8737

ONTARIO

London
Rabbi Eliezer Gurkow
519.434.3962

Niagara Falls
Rabbi Zalman Zaltzman

Ottawa
Rabbi Menachem M. Blum
613.823.0866

Greater Toronto Regional Office & Thornhill
Rabbi Yossi Gansburg
905.731.7000

Toronto Area York Mills
Rabbi Levi Gansburg
647.345.3800

Lawrence/Eglinton
Rabbi Menachem Gansburg
416.546.8770

Mississauga
Rabbi Yitzchok Slavin
905.820.4432

Richmond Hill
Rabbi Mendel Bernstein
905.770.7700

BJL
Rabbi Leib Chaiken
416.916.7202

York University
Rabbi Vidal Bekerman
416.856.4575

QUEBEC

Montreal
Rabbi Ronnie Fine
Rabbi Leibel Fine
514.342.3.JLI

Town of Mount Royal
Rabbi Moshe Krasnanski
514.739.0770

Ville S. Laurent
Rabbi Schneur Zalmen Silberstein
514.808.1418

COLOMBIA

Bogota
Rabbi Yehoshua B. Rosenfeld
Rabbi Chanoch Piekarski
571.635.8251

DENMARK

Copenhagen
Rabbi Yitzchok Lowenthal
45.3316.1850

GERMANY

Berlin
Rabbi Yehuda Tiechtel
4930.212.808.30

GREECE

Athens
Rabbi Mendel Hendel
30.210.520.2880

GUATEMALA

Guatemala City
Rabbi Shalom Pelman
502.2485.0770

ISRAEL

Ashdod
Rabbi Yosef Friedman
052.4240675

Balfurya
Rabbi Noam Bar-Tov
054.5804770

Be'er Sheva
Rabbi Avrohom Cohen
08.6233197

Caesarea
Rabbi Chaim Meir Lieberman
054.6212586

Even Yehuda
Rabbi Pinchos Noyman
054.7770707

Ganei Tikva
Rabbi Gershon Shnur
054.5242358

Giv'atayim
Rabbi Pinchus Bitton
052.6438770

Holon
Rabbi Yerachmiel Gorelik
03.6530300

Jerusalem
Rabbi Eliyahu Canterman
Classes in English
054.6823737

Karmiel
Rabbi Mendy Elishevitz
054.5213073

Kiryat Bialik
Rabbi Pinny Marton
050.6611768

Kiryat Motzkin
Rabbi Shimon Eizenbach
050.9020770

Maccabim Re'ut
Rabbi Yosef Yitzchak Noiman
054.9770549

Meitar
Rabbi Shneor Kurtz
054.5391770

Nes Ziyona
Rabbi Pinchos Feldman
054.4977092

Netanya
Rabbi Schneur Brod
054.5797572

Omer
Rabbi Menachem Feldman
050.2223770

Ramat HaSharon
Rabbi Meir Abiyov
054.5639278

Ramat Yishai
Rabbi Shneor Wolosow
052.3245475

Tel Aviv
Rabbi Menachem Gerlitzky
054.7765565

Zikhron Ya'akov
Rabbi Yosef Yitzchak Freiman
054.6631770

NETHERLANDS

Den Haag
Rabbi Shmuel Katzman
31.70.347.0222

PANAMA

Panama City
Rabbi Ari Laine
Rabbi Gabriel Benayon
507.223.3383

SINGAPORE

Singapore
Rabbi Mordechai Abergel
656.337.2189

SOUTH AFRICA

Cape Town
Rabbi Mendel Popack
Rabbi Pinchas Hecht
27.21.434.3740

Johannesburg
Rabbi Dovid Hazdan
Rabbi Shmuel Simpson
27.11.728.8152

Rabbi Dovid Masinter
Rabbi Ari Kievman
27.11.440.6600

SWEDEN

Stockholm
Rabbi Chaim Greisman
468.679.7067

SWITZERLAND

Lugano
Rabbi Yaakov Tzvi Kantor
091.921.3720

Luzern
Rabbi Chaim Drukman
414.1361.1770

UNITED KINGDOM

Edgeware
Rabbi Leivi Sudak
Rabbi Yaron Jacobs
44.208.905.4141

Leeds
Rabbi Eli Pink
44.113.266.3311

London
Rabbi Gershon Overlander
Rabbi Dovid Katz
44.208.202.1600

VENEZUELA

Caracas
Rabbi Yehoshua Rosenblum
58.212.264.7011

NOTES

THE JEWISH LEARNING MULTIPLEX

Brought to you by the Rohr Jewish Learning Institute

In fulfillment of the mandate of the Lubavitcher Rebbe, of blessed memory, whose leadership guides every step of our work, the mission of the Rohr Jewish Learning Institute is to transform Jewish life and the greater community through the study of Torah, connecting each Jew to our shared heritage of Jewish learning.

While our flagship program remains the cornerstone of our organization, JLI is proud to feature additional divisions catering to specific populations, in order to meet a wide array of educational needs.

THE ROHR JEWISH LEARNING INSTITUTE,
a subsidiary of *Merkos L'Inyonei Chinuch*,
is the adult education arm of the Chabad-Lubavitch Movement.

Torah Studies provides a rich and nuanced encounter with the weekly Torah reading.

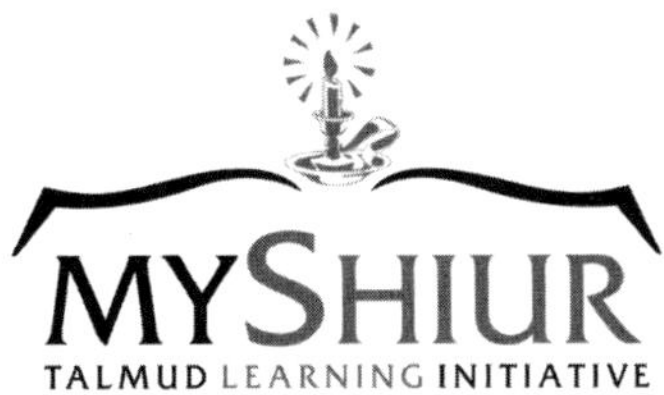

MyShiur courses are designed to assist students in developing the skills needed to study Talmud independently.

IN PARTNERSHIP WITH CHABAD ON CAMPUS

This rigorous fellowship program invites select college students to explore the fundamentals of Judaism.

IN PARTNERSHIP WITH CTEEN: CHABAD TEEN NETWORK

Jewish teens forge their identity as they engage in Torah study, social interaction, and serious fun.

IN PARTNERSHIP WITH CHABAD ON CAMPUS

The rigor and excellence of JLI courses, adapted to the campus environment.

TorahCafe.com provides an exclusive selection of top-rated Jewish educational videos.

This yearly event rejuvenates mind, body, and spirit with a powerful synthesis of Jewish learning and community.

The Rosh Chodesh Society gathers Jewish women together once a month for intensive textual study.

Select affiliates are invited to partner with peers and noted professionals, as leaders of innovation and excellence.

Mission participants delve into our nation's rich past while exploring the Holy Land's relevance and meaning today.